The Book of Pirates

By

Henry Gilbert

Author of "The Conquerors of Mexico" "The Conquerors of Peru" "The Story of the Indian Mutiny" etc.

Bracken Books
LONDON

First published 1916
by George G. Harrap & Co., London.

This edition published 1986 by Bracken Books,
a division of Bestseller Publications Limited, Brent House,
24 Friern Park, London N12 9DA, England.

ISBN 1 85170 030 7

Printed in Yugoslavia.

Contents

Illustrations

I : The Pirates who Captured Cæsar

IT was a brilliant day in summer, and the blue of the Mediterranean was answered by the fleckless blue of the sky, out of which the sun shone with all the fierceness of noon. In a rocky creek of the island of Pharmacusa, which lay a few miles off the coast of Caria, in Asia Minor, lay a long black galley, its nose of burnished copper just showing outside the entrance of the creek. With its benches of rowers who sat quietly chatting, their black oars not placed inboard, but ready to their hands, the raking mast and the huge half-furled sail, the galley had all the appearance of a vicious scorpion waiting in a cleft of the rocks for some unwary prey. Every man had a keen knife at his girdle, and in the box under his seat were stores of javelins, bows and arrows, slings and stones. These rowers were not slaves: each took part and lot in the enterprise on which they were engaged; each was a seaman and a fighter, as apt at the oar or the sail as at the set-to with knife or short throwing-spear. Indeed, this was the galley *Milvus*, 'The Kite,' one of the scouting vessels of the pirate chief Spartaco, leader of a band of sea-rovers whose name was a name of terror up and down the coasts of Asia Minor, from the Hellespont to Tyre, in Syria.

Three men sat in the little cabin on the high-curving poop, from which they had a wide view over the deck of the vessel and away to where the shores of Caria shimmered in the heat haze. They were waiting for any merchant-vessels beating up in the south-west wind from Greece or Italy, and making for Miletus or Ephesus. To pass the time away they were throwing dice, but the day was hot and the game dragged.

"Zeus!" said one, named Micio, yawning. "As well be lizards baking on a stone as wait here for ships that never come! The sea is as empty as the treasury at Samos!"

This referred to one of the most daring recent exploits of Spartaco, in violating a temple to Venus in the island of Samos, which lay some thirty miles to the north of where they were seated. The beautiful building had been ruined by fire, after the pirates had put the priests and priestesses to the sword and had rifled the treasury and temple of all the wealth given to it by generations of devout worshippers. The speaker had suggested this exploit to his chief, who sat beside him, and he rather prided himself upon his initiative.

"*Me Hercule!*" sneered the third man, a truculent, black-browed rascal named Syrus. "You talk as if you had scaled the walls of Olympus and robbed Jove of his thunderbolts! There is a greater prize than any you would have the courage for, if Spartaco here will let us do it."

"And what is that?" asked Spartaco, a little fierce-faced man with gold rings in his ears, gold chains round his neck, and flashing jewels on his dirty fingers.

"The Temple of Diana at Ephesus!" replied Syrus.

"There is booty enough there, 'tis true," said Spartaco; "but the town is a strong one and Archelaus, the governor there, is a hard man, who would not be bought over to our side except for a very large sum. And even if he agreed to take his soldiers away while we plundered, the Ephesians would fight like wild cats for their Diana."

"I like it not," said Micio. "The goddess has been good to me. I sacrificed to her when I sacked Agrigentum, and she saved me from death and capture that day, for the Sicilians fought too well."

"Pshaw!" returned Spartaco. "These gods and goddesses cannot help themselves. Until my old chief Storax of Cyprus took it into his head to sack Apollo's temple at Claros, because the god refused him the ship of the rich merchant Crassus at Chios, no captain of the sea had dared to think of trying the strength of a god. Did any ill befall Storax by reason of that? Did he not afterward sack the temple of Ceres at Hermione, and that of the healing-god, Æsculapius, at Epidaurus? What he could do others have done. Sannio the Negro took much treasure from the temple of Neptune in the Isthmus, and because the god sank two of his best galleys at Tænarus he sacked his temple there too, and at Calauria."

"But, mark you, captain," said Micio, "I think these things pass not without note, though the old gods be fallen now on careless days since the Bull-God Mithras is so widely worshipped. What happened to Storax? you ask. Was he not slain by an unseen hand as he feasted in his mountain-hold at Aspera, in the midst of his faithful men? It was an arrow of the god that slew him, of a surety, for all such deaths are from the hand of Apollo. And Sannio—what befell him at Messina? As he rode in the midst of his galleys in a calm sea, waiting for his men to bring off the senators Sextus and Glabrio, to hold for ransom, a great wave rolled in from the Narrow Strait and swamped and drowned five galleys and some four hundred men—Sannio among them."

"Old women's tales, all such!" returned Spartaco; but his words did not ring with sincerity. As a matter of fact, superstition moved him as much as it moved the wisest and basest of men in those times, when the old gods were dying and new and untried gods were taking their places. Men's minds were still affected more strongly by the old beliefs than by the new, and Spartaco could not keep down the feeling that there might be some truth in the words of his lieutenant Micio.

Syrus was quick to see the doubt in the mind of his captain and therefore laughed.

"We must look, then, for some act of vengeance upon us from the dainty hand of the goddess Venus!" he said. "Doubtless the next serving-maid from whom we would snatch a kiss will thump us heartily!"

Spartaco laughed harshly, but Micio looked gloomy. He had himself suggested the sacking of the temple of Venus at Samos, but it had been to make favour for himself with Spartaco, and he had no thought then of the possible wrath and vengeance of the goddess. Syrus sneered at him.

"Croaker!" he said. "I believe you've frightened yourself now. As for me, I fear none of the old gods while the young Mithras protects me."

He made the sign of the swastika in the air, invoking the protection of Mithras.

At that moment there came a faint, broken halloo from the look-out on the topmost rock on the shore. A quick movement ran through the men on the benches of the galley; they clutched at the handles of their long oars and looked up at their leaders for orders. Spartaco and his lieutenants gazed shoreward, and saw a man gesticulating toward the sea to the north, as if pointing to an advancing vessel.

"Jump ashore, Micio," said the captain of the galley, "and run to the northern point and see what you make of the stranger."

Micio did as he was ordered, and in the course of a few minutes returned to say that there were two merchant-galleys whose course showed that they were making for Miletus. They were heavily laden, and were therefore a likely prize.

"Give the call for the other galleys!" said Spartaco; and soon a trumpet-call, clear and high, rang out along the rocks and creeks of the island.

A few orders, and the *Milvus* had been pushed out of the creek, and, followed by two other galleys which had been hiding in neighbouring inlets, was on her way toward the merchant-ships. With their long oars rising and falling in regular beats, the pirate galleys looked like great sinister sea-monsters skimming over the bright blue waves. The oars as they struck the waters churned them into foam; the sun shone brightly and turned the tossing water into jewels which flashed as they fell; the wind sang, carrying on it the salt smell of the sea. The pirates, however, saw little of the beauty of sea and sky, sun and wind; like birds of prey, they had eyes only for their victims, and, urged by the sinewy arms of the rascals on the oar-banks, the three galleys quickly approached the merchantmen.

At the first sight of the black craft racing toward them

the traders had increased their speed, had stretched another sail, and incited their rowers to greater efforts. But the vessels were too heavily laden, and the chief merchant, a fat, pursy man, wrung his hands as he saw how swiftly the pirates were lessening the interval between the boats.

On the poop with the chief merchant was a spare young man, a Roman by his dress, with aristocratic features and bold, confident bearing. He was dressed in a white woollen tunic, with sleeves which reached to the wrists, where they were cut into a deep fringe. The garment was slackly girdled. The fringed tunic and the loose girdle were thought to be signs of effeminacy in those days. On his feet were shoes of scarlet leather. As the young man saw the pirate galleys coming nearer and nearer he laughed at the merchant's woeful cries.

"It is no use your lamenting," he said with a sneer. "If you had waited for the other merchants you might have been able to beat these rascals off. As it is, they outnumber you by three to two."

"But I wished to get the market before the others," whined the greedy old merchant. "What a loss it is! These rogues will make me pay heavily for my ransom. Oh that I had waited!"

The foppish young man turned away with a yawn. Two servants stood near, and he ordered one to ask his physician to come to him; the other he told to bring his toga, and to bid the rest of his servants to come upon the poop. Then he leaned idly against the side of the vessel and looked at the rushing onset of the first galley.

The merchant, seeing escape was hopeless, had ordered

his slaves to cease rowing, and his sailors were reefing the sails. Soon the merchant-galleys lost their way and sat motionless upon the water. Spartaco raced his galley to within a hundred yards; then, at a word, his men ceased rowing and the galley glided just within speaking distance.

"What ship is that?" came the question.

"The *Golden Fleece*, of Rhodes," was the reply, "owned by Vinius the Lydian."

"If Vinius the Lydian is there, let him come aboard," came back the order. "If he is not there, let the ship-master come to me!"

Vinius, the old merchant, thereupon got into a small boat with two of his men, and, taking his money and jewels with him, was rowed to the pirate galley. Meanwhile the young aristocrat, surrounded by his servants, sat with Cinna, his friend and physician, and, taking out a scroll from the breast-fold of his toga, began discussing its contents, as if the visit of some three hundred pirates, who thought nothing of sinking galleys and the people aboard them, was an everyday occurrence.

In a little while a boat put off from each of the pirate ships, crammed with men. They boarded the big merchant-ship, and then, after quickly going through the cargo to note its value, turned their attention to the passengers on the poop.

It was Spartaco's quick eye who singled out the young Roman gentleman in the centre of his retinue. As he went along the gangway to the poop he growled to Micio behind him:

"Here's some sprig from Athens or Rome who will pay for keeping for a while."

Gaining the poop, the pirates went toward the group. The servants closed about their master, at which movement Spartaco laughed.

"Out of the way, spaniels!" he said. "I want your lord's money, not his life."

"What is it, Phormio?" came the drawling voice of the young Roman.

The slaves made way for the pirates, who walked up to the young exquisite. The latter, wrapped in his toga with its deep purple band, looked up with a slight air of annoyance at being disturbed.

"Who are you?" asked Spartaco harshly, disliking the haughty air of the aristocrat.

The other looked at his questioner with a patronizing smile for an instant. Then, with a gesture, he turned to his friend with the words:

"Tell the fellow, Cinna."

The physician, an elderly man, looked haughtily at the pirate and said:

"This gentleman is Caius Julius Cæsar, of Rome."

"What will he pay for the lives of himself and his people?" came the harsh question.

Cinna shrugged his shoulders and looked at his master, who, however, had returned to his book. Spartaco waited for a reply, but as neither Cæsar nor Cinna appeared to think the question concerned him, and did not attempt to break the chilly silence, Spartaco, with an angry malediction, turned to Micio and said: "What are they worth, think you? From the pride of them the treasure of Midas wouldn't be enough."

Micio looked at the crowd of slaves and freedmen as

if estimating their market value, and then muttered advice to his captain.

"I'll double it—twenty talents is what I want," said Spartaco.

Cæsar raised his head, and a look of real anger was in his eyes.

"Twenty talents!" he said icily. "My good fellow, I am afraid neither of you knows your business. Any one who knows me will tell you that I am well worth fifty talents!"

For some moments Spartaco was speechless with surprise. As a rule people were anxious to get off with as low a ransom as their captors would accept, and for a prisoner to put up the price placed upon him was something unheard of. Moreover, Cæsar's valuation (equal to about £12,000 of our money) was a staggering amount. Spartaco hastened to get over his surprise and to accept the offer.

"Have it as you will," he said, with a harsh laugh. "Fifty talents you'll pay ere you see Rome again."

"I will send my people with letters to Rome," replied Cæsar. "You will ship them there at once, and the money shall be in your hands by the kalends of August."

Spartaco scowled; somehow this aristocrat seemed to be giving orders, and his captor had to obey them. The pirate growled assent and departed. In a little while the merchant-galleys were turned and rowed toward the island, where in a small bay they were anchored, and the rich gear and goods were landed to add to the stores of the pirates. Cæsar and the merchant and his people were housed in huts, which formed the village of the pirates, placed in a wide green field just below the high rock which formed the look-out of Spartaco and his band. There they would await the time when their ransoms were received. In a few hours Cæsar had written his letters to friends and kinsmen at Rome, and next morning the smaller merchant-vessel was manned by pirates, the freedmen and slaves of Cæsar, who were to take the letters, went on board, and, the wind being favourable, a course was set for Italy. The same day the pirates in one of their own galleys carried some of the merchant's slaves to Miletus, which was but a few miles away on the mainland. Cæsar also sent letters by these to friends of his in Asia Minor, particularly to Nicomedes, the wealthy King of Bithynia.

Cæsar remained with the pirates, accompanied only by Cinna, his friend and physician, and two body-servants, Milo, his barber, and Cotta, his cook. A hut was reserved for himself and Cinna, and every morning he bathed in a pool on the seashore, and on his return Milo shaved him and trimmed his nails, and then crimped and curled his hair with tongs. Then he partook of his spare breakfast of pulse and bread, which had been prepared by Cotta, after which he would walk with Cinna, discussing some point of law, or the subject for a speech or poem. At the time of his capture Cæsar had been travelling to Rhodes to study oratory under Molo, a famous orator who lived there. Cæsar was at this time only twenty-three years of age, and had the ambition of becoming a senator. He had no inkling yet of the genius which he possessed for military leadership.

About midday he would take another spare meal—for Cæsar, even as a young man, had the habit, so rare in his days, of eating and drinking little; after which, in the hottest time of the day, he would take his siesta, sleeping in his hut. At two o'clock he would take exercise by running, leaping, and throwing big stones, and at three he would bathe again, after which he rested and Cinna would read to him. His last meal would be taken at four o'clock, after which he would sit conversing or reading with Cinna, or declaiming a speech which he had thought out and noted down during the day. Soon after dark he would retire to his couch.

The pirates, observing his manner of life, used to laugh and jest among themselves about him, calling him "the dandy," "the man-woman," or "the lady." They kept strict watch upon him, but this was because of his value, not that they feared he might try to escape. As the days went on they began to have a feeling of contempt for one whose amusements, interests, and manner of life were wholly different from theirs. They found pleasure in rough and brutal sports, or games of chance, at which they quarrelled and fought, sometimes to the death, while this stranger passed his day in bathing, talking, reading, and exercising his limbs. So fearful was he of his precious health, indeed, that he kept a physician continually about him. Such a creature as this Caius Julius Cæsar, this aristocrat, was only half a man!

When, therefore, one night, into their midst, as they sat roaring out songs over their cups, the physician entered, and, going boldly up to Spartaco, said that Cæsar had sent him to tell them to keep silent, as he was about to sleep, looks of stupefied wonder gave way quickly to great guffaws of laughter at the insolence of the 'man-woman.'

"And why should we keep quiet?" growled Spartaco.

"That little white man of yours would do well with a little hardship, and a night's sleeplessness will do him good. Tell him I shall make all the noise I wish."

"You are foolish, my friend," replied Cinna. "You wish to get the ransom for my friend and master, I suppose?" The pirate assented. "My friend is a man of delicate health; sleep and a quiet life are necessary to him. If he were to die here you would get no ransom, for the money is to be lodged with the Roman governor at Miletus, and will only be given to you when Cæsar goes there in person."

Spartaco scowled; the logic of this stranger was unanswerable. "Tell your man-woman that I will keep my boys quiet," he said.

Afterward, whenever the pirates forgot their promise and were noisy at night, Cæsar sent and ordered them to keep silent, and they instantly subsided, though with muttered curses. After the first few days Cæsar spoke to several of them, getting them to talk of their exploits and leading them to reveal their true natures, in which craftiness, greed, and savagery mingled. Spartaco and Micio he particularly chose to talk to, and while he showed his contempt for their trade and their manners, and never let them forget the social gulf which lay between them, he entered into many of their games and diversions, got them to run and jump and throw balls with him, and to walk with him about the island.

The pirates could not understand him. He was frank in his manner, he laughed and jested with them, and when he chose to be so was excellent company. But they felt vaguely that he was not so soft a person as they had deemed him to be. He gave them orders as if he were their prince and they were merely his bodyguard. They resented this manner, but he was so fearless and his bearing was so lordly that they had to obey, willy-nilly. They felt that under his suavity and condescension of manner there was a determination that nothing could break.

Once Spartaco and Micio and others with them were speaking of the cities they had taken, of the slaves they held in their strongholds in Cilicia, and of the many tributes they received from maritime cities and rich merchants as blackmail, so that they should not attack those cities or capture the vessels of the merchants.

"If there was any wit in your muddy minds," said Cæsar, "one or other of you would use your powers to still greater ends."

"As how?" asked Spartaco.

"You would make yourself master of all the pirate bands within the waters of the Middle Sea, you would confederate many maritime States under your power, and—who knows?—if you had brains enough to bend the quarrels of Rome and Italy to your own ends, you could take the place of Rome herself, who hates the sea, and be master over all the lands and oceans of the world."

He was half laughing as he spoke, in spite of the strange glow in his eyes, and they knew not whether he was speaking in jest or in earnest.

"But I fear you are men of too barbarous a taste to aim so high," he went on. "Tell me, is it true, as men say, that you reverence not even the temples of the gods?"

"We care a straw for nothing," said Spartaco savagely,

incensed at the open contempt which this lord expressed for his captors, who usually experienced deference and fear in their prisoners. "And I think I would as soon slit your throat as have your money, my fine gentleman."

Cæsar laughed easily and ignored the other's anger. "If you did that, doubt not that you would rue it in a little while. What would my poor corpse benefit you? Think how you would curse yourself for a fool when you were told that fifty talents—three hundred thousand denarii—were waiting for you at Miletus, and all that you could offer for them was my poor clay! I thought you were men of business!"

"Aye, aye!" said some of the others, laughing at his mockery of their chief. "Spartaco will spare you for your money's sake, but your tongue is too free."

"Free, my friends!" said Cæsar, his eyes flashing and scorn curling his lips. "I am used to speaking my mind freely even in the Forum at Rome, before men whose shoe-latchets you are not fit to touch. Think you I should bridle my tongue for any one of your dirty knives?"

Most of the men laughed awkwardly; to take a man's life was nothing to these rough sea-robbers, but against their wills they were cowed by the utter fearlessness and pride of this Roman lord. Some found a zest in his insolence, and at any rate none of them would permit his life to be taken, unless, of course, his rich ransom never came to their hands.

Cæsar rose from the log on which he sat and, folding his toga about him, prepared to go to his own hut.

"What insolence!" he said jestingly. "Barbarians as you are, not to appreciate a gentleman's jests! Do you not know that a lord's slaves laugh or cry with him to save their backs from the whip? Not only do you threaten me with death, but you resent my jokes. For such insolence not one of you deserves less than the death of a common rogue, and, mark me, when I am free I will see to it that you all get your deserts on the cross!"

This sally excited the men to much laughter. The daring of the thought tickled their sense of the humorous. To think that this man, so much in their power, should threaten to crucify them like any other poor robber whom Roman justice thrust upon a cross along a roadside! After all, the lord could make a good jest!

Cæsar's fearlessness among these cut-throats was a matter of wonder even to Cinna, his physician, who tried to dissuade him from trusting himself among them.

"My friend," Cæsar replied, "have no fear for me. These men value me too much to injure me. They are sorry rogues, indeed, but at least they enjoy the edge of my tongue."

One day Cæsar went to a party of the pirates as they sat after their evening meal and told them he would recite an oration which he had composed. It was a revised version of the final portion of the speech which he had given in the Forum when he had impeached Antonius Hybrida for corrupt government in Macedonia. With all solemnity, while the men gaped at him in wonder, he told them that this speech had always dissatisfied him, and, more than any of his other orations, had convinced him that a few sessions with the great orator Molo at Rhodes—whither he had been proceeding when their rascalities had seized his person—were necessary to perfect him in the art of rhetoric.

Then for some time he exerted all his gifts of eloquence upon the group of wretches before him. With every addition of fine phrasing, noble gesture, and telling intonation, he strove to make them realize the force of the arguments by which he sought to prove how utterly evil and injurious to the State had been the actions of the governor in taking bribes from suitors and from merchants and in robbing travellers of their goods. But all his efforts were in vain: the pirates were not impressed in the least, and even laughed at him, and half-way through his oration many turned aside and began to play dice, or a game with small bones, called *mora*.

When he ended Cæsar looked sourly at them as they lolled in their places. Some joked about the gestures he had made; Spartaco said it seemed a lot to say about a man who had taken a few goods and trifling sums of gold; while another ruffian, supposed to be a very comic fellow, began to create roars of laughter in one corner by imitating Cæsar's motions and looks while he talked.

"Dolts and barbarians!" cried Cæsar. "It is like throwing pearls to swine or giving gold to asses to lay before you the riches of oratory such as I possess!"

"You learned men seem to do little else but talk," growled Syrus. "As for us seamen, we may be rough men, but we do much more than we talk about. Give me a man who does things, not one who mouths about what other men have done!"

"Dunce!" said Cæsar, with a scornful smile. "I suppose you will never learn that words can sway men much more than your brutal deeds with knife and javelin.

Oh, I shall take the greatest pleasure in hanging you all when I am free again!"

Saying which, he walked away with great dignity, flinging his toga about him with a lordly gesture.

The pirates laughed as he left them.

"What a fool the man is!" said Spartaco scoffingly. "He is all words. Never hath he told us of anything he himself hath done."

"I told him as much," said Syrus. "I doubt not he would turn sick to see a man killed. To talk of crucifying us!"

On other occasions Cæsar delivered orations to the pirates, and even recited some of his poems to them. He saw, indeed, that they had no appreciation for anything so strange to their way of life as oratory and poetry; but his masterful and imperious character, which knew no fear of their brutal natures, caused him to impress himself upon them in this way. And so great a mixture of pleasantry and mastery was in his bearing to these men that some began to feel the charm which in later years he exercised so powerfully over his rough soldiers in Spain and Gaul. Micio in particular felt a kind of devotion for this fearless and wonderful stranger, and often went aside to speak to Cæsar, who treated him with the haughty familiarity which a great man might show for a freedman or favourite slave.

Once Micio put to him the question which had been exercising his mind ever since the day on which the pirate leaders had talked about the sacking of temples.

"Do you think, Cæsar," he said, "that the old gods still have power to avenge themselves upon those who insult or injure them? As for me," Micio went on truculently, "I fear them not. Mithras the Bull-God is strong enough for me."

"Why do you ask, then, my friend?" asked Cæsar, with a little smile.

"Oh," was the answer, "some have said that men who have sacked temples have been slain by the gods whose fanes they had destroyed."

"Have you sacked a temple?"

"I have," replied Micio, assuming a look of ferocity designed to impress his listener with a sense of his utter fearlessness of things both human and divine.

Cæsar glanced at the man as he sat in his soiled and ragged tunic, with bare legs and feet thrust into rough leather boots. Micio had a heavy gold chain about his red, hairy neck and bosom, and thick rings in his ears. A kerchief was tied round his unkempt locks, and his face, tanned a deep red by wind and sun, wore the look of mingled craft and brutality which was common to all the pirates.

"Whose temple have you polluted, barbarian?" asked the patrician.

"We sacked the temple of Venus at Samos," was the reply, "slit the throats of the priests and priestesses, and emptied the treasury. Then we sent up the temple in fire and smoke—all that would burn!"

"You destroyed the temple of Venus at Samos!" repeated Cæsar, and his tone had something of the mercilessness of a judge giving sentence, so that Micio was stirred in spite of his air of bravado. "Of a surety the goddess will avenge herself—rest assured that you shall not escape!"

Cæsar rose from his seat and withdrew without another

word. For a little while Micio sat silent, his superstitious mind chilled by the pronouncement of doom as from the lips of an oracle. He recovered himself in a little while and laughed awkwardly.

A few days later, in the early morning, a galley was sighted coming from Miletus. The first man who jumped into the surf when the ship was pulled up the shore was Cæsar's chief freedman, Gallo, who, running up to his master, bowed to him and said:

"*Domine*, the tale of fifty talents is complete. It is in the hands of the lord Valerius Torquatus, the legate at Miletus. Shall I prepare my lord for his immediate departure from here?"

"Tell the pirate, Spartaco, that my ransom waits for him," replied Cæsar in an undisturbed manner, "and then come to me."

Within an hour the three galleys were under way to Miletus, crammed with men. The first contained Cæsar and his friend Cinna, together with the freedman Gallo and the two slaves, Cotta and Milo. All except Cæsar himself showed great joy in at length finding themselves on their way to liberty again. They had been thirty-eight days with the pirates, so hard a task had it been for Gallo and the other slaves of Cæsar to collect the sum of fifty talents. The property both of Cæsar and his wife Cornelia had been confiscated by Sulla, who was then tyrant at Rome; but Cæsar had many rich kinsmen and friends.

Throughout the preparations for departure Cæsar had sat silent on the poop of the galley, gazing upon the line of shore, from which they were now receding, as if trying to fix the appearance of the creeks and the cliffs upon his memory.

Spartaco and his two lieutenants came upon the poop. They were in high glee at the prospect of receiving so large a sum for their captive, but though Spartaco did not anticipate any trick, it had ever been his habit in these cases to make every assurance. He had known of pirates who had been lured to a place at which a ransom was to be paid, only to be fallen upon and overwhelmed by forces in hiding. For this reason he had brought with him all his men, well armed; and the money was to be handed to him on the governor's galley, at a point on the open sea outside the harbour of Miletus.

"You cannot say I have not treated you well, Cæsar," said Spartaco, with a rough laugh. "Fifty talents in a lump do not often come the way of a poor corsair, but I think I and my fellows have treated you like a king."

"I will see that your kind treatment of me does not benefit you if ever you come before the judge at Pergamum," was the smiling reply. "No word from me shall keep you from the cross."

"You will have your jest," said Spartaco, with a laugh. "Look you, if you ever happen to fall into my hands again I promise you I'll raise your ransom—'twill be seventy-five talents next time, for the sharp tongue you give us!"

Syrus and Micio laughed heartily: this was paying the Roman lord back in his own coin.

"There's the legate's galley!" said Spartaco, and cast keen eyes about the sea and away to the white bar of the harbour, against which the sea tossed up its jewelled waters, flashing in the sunlight. But there were only a few fishing-vessels here and there, and no armed galley threw back the sun's rays from its gleaming beak of bronze.

The formality was soon over: Spartaco, with a bodyguard, went aboard the galley of the legate, or governor, and the gold coins were counted out and taken in bags to the little boat bobbing at the side. The governor, a stout old Roman with a rubicund face, stood waiting impatiently while the money was being counted, and when this was finished Spartaco yelled through his hands to Micio on the first pirate galley to put Cæsar and his people in a boat and row them across. This was done with alacrity, and in a little while Cæsar stepped on board the governor's vessel.

Exiled from Rome in this outlandish province as he had been for some years, Valerius, the governor, knew little of affairs in the great city. He had never heard of Cæsar, but had supposed he was one of the old rich senators who had more wealth than wide renown. His surprise was great, therefore, when a young man of about twenty-three came toward him, dressed in a foppish fashion. Valerius welcomed him heartily, however, for his respect was according to the enormous amount of ransom which had been paid. As Cæsar stepped aboard Spartaco leaped into his own boat, and without further delay the beak of the governor's galley was turned shoreward, and the vessel was soon racing toward the meal for which the old governor had been impatiently waiting.

Valerius invited his guest to dine with him when they should reach his villa at Miletus in an hour.

"I thank you," replied Cæsar, "but I shall not dine

to-day. I will ask you to lend me four galleys and all the good fighting men you can command."

Valerius hesitated. "What do you want them for?"

"I will pay you three talents for the loan of them," replied Cæsar, "and you shall have both galleys and men back without much loss."

"If you think to take those pirates——" began Valerius.

"I do not think about it," replied Cæsar in a polite but firm tone. "I am going to take those rascals, every one of them, and string them up like crows along the coast to scare other dirty rascals away."

Valerius had long passed his fighting days: he was all for well-cooked meals and Greek wines now; but he knew a masterful man when he saw one, and without another word he submitted. Who was he to resist the will of this young patrician, with, so far as Valerius knew, powerful friends at Rome, and who, at any rate, was one for whom fifty talents had been paid? He agreed, therefore, to place under Cæsar the command of four galleys and five hundred soldiers, two hundred of whom were tried fighting men of his own guard, the others being native auxiliaries.

"And suppose you succeed in taking those desperate rascals," said Valerius "—but I don't promise that you will find it an easy task—what do you propose to do with them?"

"I will bring them here and ask you to put every one to death," was the reply.

"And do you think that will do me any good?" asked Valerius angrily. "I shall have all my merchants railing at me. As it is, they pay their tribute to this Spartaco and their galleys go free. If you crucify him as big a rogue will come and take his place, and my merchants will have to pay more blackmail."

"I am sorry to threaten these pleasing commercial arrangements," said Cæsar, with a cynical smile. "Then I will save you the trouble of punishing these friends of your merchants, and I will take them to Pergamum."

"Do that, and I shall be well pleased," replied Valerius, his good-humour returning. "Let Junius the prætor have the bother. Besides, he alone has rightly the power of life and death."

After a few more words Cæsar parted from the governor, the latter being glad to see the back of this young man who wished to disturb the comfortable relations existing between the merchants of Miletus and the pirates who patrolled that part of the coast.

Meanwhile the pirates, having returned to the island, were deep in a great carouse to celebrate the rich haul which they had so easily made. Much heady wine was drunk, boastful speeches were made, and song and jest sped the pleasant time. Even the look-out men on the highest point of the rocks had joined in the festivity and no watch was kept upon the sea. When, therefore, with the suddenness of a tempest out of the summer sky men rushed upon them from behind the rocks the half-drunken pirates were able to make but little resistance against what were found to be overwhelming numbers. Those who attempted to fight were cut down; the others were surrounded and ordered to throw down their arms.

"Who commands you?" yelled Spartaco, rocking as he stood, impotent rage in his voice.

From behind a group of soldiers came the tall, slender

figure of Cæsar, smiling, but with a cold glitter in his eyes.

Spartaco started; then he cursed vehemently for a while, and after that was silent. Micio looked gloomily at Cæsar, and then with drunken gravity he turned to Spartaco and shook his head sagely.

"He said he'd crucify us, and—and so he will!" he ejaculated.

Surrounded by the soldiers, who stood with drawn swords ready to cut down any pirate who ventured to break away or to resist, the rascals were pinioned and then were thrust into the bottom of the galleys. Only a few had escaped by flight into the inner part of the island when the surprise had come, and the number taken amounted to about three hundred and fifty. Cæsar also recovered the whole of the fifty talents which had formed his ransom.

When all were aboard Cæsar ordered the pirate galleys to be stove in and sunk in deep water; after which, setting sail before a favourable wind, he speedily made his way to Pergamum, where dwelled the prætor, or governor-general, of the province of Asia Minor.

Arrived there, he found that the prætor was away on circuit with his principal officers, judging causes in various towns. Cæsar saw his captives safely lodged in the prison in the city, though its capacity was strained to accommodate them all, and then, placing over them a guard from among the soldiers of Valerius for additional security, he set out to find Junius, who was somewhere in the east of the province.

After a little search he succeeded in finding the prætor, and having presented himself before him, he related all

NO MERCHANT SHIP COULD COUNT UPON MAKING A JOURNEY IN PEACE

that had occurred. Junius, an austere, crafty-looking person, said little while the tale was being told, but on learning that Cæsar had recovered the fifty talents besides other booty which had been seized and stored by the pirates, his eyes gleamed greedily. When his narrative was ended Cæsar said:

"Now, Junius, I have promised these rogues that they shall be crucified. Will you give me your letters directing your legate at Pergamum to execute them?"

Junius looked sourly at Cæsar, and his shifty eyes glanced up and down this masterful young man who wished to direct the prætor of a province as to what he should do. He knew that the young patrician was a scion of the Julian clan, and that he had powerful and rich friends, though at present he was hiding from possible death at the hands of the dictator, Sulla. All this, however, weighed but little with Junius; the most important thing to his greedy prætorial soul was how to obtain for himself most of the fifty talents and the spoil captured with the pirates. Like most other prætors, he had come to his province resolved to take from it all the riches he could lay his hands upon, and his fingers itched to touch the pirates' treasure.

"The matter must take its proper course," replied Junius. "Such a case must be decided with all due formalities. It must await my return to Pergamum. Meanwhile I will send a messenger with orders to my legate, Minicius, to guard the pirates and their booty with all care."

Cæsar had quickly perceived what had been passing in the mind of Junius, whose face, for all his craftiness, easily betrayed his thoughts to an observant eye. He pretended to fall in with the prætor's opinion and passed the matter off carelessly. He stayed chatting a little while on indifferent topics, so as to make it appear that the business had no real interest for him. When, however, he had taken his leave he instantly ordered his freedman to bring the horses, and without waiting for food he left the place and took the road back to Pergamum.

His decision was already taken. The man who in later years in Gaul was to slaughter thousands of barbarians without mercy took little account of the execution of two or three hundred robbers. He reached Pergamum in the middle of the next day, and after a hurried meal he gave instructions to the soldiers on guard as to what was to be done. That same afternoon most of the robbers were slain in prison: one by one they were ordered to come out into a small enclosure, and as each man turned a certain sharp corner soldiers stabbed them.

Some thirty of the chief pirates were reserved for a more formal death. These included Spartaco, Micio, and Syrus, together with others whom Cæsar had noticed to be men of more forceful character. He had these brought out and told them what he purposed doing.

"You are malefactors," he said sternly; "your lives are forfeit to the State for many crimes of murder, robbery, and violence, and you shall now meet with your due reward. You deserve, indeed, to be crucified and to hang upon the wood until you shall miserably die from hunger and your wounds. But as I have known you and dwelled with you I will grant you this grace:

you shall be crucified, but you will not be hung upon the cross alive."

The men glared at him sullenly. Death was so near to every violent man in those hard days that it had little terror for them. Some cursed him and looked about them as if they would dearly like to make one last fight for life, but the ranks of stern soldiery with wet swords in their hands gave them no hope.

"I little reckoned you were so strong a man of your word," said Micio at length. "You seemed too much the dandy, you were too clean and choice in your manners. Ah, would that I had known! I would have strangled you as you sat smiling at us. But, now, see here, Cæsar," he went on, with a mocking laugh, "I prove your words to be lying words. You said that of a surety Venus would punish me with death for having violated her temple. How now can she punish me?"

"You have not escaped the vengeance of the goddess," said Cæsar sternly. "I am of the Julian clan—of the race that has sprung from the goddess. Through me, then, she works her vengeance upon you!"

When the sun, dipping his golden face in the hyacinthine sea, shone that evening with level beams along the waves and the shore his rays threw thirty long shadows across the fields beyond the strand. The dead bodies of Spartaco and twenty-nine of his comrades hung upon the gaunt, high crosses, their sightless eyes looking at the sinking sun.

Next morning Cæsar took galley, and, resuming his interrupted journey, he went on his way to Rhodes, where, placing himself under the instruction of Apollonius

Molo, the great orator, he perfected himself day by day in the arts of public speaking.

At this time the power of the pirates of the Mediterranean was at its height. No country upon the shores of that sea was safe from their depredations for many miles inland. Ever since history began pirates had ranged the Middle Sea, but for some forty years special circumstances had afforded them the means of increasing their influence. The conquest of Greece by the Romans had thrown thousands of dispossessed and discontented Greeks into the ranks of the sea-robbers; then had come the civil wars in Rome, which had caused the Romans to overlook events passing on the sea; and, finally, the aid given by the pirates to Mithridates, King of Pontus, in his long war with the Roman State had increased their confidence and daring.

Every island in the Ægean was a nest of pirates, and their ships lurked behind numerous wooded headlands and up many a shady creek along the coasts of the mainland, from the Pillars of Hercules to the shores of Syria. Perhaps Cilicia, in Asia Minor, was the birthplace of piracy. Here was a mountainous land, shaggy with almost impenetrable forests, its coast lined with river mouths and creeks. The latter offered numerous points of refuge for the long black galleys, and the hidden fastnesses of the hills gave secure retreats where, when Roman admirals pursued them too closely, the sea-rovers could lie concealed, and where, when their power increased, they hid their captives and their plunder. Crete and Cyprus were also favourite resorts of the corsairs; but as their arrogance increased they came out boldly from their hiding-places and attempted greater things.

They still, indeed, darted forth like spiders from their holes when the watchers warned them of the approaching merchant galley; but they also formed confederacies among themselves, and, joining their forces, they attacked rich towns on the sea coast and possessed themselves of guarded places. The towns had to be ransomed by the merchants who lived in them, who henceforth had to pay tribute or blackmail to the pirates, in consideration of their galleys being allowed to go freely about the sea.

Then, also, prominent citizens or other rich men would join them, either for the adventurous life or for the wealth to be gained from booty. As a result the daring of the pirates grew more and more. The number of their galleys increased, and the richness of their gear was a thing of wonder. Their great sails would be made of red or purple cloth, the beaks and sterns of their galleys would flash back the sunlight from bright bronze, canopies of silk would be stretched along the poops, and the hafts of the great oars would be plated with silver. Thus, instead of creeping out of their hiding-places secretively to do their evil deeds, they now boldly drew attention to themselves, and flaunted their ill-gotten adornments in the broad light of day.

In certain towns they held high revel and kept up a perpetual feast, getting themselves musicians and dancing girls, and corrupting the honest people by lavishing upon them their easy gains and inviting all and sundry to their drunken revels and rich banquets.

Soon it was said that they held sway over four hundred cities about the Middle Sea, that the number of their galleys was more than a thousand, and that their ships were so swift and strong and the crews who manned them were so apt in maritime skill and knowledge of the sea and so keen in fighting that not even Rome, who boasted herself mistress of the world, could now hope to scatter and destroy them.

Far and wide the marks of their evil deeds were spread. On any morning, when the first rays of the sun shone into the lofty atrium of some lovely villa perched amid the green woods overlooking the blue of the Mediterranean, and the family of the rich Roman or Greek was just stirring, there would come a cry of terror, crisping the nerves, chilling the heart, and filling the eyes of gentle women and children with the gleams of horror: "The pirates! The pirates!"

Up from the shore they would swarm from the ships which had crept up in the half-light of the dawn, and, quickly, with hoarse cries, they would rush through the splendid rooms, staining the white marble of the floors with the blood of loyal servants, or of husband, brother, son, or father, and, rushing into the women's apartments, they would seize the ladies and carry them fainting or struggling down to their galleys, to be carried to Delos to the slave-market there to be sold, or to be kept as wives in their hiding-places, or, if they were women of patrician family, to be held until their relations ransomed them.

They extended their depredations far inland and became great highway thieves, infesting the roads about large cities and taking toll of merchants and travellers who passed that way. So daring at times were they that they even penetrated into the cities themselves, and so great was the terror which their name and cruel deeds inspired, and so weak and stupid were the men in authority, that no one dared lift a hand to punish their insolence.

Thus a band of them entered one day the busy streets of Pheræ, and, going up to the forum, where Sextilius, the prætor of the province, sat in his purple robes upon the curule chair awarding justice, they took him thence, with his lictors and servants, and kept him in a galley until his friends ransomed him. Bellinus, prætor of Africa, they also seized, as he rode along the sea-road leading from Calama to Mina, and with his guards held him captive on Mount Aspera, in Taurus, until he was ransomed.

Nothing was sacred to them, and they knew not mercy. Of children they sold thousands into slavery, for pretty boys and girls were much valued as cupbearers and servants in those harsh days. Nor was there any reverence in the minds of the corsairs. Temples which had stood lovely in the rosy light of morning and evening for a hundred years, built by devoted hands and revered by generations of pious men and women, were destroyed ruthlessly, their treasures wrenched away, their priests and priestesses slain or sold.

Especially contemptuous were they of Roman officials whom they captured. Once they overhauled a merchant ship in which was travelling a senator named Claudius. When the pirates, having swarmed aboard, were tumbling the passengers and crew into the boats to send them ashore, the senator, angry at being treated as if he were but one of a crowd, called out: "I am Claudius Claro, Roman senator!" The pirate leader, who stood by, a long, lean rascal with a sneering face, turned at the sound and began to tremble, and looked appealingly at the senator. The other pirates took their cue from this wretch, whose tricks had often amused them, and they began to slap their thighs as if with consternation. Some fell on their knees, apparently struck with terror at the disrespect they had shown him.

"Pardon us! Forgive us!" they cried. "We knew not who you were, noble lord!"

Some brought his cloak and humbly presented it to him, others fetched his walking shoes and offered to put them on. He, deceived by their manner, and being a good-natured man, cried that he forgave them. But they would not desist from their officiousness, and the cruel game continued for some time.

At length the leader, bowing humbly, said: "Do not remember this against us, noble sir. We meant one of your rank and consequence no harm. Now go you in peace!"

He gestured to where one of the men stood smirking at the head of a ladder which he had put over the side of the ship. The senator, thinking that they really meant him to go by that way to a boat waiting to take him to the land, went toward the side of the vessel, but, seeing that the ladder hung over the empty waves, he recoiled.

"Have no fear, noble sir!" mocked the pirate. "That is the way to freedom."

They began to push him toward the side of the ship, and he struggled, crying that they wished to murder him. At a furious exclamation of impatience from the chief, his men seized the wretched senator and thrust him over the side. He fell into the sea, sank, then rose, and breathlessly cried to them to save him, promising them any reward they cared to ask. But none took notice of him; not a cruel face looked over at him, and after clawing at the side of the ship for a little while, crying out all the while, his strength gave way and he sank.

However insolent and arrogant the pirates had been, they had not hitherto dared to interfere greatly with the corn-ships which went to and fro between the Tiber and Egypt, carrying corn from the fertile lands of the Nile to fill the granaries of Rome. Nor did they cut off the traders plying to the City of the Seven Hills. But about the year 78 B.C. they had become so daring as to stop the trade from Rome, and then the senators had to bestir themselves. They determined to root out the pirates from their lairs in Cilicia, and for this purpose they sent the pro-consul Servilius, at the head of a squadron, to destroy them utterly. In three difficult campaigns in the creeks and among the mountains of Cilicia he inflicted great losses upon the pirates, and on returning to Rome he was given a triumph. But the buccaneers were only scotched, not killed.

When, in the year 73, Spartacus the gladiator with his army of runaway slaves and banditti defied the power of the Roman Senate, he bargained with the pirates to help him, and along the coasts of Italy they did many deeds of destruction, while up and down the fields of the peninsula Spartacus defeated general after general sent against him. In the year 71 Spartacus was slain and the pirates disappeared for a year or two.

Then their depredations became more than usually insolent, and the senators took halfhearted measures against them. Their practice was to get a maritime allied state to lend them a fleet, which they put in charge of a general who, having burned a few pirate galleys, captured a town or two, and put some hundreds of robbers to death, would consider he had done enough.

As a matter of fact the Romans hated and feared the sea. They never had been sailors, and to the end of their history they never took to the water. Therefore they never kept up a permanent fleet, and to all intents and purposes they left the waters of the Mediterranean in possession of the wily pirates, who loved ships and the sea. If the sea-robbers had not been suspicious of each other, but had banded themselves under some leader of genius, Rome would have found it a difficult task indeed to destroy them. But the malefactors could not act in concert. Each race of seamen kept roughly to their own part of the Mediterranean, and, like the pariah dogs of Constantinople of a few years ago, any corsair found off his proper ground was roughly dealt with.

The Balearic Islanders ruled throughout the seas about Spain, the south of Gaul, and the coasts of Mauretania, a horde of Dalmatians dominated the Adriatic, the galleys of the Cretans haunted the islands of the Ægean, and from the coasts of Asia Minor to the mouths of the Nile the Pamphylians and Cilicians swept the seas in their fleets, which sometimes numbered a hundred vessels.

Toward the year 67 B.C. the forays of the pirates were becoming too bold even for the sea-hating Romans to suffer them in patience any longer. The pirates, indeed, attacked them in their most vulnerable part—their food-supply. A bad season came, when the cornfields of Italy were struck by blight and disease. At the same time the expected corn-ships from Egypt did not arrive, and soon it was learned that the bags of golden grain which had been meant for the mouths of Rome's hungry multitudes were being sold by the impudent pirates in the markets of Asia Minor and the Greek islands. Instantly there was a cry for vengeance; riots took place in Rome, and the senators found themselves compelled to undertake the destruction of the power that was striking at the very life of the State.

Fortunately Rome possessed in Pompey the general of genius who, unlike the many generals who had only tinkered at the task hitherto, would perform his duty thoroughly and make a satisfactory end of the campaign. So confident were the people of his powers that they gave him complete control of the Mediterranean for five years; he was to have under his command a fleet of five hundred galleys—larger than any that had hitherto been collected—and his authority was to overrule the powers of the consuls and prætors at the head of each of the Roman provinces whose shores were washed by the waters of the Middle Sea.

Pompey had twenty-four lieutenants under him, together with a hundred and twenty thousand foot-soldiers and five thousand cavalry. Assembling his lieutenants at Brundisium, where the main part of the great fleet was assembled, he laid his plans before them. Each man was to have a certain number of galleys under him, and with these he was to keep within a certain area of the Mediterranean, and in that area he was to search out and destroy every pirate stronghold and to burn or scuttle every galley belonging to the corsairs. There were thirteen of these divisions, which as the pirates soon found, were like the meshes of a great net, for if they fled out of one, they fell into another.

First of all Pompey cleared the seas near home, and day after day his galleys policed the Tuscan Sea, and the neighbouring coast of Africa, Sardinia, Corsica, and Sicily. Under the burning sun and over the blue waters of the Mediterranean the galleys clove their way, thrust along by the brawny arms of slaves and aided by sails. Many a pirate strove to fly, and many in their swift galleys did escape for the time; but others were overhauled. Then there would be swift manœuvring of Roman galley and pirate craft, the one to get in position for a ramming blow which should smash in the side of the pirate or splinter the oars along one side and throw the rowers into confusion. Meanwhile the corsairs, with every trick of their deep sea knowledge, dodged and turned, backed and advanced, to avoid the grim bronzed beak of the Roman ship, the deck of which was crowded with armed legionaries, from whose bronze headpieces and shields the sun flashed back dazzlingly.

At the same time the Romans shot great stones at the pirate by means of catapults, hoping to smash a hole through the bottom of the boat; or they threw lighted tow and rags, or Greek fire, in the hope of setting their enemy's galley in flames. A feint, a swift return which cracked the muscles of the sweating slaves in the rowing banks, and then the beak of the Roman galley would crash into the pirate; the oars flew in splinters, and the pirate rowers would be thrown pell-mell upon each other, with broken limbs or heads. Grappling irons leapt from the sides of the Roman ship, and then the two galleys closed in the death struggle. Over the sides of the rocking galleys on the sunlit sea the fierce Romans poured, to be met by as fierce a defence on the part of the pirates. This way and that the crowds of men would sway, while the wounded sank down and groaned, the dead dropped, and the decks ran with blood, which poured into the sea.

Discipline and hard living won the day at last. The rascally pirates, beaten to the poop, saw before them only the fierce faces and short, sharp swords of the legionaries, and behind them the sea. They cried for quarter, threw down their weapons, and were quickly thrust into irons or bound with cords ; and thus, made captives on their own boat, on which so often they had been victors and had done so many cruel deeds to defenceless prisoners, they would soon be driving over the sea toward their prison.

Or the Roman generals, creeping up in the dawn, would land their men in a woody nook and surround some stronghold or town of the pirates, and soon fire and sword would drive the robbers out like hornets from a burning nest. If they took to the sea in their galleys the Roman ships waiting for them drove them on shore again, until at last they were compelled to surrender.

So indefatigable, so unresting were Pompey's efforts that it was not long before he inspired the pirates with a salutary terror of his relentless pursuit, his hard blows, and the fighting qualities of his soldiers. Moreover, he treated his captives in a humane manner, which the pirates did not expect and certainly did not deserve. This induced many of the evildoers to submit themselves without fighting, and from these Pompey learned the whereabouts of secret strongholds and harbours, which enabled him to extirpate the pirates who had fled to them. Pompey's officers, it is to be feared, were not so humane as he was, and used to hang or drown many of the robbers who fell into their hands.

For forty days this wholesale 'round up' of pirates was continued, with such energy that it was seen that the western waters were practically cleared of the rovers. There was still a great number in the eastern seas, however, who included the most bloodthirsty and the fiercest of the corsairs. These had sent their families, treasures, and slaves into secret fastnesses among the glens and precipices of Mount Taurus, while they themselves, manning their galleys, resolved to join in one last attempt to crush their conqueror.

The fight took place at Coracesium, in Cilicia, and was stubbornly waged. Here again the pirates had no chance against the disciplined soldiers of the Republic, who, hardened by many a rough campaign, and skilled in all the devices of war craft, were more than a match for the vicious assailants of undefended towns and lonely villas and the murderers of defenceless women and priests. Seeing that their efforts were vain, the pirates ran their galleys ashore and fled to the fort which they had built. But when from their walls they saw the grim determination with which the legionaries prepared to besiege them their courage forsook them and they capitulated, offering to give up all the strongholds and maritime towns which they had fortified, together with a vast treasure and many hundreds of captives.

With the surrender of the pirates at Coracesium the campaign was over. Instead of taking five years, it had taken only three months. Pompey had indeed earned the 'pirate laurel' which many generals had pretended to gain. The number of prisoners was estimated at twenty thousand. Besides smaller galleys, Pompey seized ninety great war ships with beaks of brass, together with heaps of treasure which were found in the secret retreats of the pirates.

Contrary to the custom of many Roman generals, including Cæsar in his wars in Spain and Gaul, Pompey did not sell his captives and thus make an enormous fortune for himself. Nor did he condemn them to death. A few, the revolting cruelty of whose crimes had singled them out as of a particularly brutal character, were executed, but the rest he transferred to various inland districts throughout the Roman Empire, believing that by weaning these fierce seamen from their native element and settling them on lands which he apportioned to them on the outskirts of towns he would create in them a taste for the benefits of civil life. Some he placed in the almost deserted cities of Cilicia, others he transported to Soli, a town which had been desolated by Tigranes, King of Armenia. A large number he shipped to Greece and sent to the district of Dyma, in Achaia, which, though fertile, was but sparsely populated. Others were sent to Calabria, in Italy, where on lands belonging to the State they settled down and began a new life.

It would seem that these measures turned out to be successful in the main. It is too much to suppose that some of the pirates, finding life on shore pall upon them, did not make their way to where the blue sea lay before them, twinkling in the sunlight and beckoning with its "innumerable smiles." But not for some generations was the Mediterranean again afflicted by the scourge of piratical squadrons harrying, robbing, and murdering up and down the seaways and along the peaceful country-side.

And never again while Rome was truly mistress of the world did the pirate fleets grow to such strength as that which they possessed when Pompey crushed them.

Later, however, we shall find, as related in subsequent pages of this book, how, in the sixteenth century, there arose bands of famous pirates, splendid seamen but brutal conquerors, who defied the authority of a greater power than Rome had ever been, and whose names caused a chill of terror to sweep through the hearts of all of their generation whose business lay on or near the waters of the Middle Sea.

"PARDON US! FORGIVE US!" THEY CRIED

II: The Pirates of the Saxon Shore

I

IT was a misty morning in the spring of the year 366. Dawn had hardly broken, and toward the east the sun was trying to pierce through the swirling eddies of fog that lay over the sea and the shore. Two youths, both of about seventeen years of age, were walking along a trackway not far from the beach. Both were dressed alike, with the woollen tunic and gartered breeches of the ordinary British-Roman provincial. Each wore leathern sandals, and round his tunic a strap supporting a knife and a pouch, while each carried a stout staff. But a glance at their faces showed that they were not both of the same race. One had a round face, freckled, with grey eyes; his short hair was reddish. He was a Briton, though he liked sometimes to call himself a Roman when Italian boys were with him. The other had a long face, with a square jaw; his eyes were blue, and his hair, which was long and tied by a fillet, was as yellow as ripened corn. He was what every one called a Saxon, but the home of his forbears had been among the flat and reedy lands of Frisia, or Friesland, as we know it now.

Both lads were sturdy and well built, but they differed in manner. Elphin, the British boy, had a merry, mischievous eye; he was ever ready for a laugh or a jest, and was friendly disposed to all. Yet there was a look of determination in his glance and his jaw was strong.

Wulf, the Saxon, or Vulpius, as Elphin and every one else called him, in the Latin which all affected to know, had a reserved, fierce look in his sharp eyes, as if he were always on the look-out to resent snubs or insults. Yet when he looked at Elphin a kind light came into his eyes.

"The mist is getting thicker," said Wulf. "I guess we are not far from the river."

Elphin peered into the coiling mists around him and said: "We must go carefully here. We don't want to drown ourselves in the marsh. Hallo, it's clearing in front."

All about was the keen smell of the sea, filling the lads with an exuberance as of wine. They pushed on through the thinning mists, into which the great shafts of sunlight seemed to pierce like wide, golden spear-heads, and in a little while they stood in some bushes looking down on the shallow valley below them, two miles wide, over which the sea foamed at high tide. The sun was gaining the mastery more and more over the mist-fiends which were fleeing from his warmth and light, but the marsh was still obscured in places. Suddenly Elphin bent and pointed. "Look!" he said in an excited whisper. "It's a pirate boat! They've pushed up the creek in the mist and are landing!"

Both boys peered down, straining their eyes. Just below them, in a creek which ran into the marsh, was one of the low, open galleys, captured specimens of which they had often seen towed into the harbour of Richborough, or Rutupiæ, where they lived, two miles away on the other side of the marsh. But never had they seen one filled with its crew of fierce, bearded pirates, as now they saw them, each with a thick leather helmet on his head of long fair hair, a spear in one hand, and a round buckler on his left arm. The mist drew aside like a curtain for a moment, showing the pirates descending from their long ship and walking off into the clouds to the right of the boys, and then the curtain whirled back again, hiding them from view.

Elphin quickly took a resolution.

"The captain of the guard must know of this," he said in a quick whisper. "These fellows may be the first of a big band. We'll run on to Rutupiæ at once and tell Julian."

Without waiting for a reply, Elphin turned to the left and began to make his way toward the causeway which led across the marshes for about two miles to the hill on which Richborough, or Rutupiæ was perched. The boys had been visiting Elphin's uncle, a farmer in a village near by. This would be the last day for some weeks that Elphin would be ashore. Next day he was to join a galley for the first time. His vessel was keeping watch in the Channel for the longboats of the pirates, who, now that spring was come again, would be beating down from the sandy winding creeks of their misty land to harry and murder and rob on the fair shores of Britain and Gaul.

He glanced at his friend as he ran, and wondered for a moment at the strange look on the face of Wulf. He seemed to be dazed, and looked before him with straining eyes as if he saw something of terror and wonder which was invisible to others. Next moment Elphin almost tripped over the root of a tree, and in saving himself forgot his surprise. They reached the stone causeway, which, though covered with seaweed, they could cross almost dryfoot while the tide was out. They ran all the way. Both were silent; Elphin led the way, while Wulf followed not far behind. When they breasted the headland on which the thick-walled little town stood Wulf began to flag, but Elphin did not notice this, so impatient was he to rush into the guardroom at the main gate and tell his story to Julian, the big chief of the centurions whom he so much admired.

By this time the mists had almost gone and the sun was shining. As they reached the first of the hovels of the slaves and labourers, which were built along narrow, muddy little lanes just outside the main land-gate, Elphin noticed that Wulf was some distance behind him and seemed to be running slowly. He waited till his friend came nearer and then shouted:

"What ails you, Vulpius? A stone in your sandal?"

"No," replied Wulf, and looked up quickly and then turned his eyes away. "I have a pain in my side."

"That's through eating too much oatmeal at breakfast, or running too soon after it," said Elphin with a laugh. "You wait here till I come back. I shan't be long."

"Very well," said Wulf, and seemed suddenly to have a gloomy air about him. As he set off running again Elphin wondered why Wulf seemed so slow: he was by far the stronger of the two, and could usually beat Elphin in a race.

He had no time for further thought, for here was the land-gate, with the legionaries lounging at the guardhouse door, chatting to the Britons who brought in vegetables on their little horses. Elphin ran through the narrow main street, with its road worn into two big ruts and many holes, dodged the crowd of market women, gossiping soldiers' wives, and shopkeepers just stirring to open their booths, until he reached the other end of the road, where the water-gate gave a view over the wide sea, on which the white mists still floated here and there in wisps like wool. Most of the men on guard knew him, and soon he was telling Julian, the big, good-natured Gaul, what he had seen.

"By Jupiter!" said Julian, when he heard; "but the dogs don't lack for courage. To land in the creek almost under our noses—and at low tide!"

"But the water is deep enough in the creek at all tides to float out their boat," replied Elphin.

"All the more reason why we should send across and try to cut them off before they get back!" said Julian. "Here, Lucius, Prasutigos, Cadno, take a company of men with you—you say they counted some fifty men?" he broke off, turning to Elphin.

"As many as I could count, and judging from the size of the boat," replied Elphin.

"—— and get across the south marsh quickly. A Saxon boat landed its men in the creek to the east of it half an hour ago. Cut them off if you can, the saucy dogs! If more have come up, send to me and hold them in play till I come, or a war-galley takes them in the rear."

Lucius and his two lieutenants saluted and quickly filed out. Then Julian called in one of his sea captains and told him to take a war-galley with all speed and try to cut off the pirates in the creek.

"My lad," he said, turning to Elphin when the captain had gone, "you have shown good judgment in what you have done." Elphin glowed with pleasure.

"You go under Caros in the *Seamew* to-morrow, don't you?"

"Yes, sir," replied Elphin.

"I will speak to him about you. Go on as you have begun—keep your eyes and ears open, and your mind always on your work, and in a few years you will command a war-galley of your own."

Elphin saluted in his turn, thanked the chief centurion, who pinched his ear with good-natured gravity, and then started off to find Wulf.

But Wulf was nowhere to be found. He sought for him up and down the rising ground just before the slaves' quarters or *cannabæ*, outside the land-gate, and then went home, a mile along the rising ground further west, where his father, Cadgan, a time-expired veteran, lived on his allotment. But neither his father nor his mother had seen aught of Wulf that day. Coming back again into the castrum, he asked many who knew his half-brother, but none had seen him. It was not Wulf's habit to go off by himself in this way, and Elphin was distressed, thinking some evil had happened to his chum.

In one of the narrow little lanes of the fort, lined by the huts of the legionaries who formed the garrison at that time—the Second Augusta—he met Cadno, one of the lieutenants who had gone to intercept the pirates that morning.

"Did you have good fortune this morning, Optio?" he asked respectfully.

Cadno, a lean, long Scot, with grey eyes and wrinkled face, wind-bitten and war-seamed from long years of fighting, first as a freebooter and enemy of Rome beyond the Great Wall to the north, and then as loyal soldier of the Emperor, turned his keen looks on the lad. "Nay," he said, "they were not stopping long enough. A friend gave them the word—or they smelt us coming, or they were never there."

"I do not lie!" cried Elphin hotly. "I saw them there and so did Wulf."

"Humpf-hum!" replied Cadno. "I doubt not *your* word," he went on, emphasizing the word 'your.' He walked away some paces and then came back. "I hear ye are looking for your friend Wulf. It's the second centurion Lucius will be glad to see him when you find him."

With these mysterious words Cadno went off. Elphin stood thunderstruck. Did they really suspect Wulf of having warned the pirates? But he would answer for Wulf's loyalty as his own. Was not Wulf his blood-brother? Had they not taken the old oath of eternal loyalty to each other by drinking one another's blood? Certainly Wulf was a Saxon, by race he was one of these pirates, but—but—

As he walked slowly homeward Elphin sadly reflected, and things became a little plainer to him. Seven years before, when Elphin was a little fellow of ten, playing before his home in a narrow lane of the castrum, he had seen his father coming toward him, leading a strange little boy by the hand—a boy with a mass of blond curls, with sullen, fierce blue eyes, dressed in woollen tunic, breeches, and sea-boots, like one of the pirates whom Elphin had seen once or twice hanging on a cross by the wayside outside the fort. His father had had a strange tale to tell.

Just as had happened that very morning, so, all those years ago, Cadgan, who was second centurion at the time, had been sent to look for marauding pirates down about the marsh lands north of Dubris (Dover). Creeping along the creek heads, they had come across two boats drawn up under a guard of thirty men, the main body of pirates having stolen off inland on a swift raid, burning and plundering. Warily Cadgan had disposed his forces, and then, in a sudden onset, had completely surrounded the boat-guard and slain them to a man. On boarding one of the galleys a knife had been thrown at him from the open cabin door, and if it had not been for his quickness it would probably have pierced one of his eyes. Looking for his assailant he had found it was this little boy, who on being seized showed the fiercest spirit, tearing, biting, and scratching ere he could be bound. Some were for knocking the young viper on the head, but the lad's spirit had caught Cadgan's fancy, and he had determined to keep him, if all went well.

Then, having dressed some of his men in the garb of the dead pirates, he had placed them so as to deceive the main body of Saxons when they should return. In a storm of wind and rain, indeed, they were soon heard coming back, the booty from two or three villas slung over their backs, but they had no captives with them, as they were moving quickly. They got almost to the boats before they suspected something was wrong, but then it was too late. A shrill trumpet sounded and the Roman soldiers, closing in upon them, overwhelmed and slew them all, not one escaping. Ever since then Wulf, the little Saxon boy, whose father had been slain with the others, had been kept by Cadgan, and after a time had seemed to forget his hatred of his captors and had become almost like a brother to Elphin.

But there had always been something of a hard reserve in Wulf's manner when in the presence of strangers, as if he felt that he was looked upon as of the breed of the pirates whom men slaughtered or crucified, though, indeed, the Roman soldiers often suffered severely from death and wounds at the hands of the hardy and brave sea-rovers. Though Wulf and Elphin were great friends, Wulf never spoke of what he wished to become when he was a man. Elphin's father had said he should join one of the legions, as other Saxons and Angles had already done, though they generally were sent to serve in other provinces than Britain, to prevent treachery. Wulf never said whether he was willing or unwilling to do this, though once he told Elphin that he would prefer to go with him in the fleet—the sea was his place.

Now, as Elphin walked home he thought that, maybe, Wulf had felt that he could not allow those pirates to be cut off and massacred without trying to warn them. After all, they were his own kin, and spoke the Saxon tongue, which he still remembered, though he had rarely spoken it during these seven years. And therefore, maybe, he had run back along the causeway and warned the pirates guarding the boats and had gone off with them. Elphin was depressed to think that he had lost Wulf in this way, and wondered whether he could ever get to know whether this was really what had happened.

Next day, however, and for many days thereafter, Elphin had too much to think about in his new work to spare time even to wonder about Wulf. For now he was an apprentice pilot in the famous fleet which was under command of the great Admiral Nectarides, Count of the Saxon Shore, who guarded the coast of Britain from the

Wash right round to the Isle of Wight, against the forays and raids of the fierce sea-robbers, mingled bands of Saxons, Franks, Angles, Frisians, and Danes who were known to the Romans under the general title of Saxons, that being the name of the tribe who were the leading spirits in this confederacy of plunder.

It was a hundred years before, about the year 260, that the long low ships of the sea-rovers had first begun to be seen and feared on the coasts of Britain and Gaul along the Narrow Seas. For a few years little notice was taken of them in either province, but then the complaints of townsmen in the coast towns, or of well-to-do dwellers in country villas, and of villagers became so bitter that the Roman governors had to do something to cope with the nuisance. In Britain, therefore, a special leader was appointed, generally a man who had been a good seaman, and to his charge was committed the defence of the shores which the pirates infested. Certain coast forts were built and strongly defended, and in these were stationed the troops whose duty it was to assist in beating off the pirate bands. A fleet of galleys was built, to act as scouts upon the lonely seas, and to bring word swiftly back when they sighted the squadron of pirate craft making toward Britain or Gaul over the leaping waves. When news came that the pirates were coming the trumpet rang out, and the seamen and fighting men manned the war-galleys, which put out to sea to meet the pirate fleet and to do battle with it. On shore horsemen were sent swiftly from one fort or station to another to put the legionary officers on guard, so that if by chance the pirates broke through the Roman fleet or defeated it they would still be prevented from landing or they would suffer greatly in doing so. But of course it was not always such 'plain sailing' as this. Two or three pirate boats would creep along in the dark or in a sea mist, under the very noses of the chilled and wearied men in a patrol boat, and, having landed, they would make a swift raid inland, leaving a black wake behind them of burning villages and ruined homes and crops. Working in a circle, they would return to their boats and speedily put to sea again, laden with treasure and captives—likely looking young men and women, boys and girls, who would command good prices in the slave-markets of Paris or Bajoccas (Bayeux), Dol or Ronnenberg—and race back to the misty flats of Frisia or to the Holy Island, a nest of pirates, which we now know as Heligoland. Sometimes a keen Roman general, served by clever scouts, would come up with them before they could reach their boats, and there would be a fierce fight, with many dead on both sides. If the Roman-British conquered they made no prisoners, but the Saxon pirates were noted for their ferocity, and would capture their opponents if they could in order that they might torture or sacrifice them to their gods later.

II

THE life which Elphin led now was a hard one, but its rough living was compensated for by the excitement which every day brought forth. The *Seamew* was one of a fleet of scout galleys which policed the seas from the South Foreland to the Wash. They had to be constantly on the watch for any strange sail or rowing craft—for oars were used as much as sails in those days. They knew generally the ways over the sea by which the pirates came, and they cruised as near to this as wind and weather permitted them. As a rule the pirates waited for an east or a northeast wind; then, issuing from the numberless creeks which lined the coasts from the Elbe to the Zuyder Zee, and gathering in numbers as they went, they would sail swiftly along the coast of Frisia and Batavia (Holland and Belgium). Finally they would separate at the Rhine mouth, some making south to harry the shores of Gaul, others darting across to try their luck along the rich shores of Britain, whose country-side was studded with wealthy towns and the fine villas of Romanized British nobles, officials, and merchants.

Elphin found for the first few days that life in a galley was a misery. There were but narrow quarters on board, and the boat was continually jogging up and down over the restless waves. But use soon made the continuous movement bearable, and pride in his profession made him soon love even the hardships. He belonged to the great Guild of Gubernatori, or Pilots, which proudly bore the title, by special licence, of the Emperor Severus, who had bestowed his august name upon it a hundred and fifty-eight years before in recognition of services rendered by its pilots to his fleet. Elphin's chief was the *archigubernator*, or chief pilot, Caros, a wise old man of the sea and a rich one. It was reckoned to be great good fortune for Elphin to be chosen by so great a pilot, who, though strict, was one of the most good-natured of men. Elphin's work was to learn from his own observation and the teaching of his master every detail of seacraft—the set and race of tides and currents, the amount of water at any state of the tide in any of the innumerable creeks and river mouths along the east coast within the limits of his beat. Then, too, he had to learn all about sea-fogs, how to handle a boat when the blinding mists came down suddenly, how to sail his galley so as to get every inch of speed out of her, while husbanding the strength of her crew for any fighting that might have to be done.

The crew was composed of rowers and fighters. The former were slaves and freedmen, while the latter were soldiers or marines specially enrolled in naval legions. Sometimes the soldiers had to help in the rowing. They were under the command of an officer called a naval prefect, who shared the control of the galley with the chief pilot.

The life was very pleasant in the warm, bright weather, when the sea was quiet, the wind blew gently, and the sun was not too hot. But in the young spring days, to be watchful and alert in the fierce east wind, driving its arrows of hail or bitter rain or scud from the tops of the ice-cold waves, the galley tossing meanwhile like a cork on the choppy seas, required every ounce of manhood. When sharp storms came, and the send of the sea almost wrenched the oars from the hands of the rowers, it required seamanship of the highest order to keep the light galley from being pooped or swamped, and often it was necessary to put up a scrap of sail and run for some sheltering creek. Yet it was just in times of storm that greater watchfulness was necessary, for it was then that the hardy pirates often chose to dare the piling seas in their shallow boats, hoping to find that the more timid Roman-British sailors had forsaken their guard. Often, of course, the Saxons paid the toll of a whole score of galleys and hundreds of lives to the fiercer spirits of the storm, and their daring would end in death, their bodies and upturned boats being washed to the shore; but as often they found that the coast was clear, and, making one with the storming rain, the crash of thunder, and the vivid lightning, they would run their cranky craft upon a muddy creek-bank and add the terror of fire and bloodshed to the tempest beating upon a peaceful country-side.

Many were the fights in which Elphin assisted, for sometimes he was transferred to a war-galley forming one of a fleet sent out to intercept a pirate squadron. A pilot was not generally required to fight, but when the battle raged hotly and the pirates pressed on board his galley he had to snatch up buckler and sword or pilum and help thrust the rascals out again. So thrilled was Elphin by these encounters that often he wished he was a soldier: to match himself with some sturdy rogue of a pirate, to fence awhile with him, and then by a deft thrust to send him into the scuppers or overboard seemed to be more a man's work than to con the wind and the tides and when he saw a pirate craft to scuttle away to give warning. But all his life now was tinged with excitement and adventure; always there was the thrilling smell of the salt sea, the beat of the brave wind upon his face, and the living heave of the waves under his feet, and any shift of the breeze might bring the enemy over the rim of tossing waves on the far horizon.

Elphin began to be known to his chiefs as a young man on whom the utmost reliance could be placed, and his immediate commander, the admiral or *prefectus classis* of the Rutupian fleet, by name Varro Rufinus, gave him several special duties as marks of his favour. He sent him on various errands to commanders along the coast, stationed at other sea-fortresses, to Branodunum (Brancaster), by the Wash, to Prætorium, a place somewhere on the Yorkshire coast whose name alone remains to us, to Segedunum, on the Wall, where now Wallsend stands, and even to the capital or metropolis of the whole island, Ebòracum, or York, itself.

His visits to this bustling city were always experiences of great interest and delight. Sometimes he went by land, at other times by sea, for in those days the river on which the great city stood was like a wide creek thrusting up into the land. The stone wharves were piled with goods, busy with porters, slaves, naval men, and officers, each with his distinguishing garb to show to which fleet he belonged; the wide stream was crowded with vessels tied up to the wharves or anchored in mid-channel—broad, shallow merchantmen, made to take cargoes of corn, iron, or pottery, which, when on a voyage, hugged the shores as much as possible, and the narrow war-galleys of the fleet, deep and lank, made for speed and to dare the stormy seas.

The streets and ways of York were busier then than they generally are now. Its cobbled surface was noisy with the sound of wagons, carts and riders, its pavements were filled with the bustle of soldiery, and citizens going about their daily work. Slave women or their mistresses fingered the goods in the booths of the shopkeepers, or in the forum, or market-place, chaffered with the country dealers or the pedlars and traders, while merchants stood about in groups, buying and selling corn, minerals, or slaves. The courts in the basilica were filled with crowds of the curious and the friends of the litigants, whose pleaders or lawyers stood arguing their cases, while the judge, seated on a chair raised above them all, listened in the grave manner of judges both then and now.

York was the heart of the civil and military government of Britain ; to and from its massive gates were continually coming and going companies of soldiers in red and bronze, over the broad straight roads stretching north and west and south, singing their songs to pass the time as they tramped along—men of all builds, fair Goths and Germans, dark Moors, swarthy Spaniards, men, indeed, recruited from all the many races who owned the sway of the mistress of the world.

Elphin often walked down the Whitehall of York, and marvelled at the big houses in which many scores of clerks sat writing in the government offices of the Vicar, or Governor General, or of the Count of the Britains, or Military Governor. The men whom he saw writing in room after room kept the records of pay and service of every soldier in the big legions on the Great Wall or stationed in the garrison towns, and of the sailors and marines who manned the fleet.

All the men and women, boys and girls, going about their business or pleasure day after day up and down the streets of York thought, no doubt, that the life of their city would go on in just the same way for many generations. But on the desolate moors far away beyond the Wall, and among the dark forests and the windy, reedy plains along the Baltic and the Northern Seas there were hordes of fierce-eyed men whose hands were to scatter or slay all these people, and whose ruthless savagery was to put to fire and ruin this fair city and many such, so that we, living in later years, hardly know the places where once they stood, noisy with all their teeming life.

The Pirates of the Saxon Shore

When, after some six years of diligent work, Elphin had gained the confidence of his chief, he was one day given the sole charge of a scout galley. He was very proud of this, for he was yet very young as pilots went. On the same day he was told that he was to take one of the spies in the Government service to a place on the coast far north above the Great Wall, which stretched from the Northern Sea to the Solway Firth.

Elphin thought that this errand had been given him as a test, and he resolved to carry through his work with every care. It was a lovely morning in June when, the spy having come aboard, Elphin ordered the ropes to be cast off which bound him to the wharf in the port below the massive walls of Rutupiæ (where now, instead of the foaming green waves, the flat green land lies), and, having piloted the galley deftly through the fairway among the sands that already were slowly silting up the port, he set his prow for the north.

The spy was a dark, cunning-looking man, a half-breed Pict, by name Anko. Elphin knew that he was one of the body of Britons and half-breeds called the Corps of Arcani, or Spies, who for many years now had been stationed beyond the Great Wall, in a camp called the Castra Exploratorum, or Camp of Scouts. It was their duty to go among the turbulent tribes of Picts, Scots, and Britons in the moors and mountains beyond the Limes (or Boundary Wall) and, by appearing to be friendly, to learn any news of contemplated attacks upon the garrison on the Wall. Elphin had frequently heard legionaries who had served on the Wall say that these men gave notice of the movements of Roman troops to the barbarians in return for bribes.

Somehow Elphin did not like the look of this spy, who, however, kept very much to himself and spoke rarely. The voyage north would take four or five days, according to the wind and weather, and every night, it if was calm, they would anchor in shore to cook their evening meal and to sleep. Elphin's crew numbered seventy rowers, all armed, and all sturdy fellows who would acquit themselves well should a pirate craft happen to attack them.

Nothing untoward happened until they reached the neighbourhood of the coast beyond the Wall, when Anko became anxious that they should not miss a certain creek at which he desired to land, to see whether men whom he wished to meet were there. They reached the place on a hot afternoon, and, having run the galley into the creek and set the spy ashore, Elphin himself got on land to stretch his legs.

The place was as lonely as if it had just been created. Bushes came thick and close almost down to the water's edge, and behind these trees hid the flat landscape from sight. Away in the distance blue hills shimmered in the summer haze. Under the sun the water oozed and lolloped lazily upon the mud, and the creek held the heat like a furnace. Flies buzzed in the sultry air, and nothing else seemed to stir.

Leaving the boat under the command of his assistant, Elphin pushed through the bushes for a few yards, hoping to get into a cleared space whence he could see something of the country. He went on until he realized that he had gone farther than he had intended, when, on turning to retrace his steps, he heard cries break out at a little distance before him. He went in the direction of the sounds, and peering through the leaves he saw two men fighting. By their dress both appeared to be pirates, and they hacked and thrust at each other savagely among the bushes. Evidently they were making for the creek. In order not to be cut off, and to warn his own men, lest the pagans were in great force, Elphin fled back to the galley, and, reaching it, was about to jump aboard and order the rowers to push off, when a fierce struggling in the bushes behind him drew his attention. He turned to see the two Saxons in desperate combat on the water's edge. One was a big, tall man, bareheaded, with an evil-looking face—more evil-looking from the fact that he had shaved off all the hair of his head, and had deep blue signs tattooed on cheeks and forehead; moreover his teeth had been filed so that each ended in a point, and they were all coloured blue. His opponent was a slighter and a younger man, whose fair hair rolled from beneath the edge of his bronze headpiece. The younger man's strength was evidently no match for his enemy's, for the fierce blows of the bald man's axe on the other's bronze buckler made him stagger.

Then, suddenly, something familiar in the gesture of the younger man made Elphin start and cry out. It was Wulf. Even as he recognized his friend the bald-headed man with a mighty blow beat his antagonist down. The young man's foot slipped on the oozing edge of the creek, and the next instant the axe would have sunk into his skull. But at that moment a pilum, or short spear, leaped from Elphin's hand. Swift and hard and true it sped and thrust deep into the throat of the big pirate, from whose hands the battle axe fell with a thud. Next moment the man himself crashed to the earth in a death struggle. Elphin, running to the side of Wulf, helped him to his feet. For a moment a fierce look swept into the eyes of the Saxon; then, recognizing his friend, he grasped his hand and said breathlessly:

"You, Elphin! The gods guided your spear! But how came you here?"

"I have landed one of our scouts and wait his return."

"Who is he? Anko?"

Elphin nodded, surprised that the other should know of the spy.

Wulf gave a fierce, short laugh.

"Get back to your boat, man, and let me come with you," he said, "for my life is worth little if any of Hudda's men come to see if he hath slain me—as he would but for you."

"But Anko——" began Elphin.

"Anko will do traitor's work no more," was the reply. "Thank me for that. I sank this axe in his brain just before Hudda Bluetooth attacked me."

Without waiting to hear more Elphin ordered his men aboard, and, pushing off, they were soon upon the open sea.

"Set her nose south, my friend," said Wulf, as he sat beside Elphin on the poop. "Put oars and sails to work if you would do service to Britain, and make all speed to Segedunum to warn your general on the Wall. Though 'twill be too late, for already the Painted Men [1] and the Saxon men who keep no faith are gathering in their thousands."

"But peace hath been bought with the barbarians," replied Elphin. "Fullofaudes, the Dux ——"

"Fullofaudes bought peace with my uncle, Thorlak the

[1] Picts.

Wise, and with Fergus the Pict," replied Wulf, "and I was with them when the treasure was paid. But Thorlak is fighting in Gaul, winning land at Bajoccas, and the broken and outlawed men of no birth who were with Hudda, whom your spear happily slew, designed to break the troth and to win the Wall. Anko led the plot, which I refused to join, and I called Hudda niddering. But the plot will succeed, for there is treachery in your own fortresses and your scouts play you false."

Meanwhile the galley was making swift way to the mouth of the Tyne, urged by both oars and sail. Late in the evening they reached the first fortress on the Wall, whose ramparts were lapped by the waters of the river. There Elphin, who was known to the port admiral, Ulpius Vibius, told all that Wulf had revealed to him; and even while the Roman officer was listening to him with scornful unbelief upon his face a cavalryman leaped from his horse in the yard outside, having raced from Cilurnum, where the wall bridged the stream of the Tyne, to say that the Painted Men and the Saxons had lured the Duke of the Britons to an ambush and had slain him; that the defence of the Wall had weakened or the guards had been traitors, and that in the dawn light that morning the barbarians had pierced the bridge at Cilurnum, and after a desperate battle had defeated the garrison and were now spreading farther along the south of the Wall, pillaging the villas of the officers, conquering everywhere in spite of desperate rallies by the legionaries, and murdering or scattering the dwellers in the busy villages that had clustered beside the gates of the strong camps or forts upon the Wall.

Vibius immediately wrote out a concise dispatch

relating these matters, and entrusted it to Elphin, bidding him make all haste to the sea fortresses to warn their naval prefects on the way, and to carry his dispatch to Nectarides at Rutupiæ, as it was evident that the Picts and Scots were acting in conspiracy with the Saxon pirates, and that a big attack might be expected quickly from the sea.

"Britain is in desperate straits," said Vibius. "I will instantly send troopers to York with the news, asking for reinforcements. Do you make all speed. To save the province, Nectarides must smash the pirates ere they land to join forces with the barbarians."

III

WIND and tide served Elphin well in that swift flight southward. One after the other he warned the prefects at the forts upon the coast, and quickly the commanders there prepared for any orders that should come to them.

Elphin asked Wulf what he proposed to do, since he could hardly land at Rutupiæ except as a prisoner. For some time Wulf had been silent as if depressed by thought.

"I will join the legions," he replied. "I have made up my mind now."

"Why did you leave us?" asked Elphin. "Did you not run back to warn the Saxons that day, seven years ago?"

"I did," was the reply. "It suddenly came to me that these pirates, as you called them, were kin o' mine, and I could not bear to think that I should stand by and let them be destroyed. I ran back and told them they had been discovered; I told them who I was—Wulf Froddoson. They had heard of my father and they took me with them. But when I got to Frisia I found my elder brothers wanted me not, and looked upon me as half a Roman and an interloper. I joined myself to my uncle Thorlak, who is a good man, but he is too old now to go sea-faring any more. Those seven years at Rutupiæ have spoiled me. I think my brothers must be right: I am half Roman, and I will leave my kindred and henceforth fight for the Emperor somewhere away from Britain."

When Elphin swung his boat beside the wharf at Othona (which we now know as Bradwell, in Essex) and leaped ashore, he found gloomy and scared faces all about him. Onc or two marines leaned against a wall nursing wounds, and others stood over some half a dozen galleys which seemed to have been in a fight, for they were splintered and battered and their boards were stained with blood.

"Why, what's happened?" asked Elphin as an optio of marines—the Fortensians—who guarded the wharf hurried forward.

"Much that is bad," was the reply. "The Count has been slain in a sea fight with the pirates and we have been soundly beaten."

"Great Jove!" cried Elphin; "this is evil tidings indeed. I bear a dispatch to the Count from the tribune at Segedunum. The barbarians and the pirates have joined forces and have broken through the Wall. Besides, the Duke Fullofaudes has been slain in an ambush."

"Disaster on disaster!" said the optio, and his weather-bitten face went sallow. "Then it behoves us to bring up all our forces, for 'twill be hard to make head against the savages both from the north and from the sea."

Elphin told his news to the prefect in command at Othona, from whom he heard fuller details of the disastrous defeat of the British fleet. It seems that Nectarides had received news of an intended descent of pirates who were gathering their squadrons off the mouth of the Rhine. Either the spy who brought the news was a traitor or he had been woefully misinformed. He said that the vessels of the pirates numbered but a few, and Nectarides conceived the idea of attacking and destroying their fleet before it became larger. He set out, therefore, with some fifty galleys, and found the pirates in small numbers, as it appeared, but on delivering his attack other hostile galleys loomed up over the misty seas from the shelter of the land where they had been hiding. Desperate had been the battle on the rocking galleys; to and fro the fight had waged; pirate galley and Roman ship had been sunk or had drifted away with their loads of dead and wounded, until, finding their commander slain and their forces outnumbered, the Roman-British captains had withdrawn as best they could, losing many of their men as prisoners, and with more dead and wounded than sound men in their crews. The Saxons had not pursued them far, as they themselves were somewhat crippled; "but," ended Portumnus, the prefect, "we may expect them at any shift of wind now, and hard will it be, with half my fellows slain or wounded, to beat the fierce dogs off, elated as they will be with their victory."

The same tale met Elphin when he reached Rutupiæ, but with the added grief of hearing that this or that friend had met his death in the battle. He handed his dispatch to the legate of Nectarides, and having reported himself to his immediate chief, Varro Rufinus, who had escaped alive, though wounded, he was appointed to be captain or naval prefect of a galley, which meant that henceforth he would fight his galley, and pilot it only in case of need.

A few days after entering the port, Wulf bade good-bye to Elphin. He had taken the oath of fidelity to Cæsar, and was going with a draft of reserves to Treves, there to join a cohort fighting under the Emperor himself against the Germans. Wulf had the air of a man who had lost all he cared for in the world. He was without kin, without race. Elphin tried to cheer him up, and told him how happy many time-expired veterans became when, their fighting days over, they took the land given to them by a grateful Emperor and settled down with a native wife in some land secure in the *pax Romana*. But at the end the young men shook hands sadly, for neither felt that they would see each other in life again. And such was the case, for Wulf fell in battle two years later, fighting against the Alemanni in the forest of Elphental.

And now, one and all, the garrison of Rutupiæ, both military and marine, threw themselves energetically into the work of preparing for the attack which they knew would soon be made upon their coasts.

The summer of 367 was a terrible time in Britain. To the men of the Caint (Kent) in peaceful days the Wall and its garrison had seemed as remote as if it were in the moon, and they had got to think that somehow it was no concern of theirs, being so far off; but now they realized what its strength had meant for themselves and all Britain. Ill-news travelled apace in those days, and one disaster tripped over another's heels. Soon it was told that no part of the garrison was holding the Wall; that the barbarians had swept right along its line of strong forts and populous villages, cutting off or starving out the brave men who strove to hold a fort here and there. All they could put to the flames the barbarians had fired; they had battered down gateways and posterns, smashed the catapults and the guardrooms on the wall, looted the villas of officers, and slain all whom they had found in hiding.

Of the twelve or fifteen thousand soldiers who had garrisoned the Wall, perhaps half had been slain or had been wounded and found death later; of the others, some had fled to the garrisons in the country south of the Wall, while many had disbanded, and had sought refuge with their wives and children in remote places, throwing off all signs of having once been Roman soldiers. Some, it was even said, had become bandits themselves.

Men sighed and shook their heads as they heard all this news. Was there no general there who had brains and energy enough to grasp the situation, gather the scattered soldiers, and beat back the insolent barbarians? A little later and the news ran like fire through the land that the Saxon pirates were landing in large numbers, were joining their fellows who had helped the Picts to break down the Wall, and together they were spreading terror, ruin, and death through all the northern districts. Troopers, covered with the foam from their panting horses, dashed into Rutupiæ, Regulbium, Lemanis, and Dubris with orders from the chief general in the north to send all available forces to aid in beating back the pagans, who were threatening York itself. The soldiers trooped away up the dusty roads, and men waited to hear that at length the tide of barbarism which was blackening the fair face of the rich province was rolled back in blood and disaster; but no such news came.

Then there came hurrying from Gaul a general—Severus, Master-General of Cavalry—sent, with his suite of richly dressed officers, by the Emperor Valentinian, then with his court at Treves, on the Rhine. Severus landed at Rutupiæ, and after a day or two rode out with his staff toward Londinium and the north. Men said that now things would come right again. But they did not. Still the barbarians, Picts, Scots, and Attacotti, and the Saxon pirates, swarmed over the northern districts, and now threatened even the middle parts, the rich and densely populated valleys of what we call the Trent, the Mersey, and the rivers of the Fenlands. Presently Jovinus, another general, hurried over from Gaul, with some more richly dressed and haughty officers in his suite, and Severus, a little tarnished both in his own dress and that of his suite, came back and recrossed the strait. The Rutupians, watching from their massive walls with keen eyes on the tumbling seas, saw before the year was out the galley of still a third general, with a squadron of transports carrying troops in aid of the distressed province. The guard at the gate and the commander of the garrison received this general also with the dignity and ceremony which befitted his high rank; but they did not expect that he would be more successful than the others.

The winter came, snow and frost forcing both barbarians and Roman legionaries to keep to their quarters. But when the season relaxed a little down flooded the invaders into the midlands, and men heard with terror that the strong towns of York and Deva (Chester) had been deserted by their legions and sacked and fired by the barbarians, many poor citizens, their wives and children, finding death by the sword, by fire, or by the bitter weather, that was not more cruel than the savage Pict or Saxon.

Then came the news to Rutupiæ that a fourth general was being sent, of whom the Western Empire spoke well. But the British Romans were not impressed by rumour now. In a little while, up from a fleet of transports, rank upon rank in an endless stream, came fair-haired, great-limbed Batavians and Herulians, and then the veteran legions named the Jovians and the Victors. As they swung with a clatter of arms through the water-gate, the soldiers and citizens standing to watch them confessed that these seemed to show that at length the Emperor of the West was determined to win back the province of Britain. These men who now tramped through the street were of the pick of his troops—men who had gained the Emperor his victories against the fierce Alemanni themselves.

Then came the general, Theodosius, a short, wiry, dark man, with eyes that pierced through him to whom he spoke; a man sparing of his words, stern, almost harsh of aspect, with a jaw of granite, and every movement of his head and limbs speaking of resolution and energy.

So far south had the ravaging bands of pagans come that they had already sacked and burned villages and villas near London, and had even passed the river and reached the wide road running from Rutupiæ to Durobrivæ, which we now call Rochester. But a few days sufficed for Theodosius to make ready his troops, and then, marching out he rounded up several bands of the marauders, slew them or crucified them, and released the captives they had roped together. A part of their spoil he distributed among his soldiers, and gained a name for fair dealing by restoring what was left to the rightful owners.

Where the straight Roman road, now known as the Old Kent Road, crossed the marshy lands of what we now call Newington, a deputation from the citizens of Londinium met Theodosius and his legions and welcomed him to their city. They told him how, from their thick, high walls, they had seen the murderous bands of Picts and Scots and pirates pass by, laden with spoil, and with lines of wretched captives, and how the barbarians had shaken their fists at the citizens, and shouted threats that they would come back and burn and sack Londinium itself.

Theodosius stayed in the city for some time, sending out scouts and spies into the midlands, learning the strength and whereabouts of the enemy, and what had become of the disbanded soldiers who had left their camps and stations in the north and were now vagrants. He issued a proclamation recalling the fugitives to their duty, promising that they would not be punished for their flight if they returned ; and very soon, as the news of the strong forces which he had brought was bruited through the land, public confidence was restored, the soldiers by twos and threes came back to their banners, and the citizens began to hope that the flood of barbarism would soon be swept from the land.

The task of Theodosius was a heavy one, and only to be accomplished by energy and patience. It took him two years. The scattered Picts and pirates avoided set battles with his forces, so that he was reduced to fighting them by means of strong columns sent out in various directions, whose task it was to hunt down, ambush, and destroy the cruel raiders. So unwearied was he, and so well did he infuse his sleepless spirit into his lieutenants and soldiery, that by the end of the summer of 368 he had cleared the country south of the Humber and the Dee; and next year, by the same relentless methods, he freed the northern lands right up to the Wall, which he repaired and re-garrisoned.

Not only did he give the barbarians no rest on land, but he chased and harried them upon the sea. He got new galleys from Gaul, and, having built up a large fleet, he reorganized the crews and sent them against the Saxon pirates on their own element.

During these two years Elphin had seen much service, and being cautious yet bold he had added to the reputation which he possessed of being a good leader as well as an excellent seaman. Many had been the fights in which he had taken part, both on sea and on land, and not always had he been on the victorious side. The garrisons at the sea forts had been weakened in the efforts to check the raids inland, and the odds were often heavily against the defenders, with whom, nevertheless, it was a point of honour to attack the foe under any conditions. Thus there was often for the brave men of the sea-forts the bitter experience of defeat and of wounds suffered in vain.

Gradually, however, as Theodosius triumphed inland, he could afford to give more men to make up the sea garrisons, and then the tables began to be turned. The fleets of the British did not wait to be attacked, but under the bold and skilful leadership of Elphin's chief, Varro Rufinus, they sallied out and sought the Saxon galleys, and now it was the pirates who often had to flee, their ships wrecked or sunk, and most of their men slain or wounded or taken prisoners.

Soon the British felt that they had the mastery of their enemy: they were the equal of the pirates in seamanship and in daring, and they had the quality of dash and fire which was lacking in the colder nature of the Saxons. Toward the end of the summer of 369 hardly a pirate craft would show its nose upon the waters of the Northern Sea or in the narrows of the Channel.

One day, at this time, Elphin was called to the quarters of Varro, and found him in conversation with a Saxon who had been captured in a recent sea fight. He had formerly been a legionary, but had 'turned wild' again, as the soldiers said, and gone back to his people.

"Prefect," said Varro, "this man tells me that the pirates have a secret place in an island off the coast of Frisia, where they take their prisoners and their booty, before shipping them to the mainland. He says they will not be in great force there, and that three galleys' crews could destroy them. Take six galleys and this man to guide you. If he proves false, kill him; if he proves true, he shall get his former rank as optio in the Fortensians."

Thus it was that, four days later, Elphin found himself in the misty dawn of an autumn morning creeping up in his galley to the bare, sandy island where, as Warsa, the deserter, who sat beside him, declared, there was a certainty of rich spoils and an unsuspecting foe. Five other galleys loomed in the mist behind him, each crammed with men. At length the boats grounded at a point which Warsa said no one from the pirate huts ever visited. Noiselessly the men disembarked, and, under the leadership of Elphin, crept off among the hummocky dunes towards the village of the Saxons. The galleys were left under a strong guard.

Elphin believed that Warsa, the deserter, was not deceiving him, but to make sure of him he had him chained by the waist to two of his strongest marines, who had orders to dispatch the spy should Elphin so command them. As they went forward they could hear the sound of hammering upon wood, as if the pirates, early astir, were building a hut or store booth. At length Warsa gave a sign that they should stop, and he explained that a few steps round a group of dunes before them would bring them in sight of the huts. Elphin immediately detached four of his best scouts and sent them forward to reconnoitre.

In a little while they came back and said that the pirates, to the number of perhaps a hundred, were gathered about four new galleys which it seemed they were about to launch, and that there were some two hundred prisoners—British provincials by their dress, men, women, and children—who were being brought out from several big huts.

After speaking with Warsa, Elphin ordered his lieutenant,

SHE HAD RUN TO THE OLD SAXON CHIEF WITH HER WRISTS
CLOSE TOGETHER

a Spaniard named Herro, to take fifty men and go round behind the huts, so as to take the enemy in the rear. When these had stolen off, Elphin crept forward himself with two centurions to a spot whence, from behind a hummock of sand, he could see the open space before the huts of the pirates. Here he found that the prisoners had been ranged in regular lines of twenty or thirty along the beach, and he wondered for what reason this was done. The four new galleys were big vessels, and were standing one behind the other on a wooden slip-way, down which they would rush when the wedges were knocked out and they were given an initial push.

Some of the pirates—great hairy men, with cruel faces—stood with axes in hand guarding the captives, while others were ranged about the boats as if to help in pushing them down. On the shore before the captives, whose wan faces spoke of hunger, ill-treatment and terror, stood one old Saxon, of a great stature, lavishly adorned with gold chains about his neck and upon his shirt of mail, while his huge arms were encircled by rings of the same material. On his head he wore a steel cap, from beneath which his white hair hung to his shoulders. With this man were three others, and one of them seemed to be counting the prisoners. Elphin counted with him, and saw that every tenth person was drawn out and thrust aside. Thus there was soon a little group of some twenty persons, men, women, and children, who looked at each other and at their captors in a kind of wondering terror, fearful of what this choosing should mean.

They were not long kept in doubt. The white-haired chief took off his steel headpiece and, raising his face to the dull heavens, uttered something in a loud tone, as if it were a prayer. Then he turned to the misty sea, the waves of which lapped at his feet, and spoke to it, gesturing with his hand to the captives as he did so. When he had done, the other pirates raised a great shout as if in assent to what had been said, and each made a curious gesture with his two hands.

Then several men went forward to the captives and pinioned the arms of the twenty who had been set apart. When this had been done they took hold of them and pushed them forward to the slipway, on reaching which they forced them to lie down across the wood and began to bind them there. The unhappy victims now realized that the heavy boats were to be made to run over their prostrate bodies, which would be maimed and crushed in sacrifice to the god of the sea, on whose element the vessels were so soon to float. At this some broke loose from their captors and rushed with cries of terror this way and that, but the pirates pursued and caught them ; others ran and tried to hide among the other prisoners, but were dragged forth again ; while many from the main body of the captives threw themselves at the feet of the Saxons praying that their dear ones who were among the chosen should not be slain. Here a woman clung to her husband, sweetheart, or son, while there a mother tried to push herself in the place of a beloved daughter—all amid terrible cries of grief and tears of despair.

There was a woman who by her dress seemed to Elphin to have lately been the mistress of some rich villa. She had been chosen for sacrifice, and when others wailed and strove to fly she only turned to some one in the main body of prisoners and gave one look. Instantly a young girl sprang forth, threw her arms passionately about her mother's neck, and seemed for a moment about to burst into a madness of grief. But next instant she had run to the old Saxon chief with her wrists close together in token of her wish to take the place of her mother. But he thrust her aside: her mother had been chosen by chance, as the rite required, and no substitute could be taken. Nevertheless a victim was acceptable if she were willing, and the old pirate gestured to her to take her place beside her mother, who had already been forced to lie along the slipway. Elphin's heart was moved to see how the young girl, having bowed in gratitude to the Saxon chief, walked quickly as if with gladness, and with a beautiful smile upon her face, toward her mother. He saw the lips of the two women meet in a long kiss; then the young girl, laying her arm across her mother as if to protect her, sank down quietly as if now she were quite content.

Suddenly there came the cry of a seabird—"twee wee wee"—from behind the huts, and Elphin knew that Herro and his men were ready. He whispered swift instructions to the centurions by his side, who crept quickly and silently away. In the meantime the Saxons were catching the rest of the fleeing victims and forcing them to the slipway. But now the last were being dragged to the place, which soon would be a welter of crushed bodies, when suddenly into the thick of the men who were just getting ready to knock away the wedges under the boats there buzzed a cloud of javelins. At the same moment, with a roar which terrified and confused the pirates, a body of men seemed to rush upon them from all sides. Taken utterly unawares and surrounded by superior numbers, the pirates, though they fought desperately, were overwhelmed, and soon not one remained alive.

The British prisoners, their terror changed to gladness, surrounded their rescuers, kissing their hands and garments and shedding tears of gratitude. Some, overcome with the sudden change from fear of death to a sense of safety, clung to their dear ones in a passion of speechless thankfulness and joy.

Elphin went to the young girl who had laid herself down beside her mother, and found her bending over the body of the elder woman, who was in a swoon.

"She will soon be herself again," said Elphin cheerily, bending beside her. The young girl lifted grey eyes welling with tears, and clutched and pressed his hand.

"Oh," she said, "how can I ever tell you how grateful I am for your brave help!"

"The gods have led us!" replied Elphin. "I fear you have suffered much. But see, your mother moves. She will soon be herself again."

"Nay, sir," said the young girl; "she will never be as of old, I fear. She has seen my father and my two brothers slain by the barbarians while trying to defend us, and we prayed them in vain to kill us also."

The girl hid her face in her hands in a sudden storm of grief.

"But now you must take cheer," said Elphin. "Life and liberty are now before you, and soon we shall be at home again."

Elphin now directed food to be shared among the prisoners, a strong guard was set all round the little island, and the bodies of the dead pirates were taken away. For two days Elphin stayed on the island, collecting the large amount of booty stored there, and resting the poor captives. Then, after having burnt down the huts of the robbers, he sailed away with a fair wind, and made the port of Rutupiæ on the next day. With the four new galleys and three other galleys belonging to the pirates, his little fleet made quite a sensation as it came to anchor beside the sea-wall. Elphin received an enthusiastic welcome from the guard, whose jolly faces laughed down at him from the water-gate, and the words of appreciation which his chief spoke to him made his heart swell with pride.

Thus was Roman law and order restored throughout Britain. Cities and fortresses which had been injured or destroyed were repaired; the great frontier Wall in the north was renewed, and soon its forts resounded with the tramp of soldiers, the call of guards, the ring of the mason's trowel, and the cries of children at play. All through the Northlands the noise of life began again as men had known it before. But many were those who never came back to dig up the hoard of hard-earned riches which, at the rumour of the invading barbarians, they had buried in some secret place. The bones of the owners whitened on the wold, or the fugitives, still living, suffered slavery in some distant land. The coins remained to be turned up by the plough or the spade of later generations, to be squabbled over by workmen, or ticketed and laid away in our museums, where we may see them to this day.

For five years the fear of the fighters of Rome was fresh in the minds of the Saxon pirates, but at the end of that time they issued once more from their windy islands and marshy hamlets, and swept down in a great raid, only to be thrust back and beaten again by the vigilant and doughty fighters of the British fleet. At that time Elphin fought with even greater force than before in his strong right arm, for he fought to defend a wife and a little baby boy. He had become the esteemed friend of Lucilla the young girl, and her mother, Julia, whom he had rescued from the pirates, and when they had reached their villa home on the pleasant shores by Port Lemanis (Lympne) he had often gone to see them. Three years after their rescue from the pirates, when the mother was on her death-bed, she gave the two young people the greatest wish of their lives by joining their hands in betrothal.

For many years Elphin kept his post as a trusted and successful leader under his chief, the Count of the Saxon Shore. Then he retired and lived with his wife at Lemanis. There he died in 403, at the ripe age of sixty, a few years after his wife Lucilla. Though the times were full of gloom, happily he did not foresee the universal ruin that within the next generation was to come upon the Roman Empire, in whose downfall his own beloved country was to share.

As the years went by after the opening of the fifth century the raids of the pirates became fiercer and fiercer and the power of Rome declined more and more until at length, when every Roman soldier in the provinces had been called back to Italy to save the Eternal City from the Gothic hordes and Britain seemed to lie defenceless at the mercy of her foes, the Saxon pirates began to look upon the country as a desirable one in which to settle. Continually after this did they come in war bands, and where they could they seized land in the remoter parts of the north-east coast, between the Humber and the Forth, and settled down there with captured wives or with kinswomen from their homelands. Thus began those long years of blood-stained history called the Conquest of Britain by the English, during which pirate Saxon and half civilized Briton began between them the creation of the British race as we know it to-day.

III: The Pirate who Founded a Dukedom

THERE was a man named Ragnvald. He was a great jarl and a renowned fighter. When Harald Fairhair swore that he would be the greatest chief in Norway, Ragnvald aided him with counsel and men to conquer the land. Harald and Ragnvald were great friends thereafter, and waged many battles against the little chiefs and jarls who would not bend to Harald. As a reward for his help, Harald gave to his friend Ragnvald the two jarldoms which are called the North and South Mæris, which made Ragnvald a great man. Ragnvald married Ragnhild, or Hilda, as men called her, daughter of Hrolf Nefja. She was a fair, courteous, and gifted woman, who could speak well and also compose poetry.

As is well known, Harald made a vow that he would not cut his hair until he had made himself king of all Norway, and so long and thick did his hair and beard become that men called him Harald the Hairy. When, after the battle of Hafrsfjord, in 872, Harald had broken all his enemies and was acknowledged to be King, he went to stay with Ragnvald at his great house at Mæri, and there it was that he first washed and trimmed his hair and beard, in which, indeed, Ragnvald helped him with comb and scissors. Thereafter Harald was called the Fair-haired, and it was said that Ragnvald himself was the first to call him by that name, which the King liked.

Ragnvald had three sons. The eldest was Ivar, and he was always about the King and was a loyal man of his. He afterward was slain by the vikings when Harald went to the Hebrides, to root out the nest of wasps there who constantly came down to harry and annoy the land from which the King had ousted them. The second son was Hrolf, or Rolf, and of him we shall tell the full story. The third was Thorir Jarl, called 'the Silent,' from his moodiness. He also was Harald's man, and, indeed, married the King's daughter, Alof Arbot. The saga-men tell naught of Thorir, except that he had a daughter named Berglot, who was mother to Hakon Jarl the Great, who ruled over Norway.

Rolf was at an early age both big and strong; as to growth of body, indeed, when he was but a lad he excelled all his companions physically, being tall and broad-shouldered, slender of waist, with fine limbs and well-made hands and feet. When, at the age of fifteen, he was presented to the Thing, or meeting of freemen, and was recognized as a fighting man, his like for his age could not be found.

For three years thereafter he went a-voyaging east along the Baltic with Hrut Bersi, his mother's foster-brother, where, fighting or trading with the Letts, the Esthonians, or the Wends, he learned much, both of weapons and of war-wiles and of trading methods. When he came back it was seen that honour had grown for him and all men liked to look upon him, and at the autumn Thing, whither he rode with his brother Thorir, none could match him in fine presence or in brave apparel. So tall had he grown that he had had to get a very big Frisian horse on which to ride, because, when he bestrode one of the ordinary horses of Norway his feet swept the ground. Thus, it was told by Hrut Bersi that in their roving along the Baltic Rolf had been forced to walk where the others had ridden, and men had called him Rolf the Ganger, or Walker.

During that autumn and winter Rolf abode with his father and mother at Mæri, and at the sports which were held frequently it was seen that his *idrottir*, or attainments of body and mind, were greater than those of any other man of those parts. So skilful with weapons was he that he could cut or thrust with the sword or make sweeping blows with his axe or cast the spear as well with his left hand as with his right. So swiftly could he smite with the sword that there seemed to be three swords in the air at once. With the bow there was not found one to be his equal in both the Mæris, aye, nor in Raumsdal either: not once did he miss his mark, whether at long shot or the moving mark.

A great friend of Rolf's was Gunnar of Svarf, a man of a noble nature, generous both with treasure and food, and a rich man. He had been with Hrut Bersi and Rolf in their viking raids along the Baltic. In the spring Gunnar and Rolf said they were going sea-roving again, and began to prepare their ships. Many were the men that wanted to join them, and soon they had more than enough to fill their three skeids, or swift sailers.

Ragnvald asked them where they thought of going that summer.

"We think of going to the Finns," said Gunnar. "They are good traders and we can make much profit out of them."

"Father," said Rolf from his place at table, "do you know a man named Snowcolf in Gautland?"

"Snowcolf, Snowcolf," said old Ragnvald, as if the name were familiar. "Yes, men call him the Squinter; he lives at the Vik, but I forget his steading name. He is son of Gritgard, whom the King slew, but Snowcolf, his son, has yielded to the King."

"Then he shall yield to us also, the nithing!" said Rolf.

"What has he done?" asked Ragnvald.

"A coward's trick for which he shall get payment and over-payment. While Gunnar and I were away on an inland raid last autumn among the Letts this Snowcolf came up with three ships and set upon my ship's guard. My fellows lost half their number and had to flee. Then this Snowcolf plundered my ship of all its gear and our booty and stove it in. We have inquired far and wide who the nithing was, and at last, this winter, we learned it was he, and that he laughs over his ale when he tells the tale, thinking it a pretty trick."

"Have a care, lad," replied Ragnvald. "Get the rascal on his ships and fight him at sea."

"Why, what's to prevent us burning his house about his ears?"

"The King's command," was Ragnvald's reply. "He hath forbidden all shipmen or vikings to land with fire or sword in Norway."

"And if they do?"

"Then they will be wolves' heads—outlaws—and if they land the King's justice shall be done them."

Rolf shrugged his shoulders and said nothing; while Gunnar smiled drily and drained his horn of ale.

The Pirate who Founded a Dukedom

Now Gunnar and Rolf fare away, and southward by the land they go, past Bergen, Stavanger, and the Naze, till they round into the Vik or Great Bay, up which the Northern Sea drives and roars deep into the land through the Skager Rack. The wind served them all the way, and that was a good omen. They lay hid behind an island and stayed there all one day. When it was night they hoisted sail and stood out for land on the larboard, and at length they nosed up a creek by what men called Thrievesstrand. Gunnar bade half the men land and the other to lie by the ships, to show no light and to speak only in whispers. Then with thirty men each Gunnar and Rolf went off upland in the dark.

By and by they saw a house on a little rising, with a low turf wall round the cattle-yard. Light came from cracks in the doors. Some men went into the byres, which ran along one side, and drove out the cattle, while others pulled straw from the racks and laid it along the house walls, which were of wood. A thrall who slept with the oxen was tied up and thrown on the ground over the low wall. When all was prepared Gunnar stood by the gate in the yard and cried with a loud voice :

" Hola, Snowcolf the Squinter, come and speak to me ! "

Some one threw a great stone at the door, and then a voice was heard speaking behind it : " What do you want ? Who are you ? "

" I am Gunnar of Svarf, and Rolf Ragnvald's son is with me," replied Gunnar. " You seized our goods, scuttled our ship, and slew our men by the shore of the Letts. Come out and give us your life, or all your folk shall burn except your women."

Now Snowcolf begins to storm and bluster, saying he will make them dearly pay for any injury they do to him or his, and presently, with a great roaring shout, out of the hall rush some twenty men with arms. This was a foolish deed, for instantly fire was set to the straw piled in a heap, and by the light of this Snowcolf and his men, for all that they fought well, were struck down with arrows or spears. Snowcolf was slain by Rolf, whose axe clove his head, while Gunnar slew Thorhall Oxfoot, Snowcolf's brother-in-law, and Arnor the Long, Snowcolf's son. After that Gunnar and Rolf drove the cattle down to their ships and slept on land till it was morning. Then they went back to the house, where now were only weeping and shrilly scolding women, and ransacked it of all treasure, forcing the women to reveal what was hidden. Then they went aboard their ships, and fared southward and eastward along the Baltic, nor did they return till the winter.

Now it happened that King Harald Fairhair himself had been staying in the Vik at that time, not many miles from Thrieves-strand, and when men told him of the deed done by Gunnar of Svarf and Rolf Ragnvald's son that very night he was deeply wroth, so that none might approach him. He said that he would outlaw them at the next Thing, seeing that they had not only acted contrary to his order, but that they had committed the offence within the precincts of the King's Court. This was thought by some men to be a hard saying, seeing that Thrieves was ten miles from Heldendal, where the King was staying with his court at the house of Odd of Saltvik.

As the time of the autumn Thing approached men

wondered whether the King would doom Gunnar and Rolf to outlawry, seeing that Gunnar was brother to Einar of Balthrist, who was one of the King's greatest helpers in the war by which he had got his kingdom, and that young Rolf was son of Harald's dearest friend and counsellor. When men met at the Thing, and the dooms were about to be pronounced, Ragnvald rose from his seat and went away. The King, as he sat on his high seat, looked very angry at this. When the dooms were said, the names of Gunnar and Rolf were the very first. The King related what they had done, and very dark was his face as he spoke, and his words came forth as if each was a blow. Then he gave the doom in the set form of words.

"I doom that Gunnar of Svarf and Rolf, son of Ragnvald, jarl of Mæri, be convicted outlaws, not to be fed, not to be forwarded, not to be helped or harboured in any need.

"I say that their goods are forfeited, half to me and half to the kinsfolk of Snowcolf and the others whom they slew."

At the feast of Yule, as Harald sat on the high seat in his great rich hall at Thingness and made merry, suddenly the doorward came forward and told the King that the Lady Ragnhild of Mæri wished to speak to him. The King frowned and hesitated; but before he could command that the lady should not be allowed to enter, the lady herself, with a following of three handmaids and six men, came through the great door. She had a high look in her handsome face as she flashed her eyes toward Harald.

"Often has Harald Fairhair come to my hall," she

said, "and never once hath he been received with aught but warm welcome and quick entrance."

The King's look was sharp, but he laughed shortly.

"You are ever welcome, lady," he said. "'Tis your errand that may not be as merry as the season."

"My errand you know," she replied. "I crave your pardon for my son Rolf. You know what sort of nithing trick Snowcolf played upon him. Was he to let that pass? Was he to let Snowcolf snigger over his horn of ale as he told the tale of how he robbed the wolves of their prey? Think you, King, what would you have done at his age to avenge yourself for such a deed?"

The King's brow was dark and his eyes glowed like fire, for from few if any men had he had such blunt speech since his overlordship had given all his friends mealy mouths.

"I want peace in my land," he said. "I will mete out justice for any wrong done upon jarl or thrall. Men must no longer take the law by their own swords. The doom on your son is uttered; it is a just doom, and I will not call it back."

Many words spoke the lady, now in haughty terms, now in gentle pleading, but all were in vain. The King kept his temper marvellously, as his hirdmen, or courtiers, truly said; but his anger at her persistency was seen to be great. Yet if she was stubborn, he was firm, and would not bate by one jot the doom he had given.

Then the lady desisted and turned away as if to go. She went some steps and then turned again and sang a song which all men remembered, for its words came true.

"THE VENERABLE ABBOT LUCAS WAS SLAIN UPON THE HOLY ALTAR"

Disgrace not Nefja's namesake,
Nor drive the wolf from the land.
Thou wise kinsman of Odin,
Why dealest thou thus with my son?
Thou'lt find 'tis bad to worry
So fierce a wolf as he.
Short shrift will thy sheep get from him,
When he turns into these thy woods!

The King was furious at these threats, and swore that he would keep a keener look out than usual for the wolf's head, Rolf the Ganger. Men thought that this outlawing of Rolf, and the King's refusal to listen to Hilda's appeal, would breed bad blood between Harald the King and the family of Ragnvald of Mæri. Ivar, Ralph's elder brother, was sworn man of Harald's, and one in whom the King placed great trust, and men wondered what he would do. But Ivar said in all men's hearing that Rolf had been well served; that the King would have punished Snowcolf if Rolf had appealed to him. Thorir, Rolf's youngest brother, at this very time, came to the King's Court and was made his man, and, as every one knows, for all his glum looks he got the King's good will, and within five years married Alöf Arbot, the King's daughter, a girl not of the best looks or temper, perhaps, but one who made the King's favour a thing of surety.

Gunnar and Rolf that winter passed the time at the hall of the Scots jarl Melbrigith Longfang in Sudrland (Sutherland), where, and throughout the Orkneys and Shetlands, many Norwegian jarls and landsmen had fled to escape the overlordship of Harald. It was there that Rolf made a plan to "singe the beard of Harald," as he termed it, and next spring with a great fleet of dragons, skeids, and snekkurs, he stole eastward to Norway, and, landing his men, he led them through the Vik lands, burning and plundering, slaying all who resisted, and making a special point of laying waste the farms which belonged to Harald the King, who owned many rich lands there. Then he rejoined his ships, which had been brought round to the Ness, and, having loaded them, he sailed clean away with a vast store of booty.

When the King heard of this he raged like a madman, and swore that for all the ill that had come out of the Orkneys and Shetlands against him and his he would make them swim in a sea of blood. Many, indeed, had been the viking raids which had been made by the dispossessed jarls who had fled there, upon the lands far and wide in Norway which had once been their own, but were now given to aiders and favourites of Harald.

For the next three summers, therefore, Harald prepared his fleet, and about the time when the vikings came he would send his snekkurs to search the creeks and inlets among the islands and outskerries on the coast of Norway. But he got little gain, for there were many on the islands who thought the vikings were doing but right, and who gave them timely warning of the King's fleet being about. So the King found the vikings had fled, mostly out to sea, and all his moil and toil was done for naught.

Now it happened that one winter, at the Court of Melbrigith Longfang, where Rolf the Ganger was staying, it was told that there was a fierce wizard who lived in the dark land of Stranavar, which was a land full of strange folks and evil powers that dwelled in the Underworld. It was said that this wizard was a mighty fighter, though of small size for a man, and that he lived in a howe or mound and was named Raa. Now at the table it was told by the vikings how they had heard tell of other powerful fighters of the mound-men who had been overcome by Norse warriors. Some said it was foolish to fight such men, if men they were, and not demons or fairies; but others told of famous warriors who had fought and slain these little men, and who, having ransacked their barrows, had won much treasure.

Melbrigith, the King, a tall, lean man with a dark, narrow face, who was said to have wizard powers himself, said little while others spoke thus, and when he was asked he said that to fight the men of the fairy hills was to play with one's luck, since, even if one slew a little man, ill-luck would curse the slayer to the day of his death, whereas to aid and nourish the mound-men and to speak fair of them was to win good fortune.

Now all men had said that since the doom of outlawry had been uttered against Rolf he had become moody and short of speech, and many said that his blood was turning to gall within him. All were sorry for this, for his frankness and good fellowship had won all hearts. But it was with him as with many others who had been cast out of their own halls and from their own dear land: 'wolves' they were by name, and by long brooding they became wolves by nature.

When, now, Melbrigith had spoken, Rolf from his place at the board said: "Well, my luck can never be worse than it is. Therefore I will go see this wizard. And if he will not speak me fair I will carve what luck the Weirds[1] choose to give me from his black wizard's hide."

Next day, therefore, with three comrades, Strutharald, son of Jarl Ulf, Sveinn Skegg, and an Ostman named

[1] Fates.

Beltis, Rolf set out westward along the coast from Dunreag, where the Court was, to go to the Stranavar. As there was no horse big enough to carry Rolf, they all walked. Melbrigith was against the expedition from the first, but he did not attempt to dissuade Rolf. Nevertheless he gave him one of his gillies as a guide, a man named Crum, who was one of the small dark people whom most men looked on as uncanny.

They started early, and it was midday when they reached the valley in which the wizard dwelled. The ground was hard going, the country was wild and gloomy, with great mountains looming through the mists on each side of them and the grey soil showing bare and rocky along the high land. A clear cold stream rushed through the strath. No men appeared to dwell in that barren region, but there were many green little hills here and there. Rolf asked Crum if people dwelled in these, but Crum, who spoke little Norse that any one could understand, only shook his head. Soon they reached the place where Crum said Raa the wizard had his dwelling.

It was a green hillock on a flat terrace just above the river. The other four men stood by the water's edge while Rolf went to the wizard's hill. He walked all round it, looking for the door, but no break could he spy in the green turf. "Hola!" he shouted; "does Raa live here?"

"Aye," came a voice from within the hill, "Raa lives here, Rolf the Ganger. And what will you of Raa?"

Rolf was startled to hear his name called; but he drily replied: "If you know my name, you should know why I came."

"Aye," came the voice, in stern tones, "you come to

see if I will speak you fair, or else to carve your luck from my black wizard's hide."

"Some one hath run quickly to tell you the tale of yesterday's meadboard," replied Rolf scornfully.

"Aye, some one hath come, but having neither feet nor hands, lips nor eyes—'twas your fetch that came telling me of the black fits of Rolf the Ganger."

A 'fetch' was the guardian spirit that every Norseman believed he possessed, who warned him on occasion of dangers threatening him.

"What else did my fetch tell you?"

"That you had it in your mind to get all the dispossessed vikings of the Orkneys and Western Isles, and those dwelling on Iceland, to join in a band to thrust Harald Fairhair out of Norway or to slay him."

Now this disturbed Rolf very deeply, for it was a thought he had told to no one as yet.

"What do you advise me?" he asked. "Give me good counsel, for my way is dark."

"Keep away from Norway," came the voice out of the hill. "There is no gain for you there, only the squabbles of jarls and the plots of traitors. You will go sea-roving far and wide, even to Midgard,[1] and the lands of the Middle Sea. Remember, force of arms does not wholly rule the world, nor yet good fortune; the man of brain and crafty thinking gains more at less trouble. You are to found a kingdom which will be the equal of Norway. When you have been many years sea-roving you will be ship-sick and will yearn to settle on land. In a pleasant land that looks to the north you will found your kingdom; but not only will you gain it by the sword,

[1] Constantinople.

but by your becoming a Christian and by marrying a royal maid that is not yet born."

The voice stopped, as if there were no more to say. Rolf took a heavy gold ring from his arm and laid it on a stone before him. The voice spoke again. "I see the lands that your sons shall sway extending over all the world, in places that you wot not of; the people they rule shall be the masters of the sea, and in fame and riches none shall o'ertop them."

Rolf rejoined his fellows, and all that winter he was very quiet, often thinking, but giving no one of his thoughts.

Next summer he went south with his ships and raided and fought in Ireland, gathering much booty. The winter following he stayed with Thorfinn at Smerwick, and together they planned to go farther south. This they did, for they coasted along Valland, or France, from the Seine to the Loire, raiding and burning, so that their names became a terror to the people dwelling in those parts. As they crossed the stormy sea of Biscaya, a tempest arose, and dashed Thorfinn with four of his ships upon the rocky coast, but Rolf managed to sail out the storm, though at great peril of life. For the next five years Rolf plundered all the coasts of the Middle Sea and Spain. Many were the fights his fair-haired warriors had with the dark-skinned sons of Spain—Moors as fierce and as brave as any Norse fighters.

Once they sailed up the Guadalquivir and attacked a rich, fair city there called Seville. The townspeople fled, and the pirates overran the place, ransacking the rich houses of nobles and merchants and gaining great booty. The king of that kingdom, by name Abencerrada, learning of this insolent attack in the heart of his kingdom, quickly gathered a large army and sent it down the river, hoping to catch the pirates unawares and to burn their fleet. But Rolf then, as always, showed himself a wary leader: he had set a good guard over his ships and had his men well in hand, so that when the war-horn sounded every man left the house in which he was collecting spoil and hurried down to the riverside.

That was hard sword-play, for the fierce, dark Moslems were fine fighting men. To and fro the battle swayed, until at last both sides were weary with their efforts. Night came down, leaving the battle undecided; but the Moors had had enough, and next morning the Norsemen went on board their ships with all their plunder and many captives, and the Moors did not try to stay them.

There was no need to lay up the ships at any time while they were in the Middle Sea, for there was no winter. The vikings would, however, rest awhile now and then, and, dragging their boats up the sand in the mouth of some creek or river, they would make a camp and trade with the people of the country, or, tiring of the softening life, they would go fighting among the Moors, the Frenchmen, or Italians, burning villas and towns, or setting them to ransom, in the very places and in the very manner in which the pirates of Cilicia had acted some nine hundred years before.

At length Rolf and his men pined for the bite of the Northern air, the breath of the bitter winter weather, the fells and seas of their own homeland. So one day they dragged down their snekkurs with joyful songs and shouts into the water, and, turning the prows westward, they went before a fair wind through Nörvasund, or, as we call it, the strait of Gibraltar. Then they raced along the shores of Spain and France, hardly stopping till a storm compelled them to put in at the merchant city of Varrande, in Peitoland (Poitou), where they spared the town on payment of a scatt, or fine, of twelve thousand crowns, which the rich merchants of the place willingly paid, thankful to get off so cheaply.

When Rolf reached the dun or fort of Melbrigith, the Scots jarl, at Reay, in Sudrland, he was told news which was hard to hear. Harald Fairhair had got tired of searching in the islands and outskerries for the viking ships that never waited to be caught, and in the very summer when Rolf fared southward to the Middle Sea he had gathered a great fleet and had descended suddenly upon Shetland. There he had caught the vikings unawares, before they had had time to join together, and he had slain many before they could flee, and had burned their halls and scuttled their ships. Then he sailed southward to the Orkneys, which he cleared of vikings, so that every island was filled with the bodies of dead men, the cries of weeping women, and the reek of burning houses, ricks, and barns.

After that Harald had fared westward to the Hebrides, but there the vikings had had word of his coming and were better prepared. But all their array had availed them little: none could withstand the onslaught of the forecastle men of Harald's ships, for they were the picked fighters of all Norway. Many were the battles which Harald had fought with the vikings, both on sea and on land, and great had been his slaughter of vikings, some of whom were of high race and were chiefs of many warriors. Then Harald landed in Scotland, in the place which we now call Ross-shire, but he was not so victorious there, as the vikings had learned something of the way in which the Scots men made war, namely, by dashing out suddenly from clefts in the rocks or dark woods, and killing a few men now and then. There was one big battle, in which Harald held the battlefield, but he lost so many men that, after burning and plundering where he could, he went back to his ships and sailed away to the Isle of Man. But he got no booty there, for the people had fled in their ships, taking all their goods with them.

Coming homeward, Harald stopped at a large island in the Hebrides which he had missed when going south, and there was a large party of vikings there, who fought desperately and well. Harald had with him all his chief hirdmen, or courtmen, and warriors, and so well fought was the battle that Harald lost many of his chief men. Among these was Rolf's elder brother, Ivar, who was slain by a spear thrown by Arnfin, a son of Einar, Jarl of Stora. Harald was so enraged at this loss that he would not suffer one of the vikings to escape him, and those who fled to their ships he pursued and slew, so that not one of his enemies came alive from that fight. He mounded Ivar under a great barrow with much booty at a point of land by the sea called Howsa Head, where it stands to this day.

Then Harald went home, and as recompense for the death of Ivar he gave to Ragnvald both the Orkneys and the Shetlands as an additional jarldom. But Ragnvald said he was too old to go and be overlord in such a wasp's nest, and gave it to his younger brother, Sigurd, who, when Rolf was told all this, had but recently come to the Shetlands and, as men said, was fitting out a large fleet in order to attack Sudrland and Katanes (Caithness) when the winter should be past.

"Now I would ask you, Rolf," said Melbrigith, "whether you will stay with me and help me. For I am but a small jarl and my men are not many. But if you do not care to fight against your father's brother Sigurd when he shall come to conquer my land, do you leave some of your men with me, and I will reward them richly."

Rolf would not agree to fight against Sigurd, but he left half of his men with Melbrigith, and with the rest and a fleet of four long ships he fared south in the spring and joined his forces to those of Guthorm, King of East Anglia, who was breaking his treaty with Alfred, King of England, and was again fighting against that great and wise ruler. Guthorm was the King of the Danes who had settled in East Anglia some years before. He had tried to conquer all England, but Alfred had defeated him, and then had made a treaty with him, by which Guthorm promised to keep to his own lands and to be baptized as a Christian. But he kept not his oaths and was as faithless as the Danes ever were.

Guthorm and Rolf made their fleet ready and sailed south from the Humber to Thames mouth. Here they were joined by the great viking leaders Hastings and Thordulf, who had come from the ravaging of Flanders and France, and from vainly striving to break down the stout walls of the brave people of Paris. Together they fared up the Medway and laid their ships opposite the timbered walls of Rochester.

The Danes and Norsemen set up their tents on the land side of the town, and on the second day Rolf on one side and Guthorm on the other attempted to rear ladders against the walls. But those English townsmen were stout fellows, and, manning their walls, they threw down the ladders or poured hot water, pitch, and boiling grease upon their assailants, so that both Guthorm and Rolf had to call off their men.

Then Hastings, who had been at the siege of Paris, advised that they should build a wooden tower on wheels so that they could push it against the wall and men could leap down from its platforms into the town. They began to build such a tower, but midway in its construction the scouts came in to say that King Alfred was coming from Londonburg with a great army. The vikings did not wait to meet Alfred but instantly got on board their ships and sailed away to Benfleet, in Essex, where they had a great camp.

Guthorm had told Rolf that he might be able to carve out a kingdom for himself in England, but all that summer it seemed impossible for the vikings to make any headway against Alfred, who checked them wherever they went. The vikings got horses, but though Alfred's men were on foot they marched so rapidly that the pirates were kept on the move. At sea, also, Alfred defeated them, sinking sixteen ships and slaying all of the crews. Two days later, however, Rolf and Hastings met the triumphant fleet as it was returning to Maldon, and, having a larger number of ships, they slew many of the men and caused the remaining ships to flee.

That autumn Rolf went north again to Sudrland, but found a blackened ruin of houses, mingled with dead men's bones, where once had stood the dun and hall of his friend Melbrigith Longfang. As he strode among the charred fragments of the houses where he had passed many happy days he guessed that his uncle Sigurd had proved too strong for the Scots jarl. Soon an old Scotsman, a bard, was brought to him by his men. He had been found hiding in a cave in the wood near by. He told Rolf that Sigurd had ravaged all the north of Scotland, both in Caithness and Sudrland, and men knew not which was the crueller fighter, Sigurd Jarl or Thorstein the Red, who had joined forces with him. Melbrigith had beaten off the jarl's men for two days, but the Scotsmen and Norse in the dun were so few that they knew defeat must be theirs. Then Raa the wizard went to Sigurd's camp, to see if peace terms could not be made, but Sigurd scornfully bade the wizard begone, and spoke ill of all Scotsmen. Raa told him that though he would slay Melbrigith, the Scots jarl would be a greater foe dead than alive. Sigurd ordered a viking to slay Raa, but the wizard made the man stiff as stone and went away unscathed.

Next day Sigurd stormed the dun and cut off Melbrigith's head, saying that he would pickle it and hang it in his hall, to see whether the Scotsman were a worse foe dead than alive. He tied the head by the hair to his saddle straps, and men said that as Sigurd rode along the dead man fixed his teeth in the calf of his slayer's leg. However this may be, the long tooth which gave Melbrigith Longfang his nickname tore the flesh of Sigurd's calf, and the wound swelled, so that Sigurd died therefrom in great pain seven days later. He was buried in a great mound at Ekkjalsbank.

Rolf took the old bard with him and drove west to Barra, one of the islands of the Hebrides, where there were many vikings, Danes and Norsemen, who knew Rolf. With their aid the next summer he gained much land in the island, and settled down there. For the next three summers he stayed there living like a great chief, in a handsome and generous way, beloved of all his hirdmen, or courtmen, and served willingly and loyally by all his servants.

In the fourth year, being now thirty-two years of age, he went on a viking cruise, and had twelve well-manned ships, with all his men finely equipped in clothes, arms, and stores. At this time Jarl Erling Oddson ruled over a rich kingdom in Bretland, by Mona. Men told Rolf of this, and that it was a country where one might get much booty. Rolf accordingly sailed thither and prepared to raid through the land. He beached his ships at a place called Troedyrhos, and got horses for himself and his chief men. Now, as he was riding up from the shore, he met a fair girl, richly dressed, upon a palfrey, and with her was an old British man. The girl had a high, proud look, and was very lovely, with hair about her shoulders of the colour of beech leaves in autumn, and a white throat.

"Who are you?" she asked as Rolf came toward her. Her speech was Norse.

"I am Rolf, son of Ragnvald the Powerful," replied Rolf.

"I have heard of you," replied the girl. "My father has often spoken of you. He is old now, but he gladly speaks with warriors and men of high name and breeding. Will you not come with me to his hall, and bring your friends with you?"

Rolf went with the girl, who said she was named Nesta,

and that the Briton with her was her foster-father, Kradock. As they rode along, Rolf and the girl had much pleasant conversation together, for Nesta was a woman of understanding who could frame her talk well. Erling Oddson received Rolf with all honour, and told him that Gunnar of Svarf, who had been his arms brother, had often spoken highly of Rolf. Gunnar had gone to Iceland, where he took broad lands along Rangriver. He had a son there named Hamond, whose son was also called Gunnar. Of the famous deeds of this great man you may read in the Saga of Burnt Njal.

Erling and Rolf had much good and friendly talk together, and Rolf frankly told the jarl that he had intended raiding in the land, but that he would more willingly have peace land there, and not ravage. To this the old jarl assented, and a great feast was made in Rolf's honour, and he and his friends were well entreated.

Now Rolf and Nesta sought each other out daily, and each found pleasure in the other's company. Rolf found the girl much to his liking: she was merry, but modest, and very generous. Rolf on the fourth day asked her in marriage, and the jarl willingly consented when he had heard that his daughter loved this kingly young man. Nesta was betrothed to Rolf at once, and, indeed, the betrothal lasted not long, for they were married within a little while. Erling gave Rolf the name of jarl, and said that if he would settle in that land he should have half the kingdom while Erling was in life, and the rest should come to him when the king was dead.

Rolf willingly accepted, and stayed there all that summer and the next winter.

Next summer he went to his people in the Hebrides and stayed there till the autumn. He had to fight many battles that year against marauding vikings who landed and laid waste the islands, and when he heard that Torf Einar, his father's son by another mother, was become King of the Orkneys, and was gathering a great army to ravage all the Western Isles and Scotland, Rolf decided he would not stay in the Hebrides, and took all his people who would go with him to Bretland. By this time Erling Oddson was dead and Rolf ruled the country alone, but he found it no easy task to hold the small piece of Wales which had come to him through his wife Nesta. Not only was he assailed by sea by vikings, both Danes and Norsemen, but the Welsh Kings laid claim to his land, and there were constant forays and raidings.

Nevertheless Rolf got fame as one of the greatest fighters in the Western seas. He was, as we have said, one of the handsomest, largest, and tallest men ; a better and a stronger warrior could not be found, skilful in all exercises and wise in war-craft. He was zealous in everything he undertook, and in boldness never had his match. Both the vikings and the Welsh lords found that he was never to be caught napping, and that when he struck he struck hard. Sleepless was the watch he kept upon his piece of the coast, and while churches and farms, monasteries and granges might be going up in smoke and flame in other parts, and terrified bonders, their wives, and household folk were streaming in terror away from the terrible vikings, Rolf's land and people remained in peace, and no black weal of ruin lay across his fair country.

During these years he did not go sea-roving, finding it enough to guard his own territory. He became very powerful and had many friends, because viking chiefs heard of his renown and would often come on friendly visits; the British chiefs of the north Welsh lands also sought his friendship and counsel. Rolf lived in a large and generous way, and kept as many retainers about him as if he were king of a great land. He always had with him eighty free-born men, and in his great house at Aber-Aled there was ever meat and drink in abundance. But he would allow no man to drink without measure during the day, and at night he often went the rounds of the coast-guard to see that the watch was well kept. His full muster of fighting men was five hundred, and he never went to sea with less than a fully manned ship of thirty-two benches of rowers, and in it, when its crew was complete, there were two hundred men at the least.

He was a good man to his people. There were on his farm forty slaves, besides servants at a wage. Each slave had a certain amount of work to do in the day, and when he had finished that his time was his own, to till his own bit of arable land or to do whatever else he liked. He gave to each a certain task, by working at which within a certain time they could gain the price of their freedom, and lazy was the man who could not thereby become a freeman after two years' service with Rolf.

It was the grief both of Rolf and his wife that they had no children, but for all that they lived with much happiness. Five years they thus dwelled together, and then one summer Nesta fell ill and died. Rolf grew very melancholy after this, and drank and ate little. Often he was found drooping his head in his cloak, and nothing could cheer him.

He sat at home all that winter, but as soon as spring came he made men build long-boats and snekkurs for him, and it seemed that he could never rest or let others rest while these were a-building. He said he longed to be off sea-roving, and that he hated the land where his wife had died. When the ships were ready there was no lack of brave fellows to man them, and with thirty ships he left the land one sunny morning in April. That summer he made warfare in Scotland and England, and won for himself much booty and fame.

For the next seven summers he plundered the coasts and inland parts of France and Flanders. In his boats he threaded many rivers far into the land, and carried war and devastation into places where the name of the Northmen was only an echo and the terror inspired by their fierceness but a rumour. Sometimes he quitted his boats, hauled them across the land, and pushed them into other rivers, the country people flying before him and spreading the news of his coming. Many were the battles the vikings had with brave Frankish lords whose lands they were ravaging. Sometimes in these encounters the Northmen were beaten and had to fly to their boats, but most often they were the victors, and ruined castles and burnt villages paid for the losses the vikings had borne.

When winter came Rolf would make a camp in the bend of a river, or would seize a town or large village in some strong position. Often the lords of the French would bring strong forces against him, but so crafty and cautious was he that never was he beaten from his lair—rather the enemy had to draw off sorely wounded and broken. Sometimes a party of vikings, tiring of their lawless and unsettled lives, would seize some land and build themselves houses and till the ground, and after a time the country people would get used to the presence of the pirates turned farmers, and their daughters would marry them, and in a few years there would be a little colony of peaceful folk, and fields of waving corn where before had been the rushes and reeds of the wild river meadows, sheltering naught but teal and snipe, otters and wolves.

In the chronicle of the Abbey of Aubertin by Rille, the name of Rolf, or Rollo, often appears, and always with words of detestation and horror. One such entry runs as follows, under the year 902 :

" This year the army of the pagans wintered at Grostet, where the Ver runs into the sea marshes, and when spring came they went north and east and we thanked the Lord for this, as it seemed that they were not to descend upon our lands. But three days before the feast of St Gabriel, in the morning, into the guest chamber swept a troop of scared varlets who said that their mistress, the Lady Gille, daughter of Charles the King, was coming with her ladies and guards, flying from the town of Boudoin, in which place the pirates were ravaging. The abbot received the royal child, who, though but yet just out of her teens, showed the spirit of a woman. She had been on a visit to her foster-mother, the Lady de Chatre, at Anel, and, setting forth early that morning, she had met a multitude of terrified country people flying from before the evil and bloodthirsty bands of

Rollo and his companions. The abbot Lucas entertained the young princess and her party and refreshed them, and sent guides with them to lead them by short and safe paths upon their road to her father's palace at Limours. Next day, hearing that the pagans had come to Francoin, and were ravaging south of Seine, the most valiant lord Antoine and two knights, his seneschals Arcant and Dieudé, collected all weapon-bearing men from their own lands of Saulge and Paludes, as also some from the lands of the abbey, to the number of twelve hundred in all. The abbey men were under the command of Turold, then a monk of the monastery, who, before he adopted the habit, had been a warrior famous through all the Île de France. These were met by the lord Gogroun of Fraindre, with three hundred brave men from Dormans, Chaillon, and Nanteu, and with them came Clavice, lord of Lenné, and his retainers, who were very valiant and numerous. All these met together at the ford which is called Casserupt, and advancing, they joined issue with a band of the pagans under a king of theirs, named Eric. They smote the barbarians manfully, but night falling, the lord Antoine drew off his forces.

"During the night there arrived in the camp of the pagans all the other leaders of their hosts, who, dividing the district between them, had gone forth ravaging and burning. At the head of them was that chief of pirates and robbers, Rollo, whose vast body, greater and higher in stature than all others, is the more powerful for evil, whose footsteps sow death and ruin wherever he goes, and who these six years past has terribly oppressed our country with sword, spear, and fire. Others were

Halfden, Hubba, Gorm the Biter, and Osgood, who came with vast booty and a numerous multitude of miserable captives, women, and children. When the men of lord Antoine heard how greatly their enemies had increased in strength, their hearts became as water, and some eight hundred men threw down their weapons and fled, leaving no more than two hundred valiant souls, who prepared themselves to meet the pagans.

"Meanwhile some of the fugitives, crying aloud and weeping, had come to the door of the abbey and told of the overwhelming powers of evil which were arrayed against them, foretelling, also, that the pagans would soon be upon us. All were distracted on receiving these tidings. The abbot, in the first place, retained with himself the more aged monks, thinking that their defenceless state might possibly move the barbarians to pity. All others of stouter body and more youthful age he ordered to fly, bearing with them the sacred relics of the monastery, these being the most holy body of St Fremor and his hair-shirt and psalter, as well as the most valuable jewels and muniments. They loaded a boat with the aforesaid relics and treasures and the muniments, after which they threw the table of the great altar, covered with gold, which King Thiégaut had presented, and ten chalices, together with other rich plate, into the well of the monastery. Then, perceiving men running toward the abbey, they got into their boat and rowed away.

"The abbot and the others, putting on their sacred vestments, assembled in the choir and there performed the regular Hours of the Holy Office, after which they went through the seven penitential psalms. At this time two noble youths staggered into the church, covered with the blood of their wounds, and having cried out that the lord Antoine and his brave men had been destroyed by the pagans, they lay down on the floor and expired. Nevertheless, the lord abbot, Lucas, himself celebrated High Mass, being assisted therein by Brother Thomas, the deacon, Brother Savin, the sub-deacon, and Turot and Bapté, youths who acted as taper-bearers. Then all stood about the abbot and intoned the Litany, speaking with great fervour the prayer for protection against the bloody hands of the pirates—*A furore Normannorum, libera nos, Domine!* Hardly had the prayer been ended when a roar as of mad beasts broke from the woods and came toward the door, and into the sacred precincts burst the pagans, just as the abbot and his assistants had partaken of the mystery of Holy Communion. The venerable abbot Lucas was slain upon the holy altar, as a true martyr and sacrifice of Christ, by the hand of the most bloodthirsty king, Gorm the Biter; his assistants were also slain, while the old monks were seized and, later, tortured, that they might disclose where the treasures of the church were concealed; afterward they also were slain."

For ten years Rolf wasted and ravaged throughout the lands beside the Segene (Seine), as far as the coasts, gaining much booty, and suffering only those inhabitants to dwell in their towns and villages who submitted to pay him scatt (tribute), as if he were king of the land. The King of that country was one named Charles the Simple, a foolish king, who thought more of monks and church rites than things of war. He called his counsellors many times about him, being urged thereto by the bitter complaints and prayers which came to him from the lords, bonders, and people dwelling in that part of his dominions where Rolf was ravaging. But his counsellors either had no advice to give or the King was too foolish to follow it.

At length King Charles sent three of his chief men to Rolf where he sat with a great army of people in winter quarters in the town of Ruda (Rouen). They were well received by Rolf, who placed them at his own table and treated them with every consideration. When they had been there two days one of them, named Turpin, stood forth and told the jarl the message which he bore from King Charles. "My master sends me with these words: If you will make peace with him, and will consent to be baptized a Christian, you and your fellows, he will give you the fief of Neustria, where you now sit, and will give you his daughter Gille in marriage."

Rolf had had his spies out in the Court of the French king and knew that this proposal was to be made to him. He replied that he would consult his chief men on the matter and would give an answer the next day. Accordingly Rolf called a house-thing, or meeting of his counsellors, and they spoke of the French King's proposals. All thought it would be well to accept them. Whereupon Rolf spoke to the King's messengers thus: "Tell your master that what I have I will hold—this town of Ruda, with all the land where my men are now abiding—and such other lands as he may give me. And in consideration of these fiefs I will defend the lands about his city of Paris and along the Seine from the ravages of other vikings, or bands of sea-rovers. So, too, will I become Christian and be baptized with my friends and our men. But, first, you must send us learned men and priests to tell us something of your religion and other things which we should know. Also I will take to wife Gille, the King's daughter, so that there shall be ever peace and friendship between the King and me."

The messengers departed well satisfied, bearing many rich gifts. They told their king what Rolf had said, and Charles sent clerics and bishops to teach Rolf and his men concerning the Christian religion.

Thereupon a day was appointed, when Rolf with all his chief men rode to the King's villa at a place called St Clair, where formerly a holy hermit of that name had lived in a little cell on the side of the stream called Epte. The hermit had been slain by viking marauders some thirty years before, but the chapel which pious men had reared over his cell was named after him. There Rolf was received by the King and his chief men. The Frankish men were proud and haughty and called the vikings pirates, but the King, a small, quiet man, was all for peaceful words and courtesy. Charles and Rolf went aside, and the King and the jarl, with a priest named Turold for interpreter, had private talk together. Rolf gave his hand to the King as a sign that he wished to live at peace with the Franks, provided they left him undisturbed in the lands about Rouen and the Seine and the sea, which his sword had conquered. Thereupon the King gave Rolf the name of Duke of Rouen, and they parted with much friendliness and the interchange of many rich presents.

During the remainder of the winter the learned men taught Rolf and his men much concerning the Christian religion, for it was decided that when the spring came Rolf and his chief men should be baptized in the great church at Rouen, and that after this was done he should wed the Princess Gille, and that their sons should be Dukes of Rouen for ever. The priests told Rolf that he would have to do fealty to the King for the rich fiefs given to him, by kneeling and kissing the King's feet. But Rolf laughed when they said this, and told them that to kneel before any man or to kiss his feet was a thing of shame for Northern men and was an action only for nidderings and women. On this the priests asked whether no servant of Rolf's would do this thing for him, but Rolf said he would ask no free-born Northman to do so shameful a thing. Thereupon he rose, and his large form towered over the shaveling heads of the priests, who seemed puny, weak, and pale beside him, and he said: "I will hear no more of this slave's deed that you wish me to do. I have given my hand to your King, and I will swear on your book, the Bible, and your saints' relics to be true man to the King. But naught else will I do." With that he went forth, and the priests told the King, and the King said he would not insist upon the act of fealty. The French lords, it is said, laughed among themselves, saying that this 'Duke of the Pirates,' as they henceforth termed Rolf, was a stiff man, who reckoned his barbarous pride as worth more than the King's favour.

Some chronicles tell a foolish tale of the baptism and oath of fealty as these things took place in the church at Rouen. They say that there was a squabble, and that while the lords insisted on Rolf kneeling and kissing the King's foot Rolf refused, but was prevailed upon to let one of his men perform the act in his place. This man, it is further said, would not kneel, but lifted up the King's foot so suddenly and so high that the King on his chair was almost thrown over.

But the truth is as is written here. Rolf was said by all there, even his evil-wishers and enemies, to be one of the handsomest and noblest looking men that ever stepped along the nave of the church. He wore a red kirtle or tunic, and over this a coat of fine ring-mail. Round his waist was a belt of silver, in which were stuck a dagger with a jewelled haft and a large sword with a handle of gold. His trousers were of fine linen, with red bands of leather to the knees, sewn with small pearls. On his feet were fine shoes of Cordoban leather. Over all he wore a rich cloak of fur lined with velvet, with a golden band on the neck-strap. On his head was a fine silver helmet with a boar's head in front, the eyes of which were of sapphires. His chief men were also richly dressed, but Rolf was a head taller than any in the church, and there were many handsome lords and noble ladies there, all richly attired, and of high blood and of great race.

At the altar Rolf doffed his helmet and took the oath upon the Bible and on the bones of St Ouen, and swore to be true man to the King and to live in peace with him. What is true is that when Rolf spoke the words of fealty after the bishop the French lords did not understand the Frankish speech in which they were uttered, and therefore laughed, for their own tongue was broken Latin as spoken by the boorish people.

After that Rolf was baptized, and his chief men with him; and next day the Princess Gille was brought to him, and they spoke together, by the interpretation of a priest, and next day they were wedded, and with her ladies, her chaplain, and some French lords the Princess went to her husband's home in the villa at Rouen which he had furnished for her. Now she was but a young woman of some twenty-four summers, while Rolf was twice her age, but Rolf remembered his young wife, Nesta, and was gentle and kind to the young Princess, who lived very happily with him.

Thus it was that the pirate chieftain became a duke and the founder of a rich and powerful dukedom in France. And men found that this 'Duke of Pirates' was a good ruler and a wise one. He did not treat his province as a conquered land, but strove to give prosperity to it and to its people. He divided the land among the chief men who had helped to gain it for him, and as years went on he added to his territory, and the King gave him further fiefs. He settled the law of the province, saw that justice was done between Northman and Frank, and aided the priests to spread the softer teachings of Christ among the pirates, now turned landowners and farmers. So great was his fame and the fame of the wealth and prosperity of the country that large numbers of Northmen came and craved land of him, and settled on the holdings he gave to them. So firm was his rule and so vigorous was his arm against evil doers that the tale goes that Rolf one day hung a gold bracelet on a branch beside a public way, but no one dared to touch it, knowing that in things of justice the Duke flinched not from doing what was right. The Northmen took for wives the women of the country, and their sons and daughters spoke only their mother's tongue. Soon, indeed, the language of the North died out of the land; but the just dealing, the foresight, and the stern fighting qualities of the Northmen remain as a distinctive and splendid legacy with the people of Normandy of to-day.

IV : The Corsairs of the Mediterranean

I : The Punishment of a Crime

IT was the summer of the year 1491. There was fierce fighting about the walls of Granada, in Spain. For ten long years there had been war: the chivalry of Christian Castile was ranged against the Moslem chivalry of the Moors. It was seven hundred and seventy-seven years since the Moslems, having beaten the last king of the Goths, had conquered the peninsula of Spain, bringing its Christian peoples under their sway. But as the centuries had rolled by Christian princes had wrested from the Moorish conquerors province after province, until by the middle of the fifteenth century only the kingdom of Granada remained in the hands of the Moslems. Even this had been left in their possession only on condition that they paid tribute every year to the sovereign of Castile and Leon. This tribute was to be two thousand pistoles of gold, and sixteen hundred Christian captives, or an equal number of Moors to be used as slaves.

Then came a day when Ismael, the King of Granada, died, and was succeeded by his son, Muley Aben Hassan, a man of fiercer temper, whose blood had boiled at the pride and arrogance of the Christians when once he had seen them receive the tribute from his father. When, therefore, a haughty knight at the head of a flashing cavalcade had ridden up to the gateway of the palace, and, having been brought into the great Hall of Ambassadors, had demanded that the tribute then in arrear should be paid, the Moorish monarch had smiled with a bitter curl of his lips and, falling back upon his silken couch, had insolently replied :

"Tell your sovereign that the Kings of Granada who used to pay tribute in money to the Kings of Castile are dead. Our mint at present coins nothing but blades of scimitars and heads of lances ! "

These proud words had been uttered in 1478. War had broken out three years later. Muley Aben Hassan was now dead, and his son, Boabdil el Chico, had been made king. Town by town, by dint of furious fighting, their land had been wrested from a brave warrior people, whose knights rivalled those of the Christians in deeds of reckless daring. But all their high courage and resource was in vain : disaster dogged them ; step by step through the years they were pushed back nearer the sea, until their ancient monarchy was limited to the lovely city of Granada, climbing up its two lofty hills, one crowned with the splendid palace of the Alhambra and the other stern with the frowning fortress of the Alcazaba. About this last jewel of the Moorish crown the white tents of the Christian army were now drawn like the links in a steel chain ; troops of knights in shining armour and foot-soldiers in helmet and cuirass marched to and fro at the sound of drum and trumpet, forming to the assault of some outwork of the doomed city.

Again and again the Christians rushed to the attack; again and again the Moslem knights made desperate sallies, sweeping with death and fire into the heart of the Christian camp. Every garden and orchard became a scene of deadly contest; every inch of ground was disputed by the Moors with an agony of grief and valour. Every advance made by the Christians was valiantly maintained, but never did they advance except at the cost of severe fighting and great loss of men. In repeated charges Boabdil, the Moorish king, aided by the flower of his chivalrous knights, endeavoured to wrest away the points of vantage gained by the Christians, but always the God of the Christians seemed to be more powerful than the God of Mahomet, and again and again the Moors were driven back, their ranks rent and bloody, into the city.

Chief of Boabdil's knights, famous for his gallantry and for his lofty spirit, was Muza ben Abel Gazan, a young man of royal lineage, of a proud and generous nature, who with his nobility of race had inherited a deadly hatred of the Christians. He was a magnificent horseman, and his skill in the use of all warlike weapons and his observance of all knightly courtesies had endeared him to the hearts both of the Moorish ladies and of the youthful cavaliers.

Even the Christians who had met him in tourneys and jousts confessed that he was a mirror of chivalry and an example of lofty martial virtues.

In these last fights about the walls of Granada Muza was always the first to sally out at the head of his cavalry and the last to return. Men fighting at the point of exhaustion against overwhelming odds still found they had a reserve of strength left when his strong voice rang out near them. "Allah achbar!" was his cry. "God is great! Death to the Christians!" And those lying with glazing eyes and ebbing breath, seeing the gleaming lines of Muza's knights sweeping by with the young hero at their head, lifted themselves, and with their last words blessed and cheered him as he passed.

But all was in vain. Famine and disease began to stalk through the doomed city. The summer months of stifling heat went by; autumn arrived, but the harvests had been swept off the face of the country and no aid could pierce the Christian lines. Gloom and despondency settled upon the Moors, pent up between the walls of their beautiful city, that was now becoming a sepulchre for thousands. There were no more daring sallies from the gates, and the tuck of drum and the blare of trumpets sounded but seldom, like the last dying notes from the horn of a stricken hero. The people began to clamour. As Boabdil the King and his knights and councillors walked through the streets women threw themselves on their knees and held out their emaciated babes, crying for food for them, or men pointed to the weakened frames of beloved little sons and daughters and demanded that their misery should cease.

Boabdil summoned a council, and the despair upon the faces of his advisers gave their unspoken decision. The dreadful tale of the people's extremity was soon told by the governor of the city: "Our granaries are nearly empty; the fodder for the war-horses is needed for the men; the steeds themselves are killed for food. Of seven thousand horses which once bore knights into the field, but three hundred lean creatures remain. Our city has two hundred thousand people, every one of whom has a mouth which is ever crying upon me for bread."

The young King hesitated. He had once hoped that

relief might come from the Sultan of Egypt, or the kings of the Barbary States, but all such hope was past now: neither food nor forces could reach them. His councillors urged that he should surrender, asking what availed further defence—what alternative remained but to surrender or to starve to death in thousands?

One voice alone rose in opposition, that of Muza ben Abel Gazan.

"We need not yet surrender," he said. "Our means are not exhausted. We still have the forces of despair, which may win us the victory and crush our foes. Let us rouse the mass of the people, put weapons in their hands, and lead them against the Christians. There they will find food, revenge, or death. I am ready to lead the way into the thickest of their squadrons. Rather would I be numbered among those who fell in the defence of Granada than among those who survived to yield."

Muza's words were the words of a noble despair, but they failed of effect, for they found no echo in the minds of broken-hearted and dispirited men. It was decided that the governor of the city should be sent to the Christian King, Ferdinand, to obtain terms. This was done, and the terms proposed were merciful. They were accordingly accepted by the Moors. Muza still strove to dissuade his friends; his fevered eyes shone with the passion of despair as he urged the King not to sign the treaty of surrender; rage and indignation rang in every tone of his voice.

"Do not deceive yourselves," he cried, "nor think the Christians will be faithful to their promises, or that their King will be as magnanimous in conquest as he has been victorious in war. Death is the least we have to fear. Surrender means the plundering and sacking of our beloved city, the profanation of our mosques, the ruin of our homes, the ill-treatment of our wives and daughters; cruel oppression, bigoted intolerance, whips and chains; the dungeon, the faggot, and the fire. Such are the miseries and indignities we shall see and suffer; at least those grovelling souls will suffer them, who now shrink from an honourable death. For my part, by Allah, I will never witness them!"

These words, containing prophecies which for a hundred years and more men were to remember and to mark as forecasting the bitterest truths, were the last which Muza gave in that great council hall. He strode away gloomily through the Court of Lions and through the outer halls of the Alhambra without speaking to any. He went to his dwelling, spoke a few farewell words to his dead wife's father, Taric ben Abbu, and charged him with the care of his little son, Sidi. Then, arming himself at all points, he mounted his favourite war charger and issued forth from the city by the gate of Elvira.

A few hours later, in the twilight, a party of Castilian cavaliers, about twelve in number, were riding along the banks of a stream in the beautiful plain below the hills on which Granada stands. Suddenly before them in the gathering dusk they beheld a Moorish knight approaching, locked from head to foot in steel of proof. His visor was closed, his lance in rest, his great black steed was cased like himself in armour. The Spanish knights challenged him, demanding his name.

The Moslem made no answer, but like a panther he dashed at the nearest Spaniard, with levelled lance, spitting the man upon the spear and bearing him struggling from his horse. Wheeling round, he drew his scimitar, which gleamed blue in the twilight. He dashed at this and that knight, raining furious and deadly blows upon them, careless of the wounds he himself received, so that his scimitar gave death to others. He was fighting, not for glory, but for death. Nearly half the Spaniards fell before he received a disabling wound, and his horse, pierced by a lance, fell to the ground. Admiring his valour, the Christians would have spared the life of their adversary, but he would not have it. They withdrew a little, but he crawled after them on his knees, thrusting and stabbing with a long Fez poniard. Finding that the Spaniards would not kill him, he rose to his feet and, staggering to the brink of the stream, threw himself into its swift current, and his armour sank him instantly to the depths.

Thus died the valorous young Moorish warrior, pattern of chivalry and mirror of knighthood, Muza ben Abel Gazan.

Granada was delivered up to the Spanish King, and Boabdil and many of his people were given a kingdom in the mountains of Alpuxarras. But thousands of the Moslems left the country, streaming southward to Barbary, and settling in Tangier, Tunis, Algiers, and other towns along the coast of Africa. Then by a piece of treachery Boabdil was deprived of his kingdom and retired to the lands of his kinsman, the King of Fez. For a time the treaty with the Moors who were left in Spain—Moriscoes, as they were termed—was honourably kept. Then it was urged by a high-placed bigot that to keep faith with infidels was to break faith with God, and persecution and oppression were let loose upon them.

The choice was, baptism or exile. The mosques were closed, Moorish learning was stamped out, and the Moors themselves were beaten and insulted. They rebelled, and the rising was repressed with savage fury. Half a century of smouldering hatred succeeded. The Moriscoes feigned to be Christians, spoke Spanish, and had Spanish names; but in their own homes they spoke Arabic and were intensely themselves. The more they seemed to yield so oppression increased, until the tortured people rose in revolt again, and the fair lands of Granada and Andalusia were once more drenched with blood. The lovely valleys of the Alpuxarras, with their numerous villages, were the home of many thousands of peaceful Moriscoes. The place was one great garden of blossom and fruit, for the thrifty hands of the Moors made every inch of ground yield its produce, and their scientific methods of irrigation made the desert fertile. These lovely lands were laid waste; a fierce and bloody struggle swept through them, in which a narrow fanaticism strove with a vengeful spirit that had a hundred years of insult and persecution to wipe out. No quarter was given: men, women, and children were butchered in cold blood under the eye of the Christian leader; the mouths of caves to which refugees had fled were heaped with burning wood, so that not one of the miserable creatures survived; and so thorough was the house-to-house slaughter that whole villages which once had been the homes of peaceful and industrious people were transformed into reeking shambles in which not a living being remained.

Those who survived were doomed to slavery or banishment. Thousands spent the remainder of their sad lives with iron upon their limbs; thousands fared to

Africa, there to beg their bread in a state of abject destitution.

Is it to be wondered at that for such a crime as the inhuman persecution of the Moors in Spain there should be a fitting punishment ? The Moors while they ruled in Spain had been the most learned people in Europe. They had tolerated the Christian religion and had not oppressed their Spanish subjects. Their habits of thrift and industry, refinement and cleanliness, were known over all the continent. But when they became outlaws in none did the spirit of revenge ever burn more fiercely. The word went forth : henceforth it was to be war to the knife with the accursed Christian. Spain was the enemy, and no mercy was to be shown her. This was the penalty that Spain was to pay for her pride, her barbarity, and her ignorance.

One day, some twelve years after the death of Muza, a party of some two dozen men, young for the most part, ran a long row-boat down the shingly beach of Oran. As the stones leaped up beneath their swift feet and the waves dashed before the prow of their frail craft as it took the water none of the reckless men about her thought what might be the outcome of the adventure on which they were about to put forth. Their minds saw only the pleasant prospect of rich prizes of merchants' ships which were to be theirs, with ample cargoes of silks and spices from Persia, gold from Egypt, worked vessels and carpets from Spain, and, perhaps, occasionally, the person of some rich lord or merchant prince who would pay a heavy price for ransom. These were to be the wages if success came their way ; but if perchance they were captured by the fierce Christian Knights of St John, or by some war-galley of France, Spain, or Italy, then there would be years of misery spent beneath the whip of the slave-master as they tugged their hearts out at the heavy oar, chained with other miserable galley slaves to the bench, forced to aid their masters in fighting against their own people.

This was the first venture of their *reis*, or captain, Sidi ben Muza, son, as they had heard, of the valiant Muza, who had been one of the great heroes of their people in the old days when they ruled in Spain. Sidi was but eighteen, but already he had the name of a bold and daring mariner, as expert with the bow, the sword, and the boarding-iron as with oar and sail. Hitherto he had formed one of the crew of the galleys sailing under the flag of Hajji Reis, a reckless and successful corsair, but now, with the share of booty earned under Hajji, and the money and jewels left him by his grandfather, Taric ben Abbu, he had bought the brigantine which had just been launched, resolved to begin his own career in the campaign of hatred and spoliation against the Spaniards, the enemies of his people.

From his earliest years the mind of the lad had been impressed by his grandfather, Taric ben Abbu, with the imperative duty of revenge. The words of the Koran were continually dinned into his ears: "You shall take a vengeance equal to the injury which hath been done to you; the free shall die for the free, the servant for the servant, and a woman for a woman," and it was told him that inasmuch as injury, death, and dishonour had been done and were still being done upon his own people in Spain, so should he exact vengeance upon all who fell into his hands, belonging to that detestable and iniquitous nation.

Sidi ben Muza, seated at the tiller, directed the course of the brigantine toward the Spanish coast. The term brigantine did not then have anything like the meaning now attached to it. The pirates of the Barbary coast used the word to denote a large rowing-boat, carrying from sixteen to twenty-six or thirty oars. A mast could be stepped and a sail hoisted when conditions were specially favourable, but the boat being hardly fit for the open sea and all chances of weather it was the ambition of every young pirate to seize or purchase a galley, to be manned by Christians captured in a raid, who would be chained three or four to a bench, and would be whipped if the heavy oars which they had to pull were not served smartly enough. Some twenty-four worked the oars of the brigantine, but there were some twenty more fighters who took turns with them, who were lodged in the *rambades* or prow, and Sidi with his five subordinate officers lived in a little cabin on the poop.

Sidi knew of several inlets where he could lie in hiding, ready to pounce out on merchant galleys or lumbering sailing-ships. For some days he thus lay *perdu* in various creeks along the Andalusian shore, but nothing offered that was within the power of his little band of fifty men. On the evening of the third day, as twilight began to fall over the wide waters, the company held a council of war, and it was resolved that they should go ashore and, under cover of night, attack the tower of a Spanish lord whose estate was situated some three miles inland. Strange would it be if they could not, by the sudden terror of their attack, bring off some rich booty, together with the Spanish lord himself, his wife and daughters, for slaves or ransom.

Even as they sat, each man on his thwart, eating his evening meal of dates and bread, the look-out man came running down from the sea watch.

"Reis," said he, "there is a boat rowing from the land to the north. It is no larger than ours and has the look of a Spaniard."

Instantly there was a rush to the high rock where the look-out was kept, whence a boat could be seen being rapidly rowed south and east. The keen eyes of the corsairs, even in the fading light, knew it for a Spanish vessel, with some dozen rowers aboard, who were pulling as if for dear life.

"Maybe some escaping Moriscoes, from the speed they are making," said Sidi; "but we will overhaul them, whoever they are, and know why they are in such haste."

Swiftly the men launched their boat, and Sidi turned the nose of the brigantine to cut off the other vessel. The pirates bent to their oars with a will, for each was glad of something to do, so long as it was in the way of a chase. The other boat soon became aware that it was being followed and its crew redoubled their efforts, but in vain: the pirate boat swiftly overhauled the stranger and raced alongside.

"Hola!" cried Sidi. "What do you here at night, rowing so fast from land?"

The crew of the strange boat had ceased rowing, and now whispered together.

"If ye are Spaniards and come anigh us," came a

fierce, breathless voice," we will not be taken alive. And ye shall not all escape harmless."

"We are no Spaniards" replied Sidi, and spat at the name. "Who are you?"

"We are Moriscoes," came the reply, with some eagerness. "The lord Cuerva would sell and enslave us, and we are therefore seeking to fly."

The boats came together, and in a little while Sidi had heard all the simple but horrible tale. Don Ferdinand Hurtado de Olas y Cuerva owned much land and three Morisco villages in the district near by, and after oppressing his people, selling some of their daughters and sons as slaves, casting others into prison, and branding many fathers of families, he had at length threatened to get rid of all these pestiferous heretics within his lands. Some weeks had passed and he had done nothing to put his threat into execution, while all the poor villagers had gone in fear and trembling, wondering what their fate was to be. Then that very afternoon, into the little landlocked bay beside one of the Morisco villages had come a big galley, which at that very moment was moored a cable length from the shore. The Moriscoes saw the captain of the galley go off with several of his officers, and later they heard that they had gone to the house of Don Cuerva. Their worst fears and suspicions were now aroused, and they felt sure that on the morrow they would be driven on board the galley and taken away to another part of Spain, or even to France, to be sold into slavery.

Determined to forestall the terrible fate in store for them, some of the Moriscoes, as soon as darkness had fallen, had seized a small galley belonging to Don Cuerva and placed their wives and children in it, with a few goods, resolved to trust themselves to the mercy of the winds and the waves rather than to that of their oppressor. The women and children were now cowering in the bottom of the vessel, many of them sick and wretched, while the men told their pitiable tale to the pirates.

Sidi ben Muza asked a few questions as to the size and crew of the strange galley which was the subject of their fears, and when he had been answered he said:

"Friends, come with us. We also are Moors, and we will aid you."

The boats turned and rowed back to the creek where the pirates had been hiding. A hurried council of war was held, and it was decided that at midnight the brigantine, with muffled oars, should be rowed into the bay where the galley lay, and an attempt be made to overpower the crew and seize the vessel. A spy was sent on shore to learn what he could in the village of the Moriscoes, and then men saw to their weapons, feeling the edges of their knives and sharpening them on their belts. Extra knives were served out, for it would probably be necessary to free and arm the galley slaves, who would fight like furies against their masters. When the spy returned he said:

"Sidi Reis, matters are quite as the Moriscoes have told us. Women are weeping and men are swearing and praying. The captain of the galley is one named Don Guzman de Tormes, and he is expected back at the galley just before dawn. Some of the galley's crew are in the village, and they tell the story that Don Guzman is but a kinsman, paying a visit to Don Cuerva, and that he and his galley will depart at dawn. There are seven score fighters aboard, as it is guessed."

At midnight Sidi gave the word, and with two of the fugitive Moriscoes beside him on the poop as guides, he turned the prow of the brigantine in the direction of the bay. The oars were muffled, and so carefully did the men row that not the slightest creak could be heard as the oars turned on the thole-pins, and they entered and left the water without a sound. The night was quite dark, but still, save for a little wind that blew off shore, ruffling the waves. Soon they reached the bay, and very deftly Sidi put the brigantine into the opening and made toward the beach at the other end. Every nerve was a-stretch now, for it was of the utmost importance that the sentinels on the galley should not get warning of the brigantine before she was upon them. Men dipped their oars into the lazy waves so that the water hardly rippled. Soon a subdued hiss gave the warning which stopped all the oars but six near the prow, which continued to be worked so as to keep way upon the boat.

By now Sidi could make out the long black hull of the sleeping galley, which showed no lights. Its rows of oars jutted out on each side, raised above the level of the sea. A whispered word of command was carried down the brigantine, and, fixing their oars, eight of the rowers, with infinite care, slid over the low side of the boat into the water and with stealthy strokes made toward the galley. Meanwhile the brigantine was slowly approaching the galley under the strokes of the six remaining oars. The men on the prow were straining their eyes toward the dark galley, while the hand of each rested upon sword handle or dagger haft, as they waited for the word which would launch them over the side. The minutes seemed to go as slowly as hours.

Suddenly the clank of a falling chain sounded on the galley. It seemed too loud to be caused by the movement of a wretched slave as he slept chained to his bench. All wondered: had the swimmers gained the galley unperceived and already begun to free and arm the slaves? The moments passed slowly in the darkness and the silence. Then suddenly came a sharp cry, which leaped up fierce and hard. Was it a call of alarm, or only the cry of a sleeping slave, making one brave effort for liberty and vengeance in his dreams?

Suddenly the flash of a lantern gleamed on the poop of the galley, and voices rose in quick question and answer. At the same moment Sidi's silver whistle rang out. With a shudder the brigantine scraped the side of the galley and the pirates swarmed over the poop. Instantly there arose the fierce turmoil of fighting. The Spanish officers, though taken wholly by surprise, fought bravely; the soldiers sleeping in the *rambades*, hearing the alarm, started up and made to run along the gangway between the rowing benches, but the first were struck down in the darkness by they knew not what, and those who hesitated quickly perceived that the first few benches were empty. Then arose the dreadful cry which, once heard, struck terror into the hearts of all Spaniards on a galley: "The slaves are free! The slaves are free!"

Such a cry meant that a terrible revenge was about to be taken. Chafed by chains, beaten by whips, starved, forced to pull the heavy oars in rain, in sun, or in the freezing winds of winter, half naked, living, indeed, a dreadful daily martyrdom from which, as a rule, death alone could release them, the slaves, when once by some lucky accident they could break their fetters, exacted a full vengeance from their captors for all the misery and torture they had suffered. Rarely did one of their task-masters survive from the fight to the death which followed. Though armed merely with a length of shackle against the sword of the gentleman or the arquebus of the soldier, the result was the same.

Bench by bench the slaves were freed by some of those whom the pirates had liberated in the first instance, and while the number of the soldiers in the galley was fast being lessened, the number of their enemies was being increased. With cries of "Allah! Allah Achbar!" the Moslem slaves threw themselves upon their captors, and in the darkness a terrible scene of slaughter took place, the galley rocking on the quiet waters of the bay beneath the furious feet of the struggling men. Then gradually the sounds of fighting died down, and in their place at intervals came dull splashes, as one by one the bodies of the slain Spaniards were thrust overboard.

When day dawned Sidi ben Muza looked upon the prize which he had captured and found that it exceeded all his expectations. It was a galley the possession of which would set him up as a respectable corsair, for it was capable of holding four hundred men. Moreover, it was full of stores and arms, for it was one of the war galleys of the King of Spain, and was a prize which even Hajji Reis himself would have looked upon as a great acquisition.

Sidi knew that the story of his exploit would quickly run through the neighbouring country-side, and he determined to act promptly. At dawn he landed nearly all the Moslem galley slaves, who were now armed, and who in their new-found liberty were ready for any desperate deed against the country of their hereditary foes. The brigantine he ordered to be rowed out to sea to keep watch, and in the galley itself he left a strong guard. Then at the head of his fierce army he went inland, plundering and burning. They reached the house of Don Cuerva only to find, as Sidi expected, that the Don and the captain of the galley, having heard of the capture, had fled, expecting a visit from the victorious pirate.

After ransacking the house Sidi gave it to the flames, and then, laden with spoil, and with a convoy of men, women, and children whom they had captured from some of the villas and farms, the pirates made for their vessels. Already Sidi's instructions had been carried out and the Morisco families had gone aboard the galley, since all of them feared the vengeance which Don Cuerva would visit upon the Moslems in his territory when he returned to find his mansion gutted.

Both galley and brigantine were crammed with more people than they were intended to hold, but it happened that late in the afternoon a good breeze sprang up, and the sails being spread the voyage south-eastward to the coast of Barbary was begun. It was an anxious time for young Sidi as, followed by the brigantine, the galley made its way over the curling waves before the swift breeze. A keen look-out was kept for any hostile craft, and the sailing powers of his capture were eagerly conned. It was a great satisfaction to find that the galley was really a swift vessel. The breeze dropped when they were a few miles from Oran, and the released galley slaves had to take to the oars again. But it was with delight now that they strained their muscles to push the great craft along, for every stroke brought them nearer to the freedom for which they had yearned during many weary days.

At length, just as dawn broke, the line of faint blue hills beyond Oran could be seen lying in the sunlight. At the sight a great cry of joy leaped from the throats of the liberated slaves, and they made the galley bound forward. In a little while they came within view of the port, and then rich cloths, carpets, and tapestries were hung over the sides of the vessels, while with shouts of jubilation and the clashing of weapons and shields the crews gave notice of their success. The men on the shore, marking with keen eyes the lines of the great galley which the tiny brigantine had in tow, quickly gathered what had taken place and replied with a roar of welcome.

There were great rejoicings that day in Oran. Sidi ben Muza was received by the Dey of Oran, who, though nominally at peace with the neighbouring kingdom of Spain, was very much alive to the benefits which plunder and slaves brought to his town. After the capture of the galley Sidi ben Muza was looked upon as a prominent leader, and he never lacked men to follow him. A few days after entering with his prize, having bought sufficient Christian slaves to man the oars, he set out again, determined to add to his fleet by the capture of one or two other galleys belonging to Spain. A lucky chance, aided by his natural boldness, gained him the prizes he desired.

Fifty years or so previous to this date the Turks had conquered Constantinople, and ever since that time they had not only strengthened their position in Europe but, benefiting by the petty jealousies which raged between the States whose lands bordered the Mediterranean, they had grown to be a formidable Power. Suggestions were made every now and then that Spain, France, Genoa, and the Pope should join their forces to beat the Turk from the holy city of Constantinople, but all these Powers were suspicious of each other and nothing was done. However, just at the time when Sidi ben Muza had captured the galley an alliance called 'the Alliance of Christian Princes' had been formed by the efforts of Pope Alexander. Louis XII, King of France, and Ferdinand V of Spain joined with the Pope, and the veteran Grand Master of the Knights of St John, who from his fortress at Rhodes waged unceasing war both on sea and land against the Moslem, was appointed Captain-General of the Christian armies.

Word of this was given to Sidi by a corsair of Tunis whom he spoke in mid-ocean, and it was told him that already the fleet of the Christians was searching the Ægean for the Turkish galleys. Sidi wondered whether it would be to his advantage to tender his services to the Grand Turk, but decided that while he had but one vessel his offer would not be rated very highly. He therefore decided to visit the shores of the Papal States of Italy, thinking that as the Italian fleet was engaged farther west there would be few to guard the shores of Naples and the Roman States, and there would be a good chance of rifling a rich villa, capturing a few wealthy Christians, or carrying off villagers to man his slave benches.

A day in June, accordingly, found Sidi ben Muza

keeping a keen look-out in what seemed a lonely sea off the coast of Naples. All were on the alert, and at the slightest sign of a bigger ship appearing on the sea-line or round a curve in the coast, the corsairs were ready to show a clean pair of heels.

"Think you," said Abdullah, Sidi's lieutenant, as they stood together on the poop scanning the shore and the sea with rapid glances, "think you, captain, that the papal admiral, Ludovico del Mosca, would leave his holy master undefended?"

"That I do not know," replied Sidi; "but," he added grimly, "if I had ten full galleys I would row up the Tiber, and call upon the Pope at his villa at Briglione."

Abdullah looked with wonder at his captain, for the daring of such a thought was beyond all bounds, though in a few years' time he was to know that the words were no idle boast, but that his bold master was capable even of this exploit.

"Beyond that cape there," went on Sidi, pointing to a promontory to the south, "lies the town of Santa Lucia. There are many rich villas on the hills and beside the sea-road. We will visit the largest."

The galley crept up to the cape, and, propelled by the arms of the Christian slaves who sat chained upon the benches where but a few days previously Moslem slaves had toiled beneath the whip, the galley rounded the jutting land. A quick breath of surprise escaped Abdullah, while Sidi's face went dark. Three Christian galleys, flying the flag of Spain, were anchored off the shore.

"Three against us, captain," said Abdullah.

"But look!" returned Sidi, with flashing eyes in

which delight shone. "Their crews are swarming into the hills. The fools! The galleys are almost empty. All three are ours!"

A low whistle brought all his fighting men to keen attention, and the slave-master and his two mates with whips in hand stood ready, watching their captain for his orders. If, as they expected, it was to be flight, then there would be heavy punishment for the backs of the half-naked galley slaves. But to the astonishment of every one the prow of the galley was pointed at the nearest vessel, not a quarter of a mile away, and orders were given to ply the oars with a will.

The men on the Spanish galleys were aware of the pirate by now, but hesitated as to whether it was not one of their own ships. Those moments of hesitation were fateful. When the Spanish lieutenant, Don Amadeo, caught sight of the turbaned heads upon the poop he was no longer in doubt, but he hardly believed his eyes when he saw the pirates making swiftly toward him. Certainly his leader, Don Hurtado, and the main part of the men-at-arms were ashore on a private quarrel of the Duke of Alva, their master, but his force was still a respectable one.

The lieutenant had little more time for reflection, however, for the pirate rammed his vessel just as the Spaniard made up his mind that he could expect an attack from the stranger. The pirates swarmed over the bulwarks and a short sharp struggle ensued. The Spaniards were taken by surprise, and though some put up a resistance all were soon overwhelmed by the rush and fury of the Moslems. The lieutenant was wounded and quickly roped up, for possible ransom. Leaving a crew on the first captured galley Sidi instantly made for the other vessels, the men on which were making frantic signals to the soldiers on shore. But so fierce was the attack of the pirates that in a little while the two galleys were also in their hands, and though one or two boatloads of soldiers came off they thought discretion the better part of valour and did not attempt to board the galleys. While these events were passing the soldiers were pouring down from the hills, and the frantic figure of the Spanish commander, Don Hurtado de Mariglia, in much lace and gold embroidery and very red in the face, could be seen raging up and down the beach, at one time impotently shaking both fists at the pirates, the next moment cuffing the soldiers about him in his anger.

Very leisurely the pirates drew up the anchors, and as a wind was now setting toward the south-west they unreefed the sails, and with a hearty cheer from the throats of the hundreds of Moslem galley slaves to whom the turn of events had given freedom, the three Spanish galleys, preceded by the pirate ship, slipped gracefully over the waters and before long disappeared from sight.

If ever poetic justice was done it was on this occasion. Sidi and his Moslems gravely smiled when they heard the facts from their prisoners, and nothing of the humour of the position was lost upon the keen-witted Moors. The three galleys which the pirate had fallen in with formed part of the great fleet of the 'Alliance of Christian Princes,' which had started out so ambitiously to break down the sea power of the Turk. They had, indeed, had one or two encounters with the Turkish navy, with little damage done on either side. It happened that the great fleet contained thirty-six large bombards, with their ammunition, forty other bombards, a large number of smaller cannon, arquebuses for ships' boats, and immense quantities of iron cannon-balls, gunpowder, darts, and bullets, all purchased from Ferdinand, King of Naples. It occurred to the chivalrous and high-minded commanders of the French and Spanish fleets that as the territory of the King of Naples was thus without means of defence, it would afford a good opportunity to get possession of that desirable country. Thereupon the French and Spaniards, leaving the papal commander in the Ægean, hastened to Naples, where they landed and seized the country, the King not waiting to meet his friends, knowing that, having sold his artillery, he was powerless against them.

The three vessels captured by Sidi ben Muza had been part of the Spanish flotilla, which had been sent by the Duke of Alva to kill or capture a certain Italian lord who had incurred his displeasure, and to lay waste his territory. As it turned out, the Italian lord had a large following and was able to administer a thorough beating to the forces sent against him, so that besides the loss of the three war galleys the Duke of Alva had to smart under the sense of having had a drubbing from a man whom he had thought to catch unawares.

With the wealth he had now amassed Sidi ben Muza was able to buy five other galleys, so that when next he left the roadstead of Mars El-Kebir, as the splendid harbour of Oran is called, he was at the head of a fleet of nine full galleys and commanded a force of almost two thousand fighting men

During the next two years his name became a name of dread to every merchant whose cargo ships left the harbours of Spain, and to any others whose business led them to make voyages between Spain, France, and Italy. Nor did he limit his attentions to the sea. He had many friends and allies among the oppressed Moriscoes still dwelling in the southern parts of Spain, and by their help and his own swiftness of action and boldness of execution he carried through many daring exploits in the inland districts.

On many a night when haughty Spanish lords and their wives and daughters had sought their couches, thinking of anything rather than the Barbary pirates, they and their dependents would be roused in terror, amid the cries of fierce men and the flames of their burning homes, to find that the dreaded corsairs were upon them. No mercy was shown to any Christian who offered resistance, and soon the proud Spaniards, clad only in their night garments, were being driven, together with peasants and villagers, down toward the sea coast. Then there would be the misery of the passage, the stench of the hold adding to the wretchedness of sea sickness. Afterward the unutterable shame of the slave market, where haughty Spanish maidens and youths would be forced to stand and show their 'points' like cattle, the raucous, brutal tones of the auctioneer above their heads and the eyes of Arab dealers burning into their flesh. Then, for the men, there would be the years of unremitting labour, either at the galley oar, beneath the whip of a slave-master, or on the land, suffering the tyranny of some farmer who treated his slaves like cattle. As for the women, the more beautiful would be sunk in the mysterious depths of a harem, never more to look upon their native land. Or there would be the weary waiting for the ransom which forgetful relations in Spain would only slowly collect, while the poor captives fretted and pined amid the wretchedness of their prison.

Many were the proud hearts which broke under these intolerable conditions, many the tears, the agonies of separation when mothers, daughters, sons, and fathers were torn from each other's arms in the market-places. Some of the men, finding their captivity more than they could bear, turned renegade, denied their religion and their race, and enrolled themselves as fighting-men under a Moslem pirate. Others plotted to escape, but few ever succeeded; more often they were recaptured and subjected to horrible tortures ere they found relief in death.

In this way the sins of bigotry and ignorance committed by Spain and her rulers were visited upon her sons and daughters for many generations. The cruelties and oppression inflicted upon the Moors from 1492 until the last wretched remnants were expelled from the country in 1609–10 were paid for in the mental and physical suffering of un-numbered Christians for three centuries. The corsairs, however, did not limit their reprisals to Spaniards; every Christian nation suffered, and in the course of time so bold did the corsairs become from the knowledge of the mastery they held of the sea and the terror which their name inspired that their fleets sailed as far north as Iceland, and they brought captives for the harem and the slave-bench from the shores of England and Northern Europe.

As the years went by the name and fame of Sidi ben Muza was known for many miles inland along the coasts of Spain. The terrified Spaniards called him *Diablo del mar*, 'the Sea Devil,' so baneful a power did he wield. Every year he added to the number of his fleet, and every year the toll he took of fine vessels, rich cargoes, and captives became greater. Hitherto the Spanish Government had affected to despise the attacks of these wasps of Barbary, but at length the authorities sent one of their greatest military leaders, Don Pedro Navarro, to root out the robbers' nests. By this time great numbers of pirates haunted the ports and harbours of the African coast, but as yet they were not conscious of their power, and their forces had not been co-ordinated nor their strongholds made defensive, as was to be the case a few years afterward. Navarro, with a great fleet, put out to sea, and was able to take possession of the three chief pirate lairs—Oran, Bujeya, and Algiers—without much difficulty. He burnt many galleys and knocked the towns to pieces. He made the Dey of Algiers promise to renounce piracy in future, and in order to put a rein upon the Algerians, he caused a strong fort, the Peñon de Alger ('the Rock of Algiers') to be built on a rocky spit of land at the entrance to the harbour, where, manned by a Spanish garrison, for long it stood, the muzzles of its cannon grinning at the town and the roadstead, ready to belch forth destruction upon any sea-hawk who ventured to enter or leave the port. For some years the Moors of Algiers restrained their predatory and revengeful impulses, and the pirates elsewhere either became merchants or took their galleys and offered them and their own services to the Grand Turk at Stamboul, who received them with open arms, as goodly reinforcements to his fleet.

One of the great prizes for which Navarro had ventured

forth had been the capture of the 'Sea Devil,' Sidi ben Muza. But Sidi had had timely knowledge of the descent to be made upon Oran. Loading up his galleys with his treasure, his harem, and everything of value that was portable, he had fled long before the Spaniard had got under way, and, with his fleet of two dozen galleys, had rowed up the Dardanelles and had laid all before the feet of Bajazet. He was graciously accepted into the service of the Grand Turk, who placed a large fleet under his charge ; and then, after he had settled his wives and family in a splendid villa overlooking the pleasant shores of the Bosporus, the pirate chief had put to sea, vowed to wage war upon Spaniard, Venetian, Genoan, and Frenchman indifferently. With what success he ravaged the shores, captured the vessels, enslaved the subjects of each of those nations the histories of the Turkish fleet in the early days of the sixteenth century bear full witness. He was known to the Spaniards by the name which denoted his possession of Satanic qualities; but to the Venetian and Genoese merchants and military men he was referred to by a name which showed that they recognized his elusiveness and death-dealing characteristics : to these he was 'the Pestilence.'

After a few years Sidi left the service of the Grand Turk, though still high in favour at Stamboul, and with a great fleet of thirty galleys, which contained some six thousand fighting men, he cast about for some port which he could make his headquarters. He had tired of regular employment ; he wanted to be his own master again, and to be untrammelled by treaties, which prevented him seizing the vessel of this or that nation which happened to have entered into friendly relations for the time being with the Grand Turk.

One fine day, behold the fleet of thirty galleys ranging up before the harbour of Bizerta, that convenient port situated on the portion of the coast of Northern Africa from which so many centres and channels of rich trade could be struck at once. The shores of Sicily were just over the way to the north-east, and beyond these were the wealthy lands of Naples, Rome, Tuscany, and Liguria, with rich argosies from Genoa and Venetia lumbering along the seas. Then to the north-west were the Balearic Isles, and the coasts of that more particularly hated race, the Spaniards. What more convenient spot than Bizerta for the eyrie of this sea-hawk ?

The ruler of the territory in which Bizerta was situated was a chieftain of the Berber Moslems named Abu-Abd-Allah-Mohammed, a dignitary who had hitherto been content to live more or less in amity with his Christian neighbours in the lands of the Mediterranean. Particularly had Mohammed entered into a treaty with the rich merchant republic of Genoa, undertaking that the commerce of the Italian State should be respected by all who owed allegiance or service to Abu-Abd-Allah-Mohammed.

Now word was brought to the Berber monarch that Sidi ben Muza craved audience of him. His ships the sovereign had already seen from his high palace windows, looking like toyboats on the blue plains of the Mediterranean under the brilliant sun. Permission was given to the pirate to enter, and soon, clothed in brilliant apparel, and followed by his chief captains flashing in breastplates and helms and adorned with jewelled chains, Sidi ben Muza came into the presence, the sternness of his high-bred features softened for the moment. After the formal courtesies had been interchanged Sidi ben Muza quickly came to the heart of the matter. It was a little thing he craved: merely hospitality, in other words, permission to use the splendid harbour of Bizerta for the refitting of his vessels, and the storing of what little goods he might obtain in the course of his business.

The Berber chieftain's eyes gleamed with satisfaction for a moment and then clouded. It was the rule along the shores of Barbary that corsairs to whom kings afforded the hospitality of their ports should pay for this convenience by giving up a fifth of their booty to the ruler who provided them with this 'protection.' But, reflected Mohammed, what would Genoa say if he sheltered this prince of pirates, this 'pestilence' whose ravages had wrought destruction among the wealth of the merchants of Genoa, to say nothing of those of Venice, the Papal States, and of Spain?

However, Mohammed thought the proposal was worth the risk of anything the Genoese could do, and he therefore graciously granted the use of the harbour of Bizerta to Sidi ben Muza.

As time went on Mohammed found that the benefits derived from sheltering the corsair were very substantial. Much booty was captured by Sidi, and a fifth of all this fell into the hands of Mohammed, besides a certain number of the fairest Christian female captives. Meanwhile Mohammed pretended that he was dealing quite fairly with his Genoese friends. One merchant bitterly reproached him with harbouring a pirate contrary to the terms of his treaty.

"You want benefits whichever way you turn," said the Italian, a merchant prince of Genoa named Messer Alfredo. "You take your harbour dues from us when we put into your port with our cargoes, and if, when we leave your roadstead, we fall into the hands of the Devil of the Sea to whom you give shelter, you take a fifth of our goods. You ask too much, your Highness, and their Graces the lords of Genoa will require an account from you."

Mohammed affected to treat such threats with contempt and some indignation; but one morning he and his town were awakened by a round shot which crashed into the courtyard of his palace. It came from the sea, where a great fleet of Genoese galleys was crowding up. After Mohammed had had the cannon-balls hopping about him for an hour or more, smashing up his town, shivering his walls, and bringing all his terrified harem on their knees before him, he felt very much inclined to parley with the Genoese and to promise whatever they wished of him. But they gave him no chance of pledging his soul to anything. When the Genoese commander thought he had sufficiently shaken the courage of Mohammed's few hundred men-at-arms and whatever corsairs were in the town, he landed a large force of soldiers and crossbowmen, against whom the townspeople made little opposition.

In the inner harbour were found half a dozen galleys of the redoubtable 'Sea Devil,' but Sidi ben Muza himself was away with most of his fleet. The corsairs who had been left behind had fled inland, taking Sidi's harem and his treasure with them. The Genoese burnt the galleys, plundered the town, and pursued the fleeing Mohammed and his crowd of houris for a while. But then, thinking that their comrades were getting more than their due share of booty, the pursuers gave up the chase and returned to finish plundering the town. Later, with some hundred or two Christian captives, the Genoese took to their ships again, leaving Bizerta but an empty shell.

If the Genoese thought they had inflicted any great loss upon Sidi or put any fear in his corsair's heart they were greatly mistaken. In the very week during which Bizerta had been captured a fleet of rich merchant vessels, convoyed to Egypt by four war-galleys of the Genoese, were set upon by Sidi at the head of some fifteen pirate galleys, and after a stiff fight two Genoese war-galleys were sunk and all the remaining vessels were captured. There was much wrath and indignation by reason of this affair, for it was the richest fleet that had sailed from Genoa that season, and the merchant lords who owned it had believed that Sidi was at that time occupied in repairing his losses at Bizerta.

Three weeks later an event occurred which put terror into all Christendom. It seems that the Pope was in the habit of visiting the villa of Signor Velturo, one of his noble friends, at Cesennio, a place on the shores of the Mediterranean near Civita Vecchia. His Holiness was fond of the sea air, and one day, accompanied by two cardinals, his host, and a bodyguard of a dozen soldiers, he had set out upon a palfrey to visit an ancient place along the shore where some treasure of the old Etruscans had lately been dug up. The country through which they passed, after leaving the fertile lands around the villa, was a desert of undulating heath, overrun with lentiscus, myrtle, and dwarf cork-trees, the haunt of the wild boar and the roebuck. There were also ruins in places, in which were the cavernous holes of old tombs or underground vaults under houses, and robbers had been known to make their lairs in such spots.

As they ambled along, the Lord Velturo in front, followed by the Pope and the cardinals on mules, with the soldiers behind on foot, Velturo called attention to a galley which could be seen at some distance out at sea.

"I suppose that is one of your Holiness's galleys watching the coast," said Velturo; "but I thought that Lodovico, your admiral, always ordered his captains to watch in pairs."

"I have no doubt the other galley is not far away," said the Pope.

The party had almost gained the outskirts of the little village of Piano d'Orno when suddenly from some old ruins beside the rough track several men rushed forth. There were about a dozen of them, and while some fought with the soldiers, others grasped the reins of the cardinals' mules. Suddenly one cardinal, who loved to appear in rich and splendid attire, was seized bodily by two ruffians and rushed off in the direction of the beach a quarter of a mile away. Hereupon the other robbers, who evidently thought that their fellows had secured the Pope himself, fled, leaving one of their number lying dead. Running down toward the sea, the Pope and his friends were just in time to see the cardinal bundled into a boat, which was immediately pushed off and rowed away to the galley they had noticed.

"The rascals! the ruffians!" cried the Pope. "It is a pirate galley! What has become of my guard boats?"

On making his way quickly to Rome, the Pope learnt that the wretch who had made this daring attempt to carry him off was Sidi ben Muza, who had also sunk one of the galleys stationed to keep guard off the coast, and had captured the other. All Christendom shuddered when it heard how near it had been to losing its spiritual head, and the terror of the name of the 'Devil of the Sea' grew greater than ever.

For some years thereafter Sidi ben Muza carried on his depredations through the length and breadth of the Mediterranean, his following growing every year, and his bold exploits becoming more daring and successful. Many expeditions were sent out against him by Genoa, Venice, Spain, and the Pope. Sometimes these fleets succeeded in vanquishing some of the galleys belonging to the corsair, but any such success was always followed by some particularly bold stroke against his enemies which brought the balance again in his favour.

At length the Grand Turk, Soliman the Magnificent, sent for Sidi and told him that he wished him to assist in the campaign which he, the Sultan, was about to undertake against the Knights of St John at Rhodes. Long had these valiant Christian fighters—'soldiers and sailors too'—been a thorn in the side of the newly won empire of the Turks in Europe. They waged an unsleeping war against the infidel, and so brave, so skilful were they both by sea and by land that the Moslem rarely succeeded in worsting them.

The Knights of St John were no carpet warriors.

They had a noble history reaching back to the time of the Crusades, and they first appear as the Knights of St John of Jerusalem. They had always been enemies of the Moslem, devoting themselves to the destruction of the Mohammedan faith. In 1291 they had been beaten out of the Holy Land, and had been compelled, much against their proud will, to accept hospitality and charity in Cyprus. There they still carried on their unwearied feud against the Moslem. They were all men of high lineage, and recruits came craving admission into their order from every princely and noble family in Europe.

In 1310 they left Cyprus and seized upon the isle of Rhodes. There they grew and flourished. They fortified the island until it was practically impregnable; they added yearly to the number of their war-galleys, obtaining wood from the forests of Asia Minor, and slaves to row upon their benches from the Moslem villages which they raided. An ancient enemy of theirs, the Sultan of Egypt, came and besieged them, but after forty-two days' ceaseless fighting he was beaten off, and constantly thereafter they warred against him and his fellow infidels.

If the Knights fought with fury against the infidel, their hatred was answered with as great an animus by the rulers of the Moslem world. In 1480 a Turkish fleet, with a great army, made what the Grand Turk thought would be an overwhelming assault upon Rhodes. Both sides fought with desperate bravery. The Turks pressed on, losing terribly, but still undaunted. At last the victorious janissaries, the flower of the Turkish army, fought their way to the top of the fortress wall; but then the exhausted Knights, making one final rally under their indomitable old chieftain, Pierre D'Aubusson, cut the foe to pieces, and again the standard of the Cross floated proudly in the breeze. Sixty-five days had the terrible battle raged. Three thousand dead janissaries were piled in the ditch into which the Knights' last charge had flung them; six thousand of the Moslems altogether had already been slain, and there were fifteen thousand lying wounded in the camp of the Grand Turk. The Turks retired baffled, to try to forget their defeat and to await another favourable opportunity.

The renown of the brave defence of Rhodes rang through Europe, and young scions of noble families flocked thither to fill up the thinned ranks of the Knights. All Europe was proud of their deed. Unfortunately the kings of Europe did not emulate the noble Knights in sinking all national jealousies and joining forces against the common foe. If the Christian Powers had had sufficient nobility of character to do that they could have swept the intruding Turk out of Europe, and thus centuries of tyranny, torture, and wrong would have been saved.

For forty-two years the Turks nursed their resolution to avenge their defeat, and at length, in 1522, one of the greatest of their monarchs, Soliman the Magnificent, resolved to make a final effort to expel the Knights from Rhodes. It was a long and bitter struggle, in which all the forces of the Moslem world were united to pluck out this thorn in the side of the conquering Turk. The operation was successful, though the price paid in blood and the lives of men was enormous. On December 24, 1522, Soliman the Magnificent, having received the

THE NAME OF THE 'DEVIL OF THE SEA' GREW GREATER THAN EVER

capitulation of the fortress from the hands of the vanquished Knights, made a triumphal entry into the town. Yet the Sultan had a great heart. When the noble leader of the Knights, Villiers L'Isle Adam, in battered and broken armour, was led toward him, he said: "It weighs upon me somewhat that I should be coming hither to chase this aged Christian warrior from his house."

A week later the Knights of St John left the island whence for over two centuries they had waged victorious warfare against the Moslems, and retreated to the rocky island of Malta, where they were to make an equally glorious name for themselves.

At the same time Sidi ben Muza was made governor of Rhodes by his master, the Grand Turk, in recognition of his numerous and worthy services. There, for many years, 'the Sea Devil' ruled with great renown, and the place that had once been a bulwark against the infidel now sent out powerful fleets and expeditions to the great loss and undoing of many merchants, nobles, and princes of Christendom.

II: The Pirate with the Red Beard

IT was a morning in June. Already the sun had risen, and its low light blazed through the leafy screen of woods which topped the hills beside the sea. Away to the west lay the waters of the Ægean, gently heaving, stretched out to the misty horizon. A long point of high land jutted out into the deep, its steep sides clothed with dense, dark woods as with a lovely green garment. Farther out, lying like purple patches on the deep blue floor of the sea, lay islands. Closer in, but still at a great distance, was Cos, with its great ridge of tree-clad hills; nearer to the land was Istros, a tiny speck; while still further to the west could be seen the faint lines of Astypalæa. Due north from the wooded point lay another long stretch of shore, forming the other side of the deep bight or bay which ran like a fjord into the Caramanian land.

Down on the shore, north of the wooded point, a big fire was burning, and some twenty or thirty men were reclining about the cooking-pots. Pulled up well above the water was a brigantine. All the men were young, and all had the look of seamen. They wore the loose trousers and long open tunic of Moslems, and in their belts were stuck knives, while bows and arrows hung at their backs.

Three of their number sat some little distance apart, talking earnestly. One, evidently the leader, was a young man of a thick-set frame, with a bullet-like head, and his face had the look of a master. His eyes were cruel, his lips thick and jutting, and the gestures with which he emphasized his words were rough and imperious. On his chin was a short red beard.

"I tell you, Kara Hassan," he cried, "you haven't spirit enough for this business. What if we are so near the nest of those great robbers, the Knights of St John? Have they not throats to slit, wealth to be looted? There is no risk from those at Rhodes, I tell you. We shall but run the brigantine up the river, then creep up to the village, and Kmitri and his money-bags will be ours."

"Have it as you will, then," said Kara Hassan, with a smile and a shrug. "When ever was Uruj, son of Mohammed, persuaded that his will was not to his advantage?"

Uruj made no reply to this remark, but told Kara Hassan, who was his lieutenant, to get the men into the boat. "The earlier we reach the village the better," he added.

In a few moments the brigantine was run into the sea, the last stores were thrown in, and the men pushed off. Propelled by strong young arms, the little vessel skimmed over the water toward the mouth of the bay. As she ran by the last spit of land and came out upon the broad bosom of the Mediterranean a fierce imprecation broke from the lips of Uruj, while Kara Hassan, his lieutenant, shrugged his shoulders, but his face went grim. Right before them was a great war-galeasse, the cross of the Knights of Rhodes floating from her peak, and on her side in great proud letters was her name—*Our Lady of the Conception.* Too well did the occupants of the pirate boat know what they might expect from the mail-clad knights whose fierce faces looked at them from the poop and the prow of the Christian vessel. The only hope for the pirates was flight, and that possibility might be a remote one.

Out on the open sea there was a good breeze, and Uruj, ordering the sail to be set instantly, put up his helm and scudded before the wind, while at the same time his men strained at their oars. The little brigantine was a swift vessel, and for a while the crew thought they would succeed in showing an enemy a clean pair of heels.

"The lumbering Knights may learn now how to manage a boat," sneered Uruj, who was already certain of the superiority of his sailing powers.

If it had been merely a question of sailing it is possible that Uruj and his friends might have made good their escape, but the Knights on board *Our Lady of the Conception*, seeing that the brigantine was running away, commanded the oars to be put out. *Our Lady* had twenty-six oars a side, and at the loom of each sat nine Moslem slaves, each bare to the waist. The boatswain's shrill whistle gave the signal, and as if pulled by one string fifty-two great oars dipped into the sea together. The breeze was not a strong one; the surface of the sea was smooth, and well suited, therefore, for rowing. Now *Our Lady* began to hasten indeed. The boatswain and his mates, walking up and down the gangway dividing the two banks of oars, applied their thonged whips without mercy to the backs of the bending slaves, whose flesh was already wealed and broken from old blows half healed. Those hard days knew little mercy for the conquered, and the rowers were beaten in order to get the greatest amount of work out of them. If any slave fainted under the day-long toil or the pain of the blows a piece of bread sopped in brandy was placed between his lips to rouse him to consciousness, but even then no respite was given him, for he had to pull at the oar again at once, and if the men next him on the bench felt that he was not pulling at full strength there were fierce words and bitter insults from fellow-slaves, who feared that the boatswain's whip would punish them for the slowness of their oar.

Fathom by fathom the great war-galeasse overhauled the little brigantine, whose crew now broke out into useless curses and imprecations, as they saw the gilded beak coming closer and closer as if it would ram and sink them. As the men pulled with desperate strength at their oars they could see the decks of the approaching vessel—could see the boatswain and his two mates walking up the narrow gangway between the oscillating rows of half-naked slaves, and could perceive the upward fling of the thick leather whips. They knew too well the fate reserved for them if they fell into the hands of the Knights. Therefore they pulled as if they would crack their heart-strings, so that the brigantine raced as never before over the long smooth waves. But it was all in vain. In spite of their desperate efforts for freedom, the strength of some twenty men could not avail against that of four hundred and fifty-two, slaves and driven though they were.

Already the pirates were gasping and the oars were jerking wildly as their strength oozed away. The beak of the galeasse was almost upon them when, uttering a fierce curse, Uruj cut the line which held the sail, and down it fell in token of surrender. There was no use in fighting: every one of the crew would have been slain without hesitation. As the great ship's nose swerved to avoid striking them, the pirates could see the haughty faces of the Knights looking down at them, and the oars held over their heads by the galley slaves as the great vessel went on a little way seemed to threaten to beat them under the sea. A cry of rage burst from the throats of the pirates; many turned and cursed Uruj as he sat with baffled looks of fury, gnawing his fingers, while Kara Hassan smiled in a sickly manner beside him.

"Hook their boat to and iron the rascals!" came the command in a high, well-bred voice from the forecastle or rambades. Great boat-hooks leaped out and held the brigantine as in the grip of a vice. Each pirate was dragged aboard the vessel, and the smiths stood ready with shackles, which they clipped upon the wrists of the captives. Then, with a run, the prisoners were forced along the gang-plank and down a scuttle into the hold. Here they would have to stay until they were needed to take their places on the rowing benches. There were others in the dark hold: several Moslem villagers who had recently been captured, and a few seamen who had been taken off a trading-boat. One who lay where Uruj had been flung had been wounded in a scuffle and lay groaning.

For a time the pirates were too depressed to talk, but in a little while their anger awoke, and they turned to Uruj and vented their wrath upon him.

"You call yourself a pirate and a sailor," said one. "Kara Hassan was right. None but a fool would have ventured on the coasts of Caramania where he could run slap into the Knights of Rhodes."

"I hope Uruj is the first to be chained to the oar bench," said another. "He got us here and it's his due to get the first taste of the whip."

"And may it bite deep into his flesh and search his vitals!" snarled another.

"Hold your peace, fools!" said Uruj. "One would think you were children to hear you weep."

But they continued to revile him until the tossing of the galeasse and the noise of a rising storm made them desist. In the close, dark hold they lay in gloomy silence, while they felt the ship rise and fall on the great waves as she fought her way in the teeth of the gale to shelter under the lee of some island.

Besides the thud of the seas on the wooden sides of the vessel, the roaring and whistling of the wind, and the creak and strain of timbers and cordage, there were other sounds which added to the pirates' fears. These were the occasional piercing shriek of some slave as the knotted thong of the whip bit into the flesh as a spur to greater effort. There were also the imprecations of the boatswain and his mates, as with many coarse insults they walked the gang-plank between the rows of half-naked rowers, who, with panting breath, straining hearts and bloodshot eyes, swung to and fro like a horrible human machine.

As Uruj and his men sat in the noisome hold, with only a plank between them and the sounds above, they realized what was soon to be their fate. All day this was their experience, until just after nightfall the galeasse came to anchor under the shelter of the island of Castel Rosso, at the entrance to the Gulf of Satalie. Here the vessel was in comparative safety, the turmoil of the storm and the struggling oarsmen ceased and very soon the only sounds to be heard were the moans of dreamers, or the clank of a chain as some sleeping slave moved to ease his cramped limbs on the oar bench where he sat day and night without change.

Meanwhile Uruj had discovered that one of the bolts of his manacles was loose, and now, by straining and pulling, he was endeavouring to release his hands. His comrades slept around him while he worked and sweated at his task. Presently his experienced ear caught other sounds: the wind was veering, and was beginning to blow into the anchorage where they lay. The ship pitched and heaved and he knew that very soon the captain would have to move the vessel from her dangerous position, or she would drive upon the land. Then Uruj's chance of escape would vanish, and his fate would be to live the life of torture the sights and sounds of which had been about him all that day.

He still tugged at his imprisoned hands, bruising the flesh and crushing the bones. Suddenly the ship gave a mighty leap and stagger, which shook her in every timber: Uruj knew that she had dragged an anchor. Next moment a harsh voice rang out overhead:

"Oars out! Oars out!" heavy footsteps ran down the gang-plank, and the crack of whips sounded, as the boatswain and his mates drew their thongs over the bodies of the sleeping galley slaves.

Uruj knew that it was now or never. It was likely enough that more than one of the slaves would never wake again, having found release in eternal sleep. Then there would be a call for others to take their places. He might be dragged from the hold, and the dead slave's body having been thrown overboard, his own legs would be shackled in the chains which had gripped the limbs of the dead man, and thus he would suffer until death, perhaps only after many years, released him in his turn.

One final wrench and his hands were free. His companions still slept, and Uruj stepped over their prone forms and made his way in the darkness to the scuttle. He groped his way up to the deck, where he could see the haggard bodies of the slaves beginning their hateful swaying, as they pulled at the oars in order to get the ship out to sea. Watching his opportunity, he darted out when the boatswain was farthest from him, and then, climbing over the bulwark, he dropped into the water. He saw dimly the startled looks in the faces of the first row of slaves before whose bench he had to run in order to escape. They seemed to think he was some ghost or evil spirit. Next moment his body was swirling in the eddy made by the vessel as she turned and was pulled out of the anchorage.

Strong of body though he was, the water seemed to freeze him ; but with quick, firm strokes he made for the shore, a mile away. After what seemed an endless struggle he reached it, and having lain some moments exhausted upon the beach he crept into a shed where fishing-nets were stored. Here he wrung out his wet clothes and then, weariness overcoming him, he slept till daybreak. Soon the sun rose up in all its strength, and in its rays Uruj dried himself. He betook himself to the port and mixed with the sailors lounging there. During the day he managed to get service on a boat belonging to a Christian, which was carrying merchandise to Egypt. They got away next day, and two days out were set upon by a brigantine, filled with riff-raff from the port of Cadros. Thereupon Uruj fought so well that his Christian master was high in his praises, and when they had put the pirates to flight with several broken heads among them he called Uruj to him and made him great offers to enter his service as a permanent hand.

" You are a man of mettle," said he ; " and should be able to earn command of a merchant vessel in a few years."

Uruj said he would consider the matter. No doubt there were many ways of making profit out of the cargo committed to one's care, but the slow gains of honest and humdrum business did not commend themselves to him. He loved the free and reckless life of a corsair, was glad when there was prospect of a fight, and yearned for the wealth which a successful piratical raid would give a bold fighter and a good seaman.

Arrived at Alexandria, Uruj told his Christian master that he had decided to offer himself as a mariner to the Sultan of Egypt, since he preferred a life in which there were prospects of advancement under a great admiral, and where there was fighting to be done.

" But how can you, who are a Christian, join the navy of an infidel, whose ships fight the galleys of the good Knights of St John ? " returned the merchant. " Are you not a Christian ? "

" My father and mother were Christians," returned Uruj with a laugh. " But I have a score to settle with the Knights. They are too proud, and respect not a poor man's possessions."

The Christian merchant left Uruj in disgust and the

latter betook himself to the admiral of the port, who, when he heard Uruj's request, instantly sent him aboard the *Hissar*, a vessel which belonged to the Sultan, and which was just setting off for the coast of Caramania, there to cut wood for shipbuilding. Uruj liked not this prospect of hard work, but decided to accept the service, since it might lead to a post on the war-galleys a little later.

The forests of Caramania were the stores whence was drawn the wood required for shipbuilding both by the Sultan of Egypt and the Knights of Rhodes, so that the vessels of both these Powers were constantly meeting each other when engaged in their business of cutting timber. If, therefore, Uruj was looking for hard knocks he was in the very service where he could most easily find them. The Caramanian coast had already proved disastrous to him in his first venture as a pirate, and it was to bring misfortune to him once more.

The *Hissar* went on her way to her destination, but never reached it. On the very morning when she was making for the point of land where a party of men were to be put ashore to cut wood a big war-galley of the Knights of Rhodes emerged from a bay and attacked the Sultan's ship. From the first the Moslem crew was outmatched, outmanœuvred, and outnumbered. A feeble fight was put up, but the Christian Knights were not to be baulked. Hooking the ships together, they poured over the Moslem's bulwarks. As they came over on one side Uruj and some others of the crew dropped into the sea on the other, and struck out for the shore, which was some two miles away. The sea was rough and it required a strong man to swim the distance.

Alternately swimming and treading water, Uruj slowly made his way to land and waded ashore, possessing nothing in the world but what he stood up in. He did not wait to see whether any of his comrades had also managed to reach land, but having wrung the water from his garments he scrambled up the rocks and made his way inland.

He tramped some miles before he saw anyone, and then it was but a poor shepherd. From him, however, he received a meal of goat's cheese, bread, and a drink of sour whey. He entered into conversation with the man as he sat eating, and learned that he was only some twenty miles from the town where dwelt the Governor of Caramania.

"He is brother of the Defender of the Faithful," said the shepherd, "and is rich and powerful beyond all other rulers in these lands."

"What is his name? Has he any ships?" asked Uruj.

"His name is Khorkud, and he has some ships, as I hear," was the reply. "They fight the Christians, and men do say that he likes to hear of brave men who know how to sail ships, and how to make war upon the proud men of Genoa and Venice."

This was good news to Uruj, who instantly resolved to go to the Governor and offer his services to him. By next day he had made his way to the town where the Governor was living, and though the guards at the gate of the palace mocked his dusty clothes and rough appearance, his bearing of command and his masterful manner forced them to carry his request to the Governor, who, after some time, sent out an officer to interview the 'man of the sea' of whom the guards had spoken.

Uruj was very short with the richly clad officer who haughtily inquired the object of his desired interview with the Governor.

"I learn that your master wants men who know the sea and how to sail and fight ships," said Uruj, with threatening eye and impatient words. "Tell him I have known the sea since I was a child, that I have commanded my own ship, and that I am prepared to enter his service. If he does not need me, the Venetians or the Genoese would be very willing to have a good fighting man such as I am."

The officer was somewhat impressed, and went and informed his master of the manner of man who wished to see him. The Governor thereupon ordered Uruj to be brought to him, and questioned him as to his experiences and what he could do. He was struck by the fearless, almost brutal air of the man, who, while yet young in years, had the masterfulness of a born leader of men. This was what Uruj said:

"My name is Uruj. My father is Mohammed, a great sailor of Mitylene. I have known the sea and sailed in brigantines and barques since my hands could hold a rope or an oar. I can fight and I can sail a ship, and whether it is galley-slaves or free companions, they have to obey my orders and I can get the last ounce of strength out of them. You, my lord, want good sailors and fighters. The Christian captains have it too much their own way; they have the knowledge of the sea which your Moslem captains too often lack, and therefore you lose many vessels, and hundreds of your sailors are rowing in the

Christians' galleys, their backs wealed by the whips of the unbelievers. Give me command of a war-galley. I have the way of the sea equally with these Christian captains, and I will make head against your enemies."

"How many vessels of your own have you commanded?"

"But one, and that was taken from me by the Knights of Rhodes, whom may the devil seize and the Grand Turk burn out of their holes ere long. But I have sailed my father's boats, and served in those of others ever since I was a boy. I know I can do great damage to your enemies if you will give me a galley and force enough to capture merchants' ships and to fight war-galleys if need be."

The Governor said he would consider his proposal, and sent him to be lodged in the house of one of his officers. In two days' time Uruj saw Khorkud the Governor again, who gave him a letter to an inferior governor, the Basha of Smyrna.

"You will take this letter to the Basha," said the Governor, "and he will furnish you with a galley. Pick your own rowers and your own fighters. Use dispatch in all you do, and see that others use the same energy in carrying out my orders. If you are successful and do not lose my galley, I will advance you still farther. Whatever prizes you take you will give me half the value of the cargo and the slaves. You are to make war upon all Christians, no matter of what nation, and if they dare to fly the Crescent instead of the Cross, hoping by that base fraud to escape you, see that they are punished severely."

Uruj thanked the Governor, promised to fulfil all the terms of their bargain, and made his way swiftly to

Smyrna. Here, using the driving power of a strong personality, and the name and influence of Khorkud, Uruj at length succeeded in getting the ship, the equipment, and the men, both sailors and slaves, necessary for his purpose. The Basha of Smyrna, it is to be feared, was not very enthusiastic about the matter; Khorkud had simply commanded his satrap to bear all expenses, and whether he would ever see any return for the five thousand ducats he had spent out of his private purse in carrying out Khorkud's orders the Basha was very doubtful. Certainly he got Uruj to promise to give him a share of all his captures, but, as the Basha reflected, Uruj was doubtless as much a rogue as any other pirate, and if he did not lose his galley would probably keep no bargain that it was not to his own advantage to keep.

At length one morning, the delays and subterfuges of the Basha having all been overcome, Uruj found himself on the poop of as well found a galley as ever breasted the seas. It stole out from the port of Smyrna without any particular notice being paid to it, but it bore a man whose fame was to ring throughout the Mediterranean for several years, only to be eclipsed and overshadowed by the name of a greater man, that of the younger brother of Uruj, whom already he had thoughts of asking to join him.

But first he had to prove himself, to show Khorkud and the Basha of Smyrna that he was no self-glorifying seaman, whose talk was far bigger than his deeds. As he slipped out between the heads of the port and put the ship's nose toward the open sea he reflected that the Caramanian coast had meant disaster to him already on two occasions, and though it had also got him the command of this war-galley—the *Fatima*—he resolved that he would give it now a wide berth and seek his fortune where the Knights of Rhodes were less in evidence.

Accordingly he made for the seas west of Italy, through which plied the merchant vessels of Genoa, Florence, France, and Spain. His first season was very successful. When two weeks out of Smyrna he saw, creeping in the shadow of the western cliffs of Sicily, a Spanish merchant *nef*, or sailing ship, making for Syracuse. He instantly gave chase, and, aiding his sails with his oars, he quickly overhauled the lumbering merchantman.

Scared faces looked over the bulwarks into the galley packed thick with Moslem fighters and Christian slaves, and a flight of arrows stuck in pirates and rowers indifferently. Uruj lacked restraint and caution, and generally relied on the rush and force of a sudden attack. The pirates had already dropped their sail, and had thrown out grappling irons, with which they hooked themselves to the Christians' bulwarks.

"Now, lads," shouted Uruj, "aboard with you and the fat cargo is ours."

At the head of his men he sprang on board the other ship. As he lighted upon the deck a burst of shot rattled among his followers from a small culverin which was placed at the break of the poop, and at the same time some dozen men-at-arms who stood behind it launched their crossbow bolts at the swarthy crowd. Many were hit and fell, cursing their assailants; but next moment, with a rush and a yell, Uruj had thrown himself at the Christian soldiers. These were well backed by the crew of the ship, who, from the poop, threw missiles

WITH ALVAREZ I WENT ON THREE CRUISES WHICH WERE VERY SUCCESSFUL

down at the pirates. The fight raged fiercely for some time, and many of the pirates were cut down. Finally, however, Uruj with some half-dozen picked men managed to secure a footing on the poop. Once this was done, the crew threw down their weapons or leaped overboard, and the soldiers, taken in the rear, were either killed or captured. When all was told, the pirates found that they had lost a dozen men killed and ten wounded, but the prize was worth the cost. It carried not only a rich cargo of cloth stuffs and general merchandise, but bore vessels of plate, both gold and silver, as a present to the King of Naples from the King of Spain. There were, moreover, several passengers of high rank with a following of servants, all of whom could be held to ransom at large sums.

During that summer and autumn Uruj kept in the waters which had thus yielded him so good a catch, and succeeded in taking several other fine prizes. When winter with its storms approached he took his ship to Alexandria, whither he had already sent his prizes and prisoners. He forwarded to the Governor of Caramania the share of booty which was due to him, but did not trouble about the portion promised to the Basha of Smyrna. So long as he kept in the favour of Khorkud, the Governor, he could afford to ignore the inferior man.

At the same time Uruj sent a message to his younger brother, Khizr, asking him to join him in the spring. Khizr was a man of a different type from Uruj, and he took some time to consider the story and the proposal which his brother's messenger had brought him. Uruj was headstrong and fiery, with no great endowment in the way of brains. He was the fighting man pure and simple, bold as a lion, but with little cunning or wariness. Khizr, on the other hand, was a man of cool judgment, shrewd and keen in his knowledge of men and matters, not given to brutal outbursts of rage as his brother was, though not likely to be more merciful. He also had taken up the trade of piracy, running his ship from his native harbour. He had had more success than Uruj, as was to be expected, and his help as partner would be of the utmost assistance to Uruj.

Khizr took two days to consider his brother's proposal. On the third day he called the messenger into his presence and said :

"Tell your master that he will need a store place at which to refit his ships. Let him meet me at Jerba, by Tunis, three days after the new moon in the first month of spring, and I will bring all my ships and join him as he wishes."

When Uruj heard that his brother had decided to join him he was greatly pleased. He knew something of his own limitations. "Khizr was always the thinker—never the blow before the thought, as with me," he said to himself ; "but when Khizr had thought how best to get his blow in, it was often more shattering than mine. Together we shall get power, and go far."

Khizr had entered the service of the Grand Turk Selim as a captain of one of his war-galleys, and it was rumoured that the Sultan thought very highly of his seamanship, his sagacity, and his qualities as a councillor and a leader of men. Already Khizr had got the nick-name of Barbarossa, or "Red Beard," from the colour of his beard, which was to carry the fame of both brothers far and wide throughout Europe for the next generation.

Jerba is an island lying off Tunis. It was an excellent place from which to tap the trade-routes of the Mediterranean, since it was within easy reach of the narrow seas by Italy and Sicily, through which all merchantmen had to pass to enter either half of the Middle Sea; it was, moreover, within striking distance of the coasts of France and Spain, and within hail, as it were, of the forces of the Grand Turk about the Dardanelles. The island had been wrested from the Bey of Tunis by the Spaniards some seventy years before. They had built a fortress on its desolate, sandy soil, but their occupation had never been a strong one, and soon they had deserted it, leaving the fortress to the owls and the bats and the echoes of the sea winds.

At the time appointed Khizr Barbarossa, with some three galleys, appeared and cast anchor off this island, and on being rowed ashore was met by his brother, who embraced him warmly. Khizr found that Uruj had lost no time in putting the fortress in repair. Huts had been built for stores, and strong places had been prepared for the prospective crowds of captives.

"Brother," said Khizr, after he had seen these things, "we must approach the Bey of Tunis and get his protection and permission to stay here."

"Protection and permission!" said Uruj, scoffingly. "Who is the Bey that we should truckle to him?"

"Brother, he is very useful," was the reply. "You cannot keep your captives here for ever. We shall want a place to sell those whom we cannot use in our galleys, we shall want some one to hold those whom we put to ransom and to see that the full ransom is paid. When we are both at sea we cannot attend to these things ourselves. Again, we shall want a market in which to find buyers for our spoil. No merchants will come here."

"He will make us pay well for these conveniences," growled Uruj.

"He will demand a fifth of all our booty," was the reply. "It will be a stiff price to pay, but what can we do? As yet, brother, we are unknown, and perhaps the Bey's forces could thrust us from this place and destroy us and our ships. We must speak fair, brother, while we are weak. When we are strong—well, we will do what we will, then."

Khizr went to the Sultan of Tunis and begged leave to have harbourage in his dominions, with liberty to sell spoil in any of his ports and markets. The Sultan received him graciously, by reason principally that Barbarossa was a favoured captain of the Grand Turk Selim, and was pleased to grant him the favours he asked, on condition that a fifth of the value of all goods, commodities, and captives landed in Tunis was paid into the royal coffers. The treaty was drawn up by the Sultan's vizier, and signed both by him and Barbarossa.

Immediately after this the brothers set to work. They had three good war-galleys, and two or three smaller galleys and brigantines. For the present season—the spring of the year 1512—they decided to rely on the three war-galleys—the *Sea-hawk*, the *Shark*, and the *Sword of Allah*—and one morning, under their respective captains, these vessels put to sea. Uruj commanded the *Sword of Allah*, and Khizr the *Sea-hawk*, while the third galley was captained by Uruj's former lieutenant, Kara Hassan, who had been captured at the same time with Uruj by the Knights of Rhodes. After serving some time on the oar-benches, Hassan had managed to escape from Rhodes while ashore, and having made his way to Alexandria he had been met by Uruj one day in the 'Street of the Quay.' Uruj had immediately yielded to Hassan's appeal to be taken into his service, and had with Khizr's consent been placed in command of one of the fighting galleys.

Pulling easily along the Straits of Marsala, the pirates suddenly perceived away on their lee a big sailing vessel, or nef. This was a ship similar in all respects to the caravels in which Columbus sailed when he discovered America, and which took Pizarro and Cortés across the Atlantic to their conquests of the wonderful lands of Peru and Mexico a few years later. The ship met with by the corsairs was a three-masted vessel with a very high forecastle and stern-castle, and correspondingly deep in the waist. On her foremast she carried one square sail, the mainmast had mainsail and maintopsail, and on the mizzen was rigged a lateen, or triangular, sail.

As the giant sailing vessel came lumbering toward them the keen eyes of the pirates, straining to note every feature of their foe, saw that the arms of Naples were painted on the bellying mainsail, and soon they saw her name upon the prow—*La Galera di Napoli.*

"A rich prize!" said many a pirate, as he loosed the knife in his sheath and clutched the handle of his sword, while his eyes glistened, and he yearned to get at close grips with the men swarming upon the decks.

"A rich prize, truly," said others, "but too big for our eating, I fear!"

"Nay, nay," said others who had sailed with Khizr or Uruj; "if you say that you know not our leaders. They will baulk not at this; they would not baulk at two such. Pity the sun is so near the setting!"

A shrill whistle sounded from the poop of the galley where Uruj sat, and every face turned expectantly at the call. It meant "Prepare to attack." Two more shrill calls sounded, and with whips at work the boatswains ran up and down their gangways as the three galleys raced over the waves toward the oncoming nef. Skilful handling was required as the galley met the giant ship, but good seamanship was not wanting, and while the great oars on one side were lifted as by one man at the word of command, the grappling irons were thrown and two of the galleys were securely hooked to the nef. The galleys swung round to the way made by the nef, which still sailed lumberingly on. The iron hooks held fast in spite of the efforts of the Italians to cut or knock them off, the crews hauled upon the chains which held them, and in a few minutes, while stones and arrows flew among the pirates, the beaks of the galleys were grinding the sides of the nef. One galley was on each side of the big ship, while the third, the *Sea-hawk*, was held in reserve.

Then the pirates by means of short ladders, or by scrambling on each other's backs, attempted to climb the sides of the nef. But the crew of the *Galley of Naples* were good fighters. They numbered three hundred, and so were about equal to the number of pirates. With stones and arrows and crossbow-bolts some shot into the mass of pirates just below them, killing the slaves on the rowing benches, though many of these were of their own religion, and maiming and wounding indiscriminately. Others thrust back the swarming forms that pressed to the bulwarks, hacking off hands, fingers, or arms, stabbing their sword points into fierce Moslem faces. Oaths and curses, cries of fury, calls upon the saints or upon "Allah!" and "Mohammed!" mingled with the groans and shrieks of Italian sailors as they fell back into the scuppers dying or wounded, and of the pirates as they sank into the mass of their fellows pressing on behind them.

The captain of the *Galley of Naples* had hoped that the wind would hold and thus keep his vessel going through the water, but as the sun sank slowly into the waters of the west the breeze dropped. The red light touched the faces of the combatants and bathed all the vessels in the colour of blood, and those passengers who ventured up from below to see how the fight was progressing went sick at heart to see this omen of disaster. Strive as the pirates would, the swiftly falling darkness found them still on their own galleys, having succeeded nowhere in making good a footing on the decks of the great sailing vessel.

Darkness came down, the galleys drew off, and men nursed their wounds and got what comfort they could. The captain, crew, and passengers on the nef prayed for a strong wind, but the night was still, the stars sparkled in the heavens, and the moon silvered the lazy wavelets. Peace was in sea and air; the warm air fanned fitfully the cheeks of the affrighted passengers when they ventured on deck, and the splendour and quiet of the night spoke nothing of murder and of worse than death that lay an arrow-shot away on both sides of the great ship. There were men and women of noble family on board the *Galley of Naples*. The ladies bore themselves like brave women, while such of the men as were soldiers had aided in the fighting that day ; and all night the women were upon their knees praying for aid to come before the dawn—for a strong wind from a merciful heaven, or a great force of Christian ships which should put the monsters of piracy to flight. Many tears were shed as the prayers were uttered, for all knew the certain fate which would befall them if defeat was theirs when daylight came. No longer would there be life for them among the groves of their pleasant villas amid friends and kinsmen of their own race under the sweet skies of Italy, no longer liberty to walk or ride with gallant cavaliers who deferred to their every wish and courted them with every mark of devotion. Instead, retained by their captors, or sold to some rich pasha, they would be for ever immured between the walls of some harem in a twilight atmosphere amid barbaric splendours, as much dead to all their natural world as if their bodies were at the bottom of the sea.

The day dawned faintly through the clammy mists, and wearied eyes on the deck of the nef looked over the side and saw the long low galleys looming through the drifting vapours like immense scorpions ready to pounce on their prey. The light strengthened, the sun's beams touched all three ships with a yellow glow, the mists drifted away, and then the pearly light of day was all about them. Men on the nef snatched hasty mouthfuls of food, for they saw the galleys moving, and they knew that the fight would quickly be renewed.

The corsairs now decided to attack with all their forces at once. Uruj and Khizr would grapple with the nef to port and starboard, and when they had closely engaged the enemy and drawn his attention upon them Kara Hassan would range his galley at the stern and board the nef there.

The men on the nef observed the galleys separating after the leaders had taken their last counsel together, and saw the great oars bear them nearer and nearer. Then came the grinding of the timbers of the galleys against the sides of the nef, the gripping of the iron hooks on shroud and bulwark, and the fierce cries of "Barbarossa! Barbarossa!"—a cry that was new to the ears of all the Italians on board the *Galley of Naples*, but one which was to echo upon those waters for many years to come, paralysing the arms of many brave men, and striking terror into the hearts of women, for always it was to mean a fierce and overwhelming attack against which nothing could stand.

This time there was no denying the corsairs. Distinguished by coats of mail, Uruj and Khizr led the way, and by an attack in force in the waist of the nef they gained a footing on the deck. Then came the dreadful press of battle. Men gave and received mortal blows, while above the clash of arms and the fierce faces of the combatants shone the sun, its light glinting from the dabbled sword-blades as they rose and fell, and striking the little waves that heaved peacefully upon the sea. From the slippery decks rose the fierce cries of men, calling upon the saints in heaven or on the name of God, and replied to by the fiercer shouts of " Allah ! Allah ! " " Barbarossa ! Barbarossa ! " Below in the dark cabin lay and knelt half fainting women, their pride of race and usual haughtiness of mien fallen from them, weeping and praying and clinging in frantic terror to each other as the sounds of rushing feet, falling bodies, and roaring voices came to them through the deck.

The Christians fought stoutly. Many a merchant and scholar who knew better how to wield a quill pen than a sword proved himself a man that day, and foot to foot they dared the scimitar in the deft hand of a Moslem pirate whose life had often depended upon his knowledge of sword play. Many a Christian found death, but only after a hard fought struggle in which he made up for his ignorance of arms by reckless bravery.

At length a cry akin to horror arose : " They come over the stern ! To the stern, lads, and beat them off the poop ! " It was true. Here was a swarm from the third galley pouring over the high bulwarks of the sterncastle, and the men of the weak guard that had been stationed there were dead or dying. At the same time the corsairs to port and starboard made another determined onslaught. The Christians, disheartened by the sight of the new foes running down from the stern, had little further fight in them and soon were overpowered. The dead were cast overboard, as well as those whose wounds were severe ; while those who still lived were manacled and thrust below.

It was found that the corsairs had suffered severely in killed and wounded, Uruj Barbarossa himself having been badly cut about by a Spanish cavalier who had run his sword into the pirate's breast, only to find death himself immediately afterward by a blow from an axe. Khizr, however, was almost untouched, and took command, while Uruj lay by, weak from his wound, but uttering maledictions on all things Christian.

The decks were washed down, the wounded looked to their hurts, and food was served out. Then, when the great nef was being towed by the three pirate galleys toward the port of Tunis, Khizr Barbarossa, dressing himself in his richest garb, went with a chosen body of his chief men to see the captives of high degree who had fallen into his hands. The ladies, white and still, sat crouching together, rigid with horror, and received his courteous salutes without a sign, while the Christian gentlemen looked on with flaming eyes, furious at the fate which had thrown their ladies and themselves into the hands of these fiends.

After having seen all the booty, both in captives and in rich goods, which the taking of the nef had brought to them, Khizr went and told Uruj, pointing out how rich and famous this achievement would make them, and thereby instilling some patience into the savage mind of his brother.

Arrived at Tunis, with banners flying and the galleys and nef decked out with flags and with rich clothes and tapestries hung along their sides, the pirates towed their prize into port, to the accompaniment of trumpet blasts and the cries of the seamen. Crowds swarmed along the quays cheering them as they entered. When they had tied up at the landing-place, mules and horses were quickly procured and the captives landed in procession. First came some of the leaders of the pirates, then, mounted on mules, four beautiful Italian girls, followed by two noble Spanish ladies of high birth, seated on richly caparisoned Arab chargers. Sad white faces had these women, for they knew that they were doomed for life to dwell in the tomb-like recesses of their captors' harems. Then came other captured women on foot, followed by the male prisoners and the crew of the *Galera di Napoli*. The Sultan of Tunis with his suite watched the procession from the walls of his palace, and was highly delighted at the sight, and at the prospect of receiving his fifth share of such rich booty.

"See how Allah rewards the brave!" he cried to his followers. "These Barbarossas are lucky and gallant men. We have done well to give them the protection of our port and the countenance of our approval."

Great was the fame of the Barbarossas throughout the coasts of Northern Africa when the news of their success was told. And bitter was the wrath of many noble families of Spain and Italy when it was learned that some of their noblest and most beautiful kinswomen were lost to them for ever. Their men who had been captured could be ransomed, but there was no ransom for the women. Merchantmen and sailors cast a warier eye over the sea as they plied to and fro in their voyages, and the prayers and gifts to the various saints in whom travellers placed faith were redoubled.

When Selim the Grand Turk heard of the deed he remembered that Khizr had shown very great gifts of seamanship during the year that he had commanded a war-galley for him, and this capture of the great Neapolitan nef showed that the pirate was a man to be honoured and encouraged. The Sultan thereupon sent an officer of his Court to the camp of the Barbarossas at Jerba with a certain document and the present of a great pearl. The document granted Khizr the title of Kheyr-ed-Din (pronounced Hare-Uddeen), which means "The Protector of Religion." Seeing that Khizr was the son of Christian parents, and probably had no more religion than was profitable to him as a pirate, this was an absurd name to give him. Nevertheless it is one which stuck to him, and under it he won renown far and wide, and the Turks still honour his name as that of one of their best and boldest leaders.

While Uruj lay on his bed in pain, Khizr and Hassan Ali went abroad with their galleys, and by attacking only when they were evenly matched with the enemy or were in superior force they won many more prizes during that season, thus increasing the reputation of the Barbarossas and adding to their wealth. When the autumnal storms swept the seas, driving with furious gusts and mighty waves upon the shores of Africa, the pirates laid up their galleys, and Khizr and Uruj, the latter of whom was getting better of his severe wounds, began to plot what they should do when Uruj was well again.

"I have decided," said Uruj, "to seize Bougie from the Spaniards. It will make another store place for us, and, besides, the fifth share which we have to pay the Sultan of Tunis is something I would willingly save for ourselves. If we wrest Bougie from the Spanish commander there, we shall be independent of the Sultan of Tunis."

Bougie was a coast town in the country of the Kabyles, far away to the west of Tunis. It had been captured from its Berber lord two years before by the famous Spanish general Pedro de Navarro. Unfortunately, the dilatory methods of the Spaniards had prevailed here, and not only was the building of the fortifications of the place not pushed on with energy, but the garrison left in the town was very meagre. The soldiers worked at the walls with trowel in one hand and sword or cross-bow in the other. At any moment a cloud of Arab horsemen might sweep down from the defiles of the hills round about the town and attack the garrison, which was not strong enough to inflict a crushing punishment on the marauders. Meanwhile, the number of the Spanish soldiers was slowly being reduced, and urgent appeals were sent to Madrid asking for reinforcements and supplies.

When spring came round and Uruj found himself in fit condition to lead his men again, the capture of Bougie was the first business he attempted. His brother Kheyr-ed-Din tried to dissuade him.

"Why do you not surround the place, brother," he said, "and let starvation work your will upon the garrison? They rely upon the reinforcements and food to be sent from Spain. Intercept them, and then sit down before the town, and in a little while the place will be yours."

"Nay, I like not such methods," replied Uruj impatiently. "I will beat the wretches out of the place. But first we will lie in wait for the convoy from Spain."

One fine morning, indeed, the captains of three Spanish ships which at last were bringing reinforcements, stores, and food for the garrison at Bougie found themselves within a few miles of their destination. The rocky coast of Africa was on their starboard, and a few hours would find them in the little harbour of Bougie, safe from the villainous hands of any pirates—the "Devil of the Sea," for instance, or those new miscreants, the Barbarossas. Thus men and captains were congratulating themselves, when suddenly a cry came from the look-out man on the foretop of the leading vessel: "Galleys on the port bow!"

Men ran to the side to see the stranger galleys, when a shout came from another of the ships: "Three galleys astern!"

Almost before the words had left the sailor's lips another cry arose: "Galleys ahead!"

As the moments passed men grimly looked upon the foes creeping rapidly toward them and counted their number—eight in all, each galley crammed with at least two hundred fighting men. Quickly the Christians counted up the chances against this overwhelming force, and the Spanish captains cursed the meanness of the dockyard authorities and the military commanders, who together stinted them of guns, ammunition, and men. Notwithstanding that there were some men-at-arms on board who were to reinforce the garrison at Bougie, the Spaniards had no hope against the numbers of the pirates; yet, like brave caballeros, the captains resolved to sell their lives or liberty very dearly, and accordingly the trumpet rang out the signal for each man to go to quarters and prepare for the battle.

The struggle was a fierce one, but the Christians were hopelessly outmanned. Soon one vessel was swept of its fighting men, and the crews of the two others immediately cried for quarter. When all had been disarmed the prisoners were tied up and cast into the hold, and the ships were triumphantly towed to Jerba.

Uruj Barbarossa now prepared to capture Bougie being excessively eager to get possession of the town. Again Kheyr-ed-Din counselled siege and patience, but Uruj, hotheaded and reckless, would have nought of either.

Thereupon, with a select band, Uruj sailed in one galley to Bougie, determined to rush the fort and thus to show his over-cautious brother how easily the place could be taken. He landed at the head of fifty of his best men, and, approaching the half-finished walls of the fortress, he planned an attack at what seemed the weakest part. When all was ready the pirates sprang forward amid cries of "Barbarossa! Barbarossa!" If they had been less impetuous they might have seen the sun flash from the helms of the soldiers who, crouching low behind the walls, awaited their onset. Suddenly when the first of the pirates was on the point of springing upon the rampart two sharp words of command rang out from the Spanish commander. Instantly the soldiers leaped up, and poured a volley into the advancing pirates.

Men fell right and left, or sprang up in their death agony. So unexpected and so immediate was the attack that the pirates paused for an instant and looked at each other and to their leader. To their consternation they saw that Uruj also was down. Some ran to him, and found him cursing fiercely and pointing to his left arm, which hung helpless in his sleeve. They carried him out of the range of the arquebus men, and then the corsair among them who had some knowledge of such rough surgery as the pirates allowed to themselves found that Uruj's arm below the elbow had been shattered by a bullet.

"Can you patch it up? Is it only split?" asked Uruj impatiently.

"Nay, captain," was the reply, "the bone is in a hundred little pieces. 'Twill have to come off."

"Off with it then, in the fiend's name!" said Uruj.

Without more ado the arm was taken off at the elbow by means of a sharp knife. The arteries were bound up and Uruj was carried to the galley, where he lay cursing his ill-luck and his wound. When he was borne into his dwelling at Jerba and Kheyr-ed-Din came to visit him, the younger brother smiled sardonically, but it was not his character to boast his confidence in the ill fortune which he knew would accompany his brother's rash and ill-considered attempt.

For the remainder of that season, and indeed for the next two years, the brothers Barbarossa confined their activities to the sea. Every month found their success attaining greater proportions, and the strings of their captives and the bales of their booty became a common sight in the streets and on the quays at Tunis. The combination of craft and reckless daring possessed by this partnership of the pirate brothers was an exceptional one, and when the tales of their depredations were told howls of rage at the losses inflicted by them sounded in every harbour and in every merchant's counting house from Seville to Brindisi, while pride and delight rose in the heart of every Moslem, in the streets of Constantinople as in the skin tents of the Berbers.

At length Kheyr-ed-Din determined that the partnership was too wealthy and too powerful to pay any longer the tax of one fifth to the Sultan of Tunis. He broached a certain project to his brother, and Uruj, convinced at last that his method of attacking Bougie was not the most promising, left the conduct of the next attempt to gain a coast place of their own in the hands of his younger brother.

The place whose capture Kheyr-ed-Din had determined to attempt was a coast fortress in the hands of the Genoese, who had garrisoned it with five hundred sturdy Genoese soldiers. It was named Jigelli, and stood not so distant from Tunis as Bougie, though in the same direction. It was a strong place and only a madman, or the elder Barbarossa, would have attempted to take it by assault. The methods of Kheyr-ed-Din were much slower than those of his brother, but they were better calculated to end in success.

One day, into a black-tented village of Berber nomads some miles in the depths of the desert came a cavalcade of well-dressed men who looked like merchants. But they were not men of the ledger and the steelyard: it was Kheyr-ed-Din, with thick, heavy jaw, round, stubborn-looking head with curly hair and beard, and the masterful yet thoughtful look of a leader of men. Behind him was a company of his captains and principal warriors. He was led to the chief of the village, a man of reverend aspect, tall, with white hair, and the manners of a king—Ibn Abbas, chief of the Berbers of the Plain of Sbakh. Very courteous were Kheyr-ed-Din and Ibn Abbas to each other as they exchanged greetings, but soon the business of Barbarossa was revealed: would Ibn Abbas, for a certain consideration in gold coin and in booty, join with his friend in an attack on the strong fortress of Jigelli ? While Barbarossa laid siege from the sea, would the tribesmen of Ibn Abbas sit down about the Genoese on the land ?

There was a little haggling, but a bargain was soon arranged, and Kheyr-ed-Din rode back knowing that, whether it took a long time or a short one, Jigelli was as good as taken. A few days later, Pietro Bembo the Genoese commander, standing upon his battlements, saw that what had been rumoured was now coming to pass. As far as the eye could reach among the hills toward the desert to the south were to be seen hordes of Berber tribesmen, shouting words of scorn and brandishing their weapons at the black mass of the fortress.

A few tents were pitched at the foot of the hills to shelter the Berber chieftains, but the remainder of the host encamped in a semi-circle just out of range of the guns of the port. The seashore was left empty, but the Christian commander, casting his eyes to sea in the gathering twilight, saw the galleys of the pirates lying off the coast. Certainly his enemies were gathering closely about him. Yet, as he looked up at the golden folds of the Genoese flag, the brave commander resolved that, whatever fate was to be his, he would never yield either to these land pirates, the Moslem raiders of the desert, or to the sea robbers, the renegade Barbarossas.

There were said to be twenty thousand Berbers who sat down before the fortress, resolved to starve out the little garrison, as their chiefs had agreed with the great Kheyr-ed-Din. And when many days had passed in the brilliant sunshine and heat of the Mediterranean, there seemed little prospect of any succour coming to the soldiers cooped up in their walls.

At length a soldier named Guido Candilia offered to go out disguised as an Arab and try to creep through the host of enemies and take a message to the commander of the Spanish forces at Bougie, who might send a swift galley to Genoa telling the fathers of the State there of the deadly plight of the garrison at Jigelli. The soldier knew something of Arabic, and the commander and his officers went to much pains to disguise the bold fellow and to instruct him as to how he should proceed in his dangerous task. Then one dark night, with a precious note concealed in his clothing, he was let out through a sally port and disappeared in the gloom.

Three days passed in much anxiety and doubt. Would he be able to find his way through the hordes of fierce tribesmen? Would he be able to pass their keen eyes without detection, or to escape without a sharper challenge than his poor knowledge of desert Arabic could satisfactorily meet? These were the questions which Pietro Bembo, the commander, asked himself and his captains. When the fourth morning broke without sign from the enemy that they had discovered the fugitive, the garrison began to hope; spirits rose generally, and a man or two, thinking of home and the sight of comrades coming in rescue of them, even whistled a snatch or two of a song.

The morning passed, during which an attack was delivered by the pirates of Barbarossa upon the defences of the sea-gate. It was not a stubborn attack, and was delivered chiefly for the purpose of learning whether the garrison was still as determined as ever in their defence. Then came the hot hours of the day, when, as a rule, even hatred and murder slept, and quiet descended upon besiegers and besieged, except for the sentinels who kept wary watch on both sides. Suddenly, with a thud, something fell from over the wall into the courtyard of the castle where soldiers lay dozing in the shade. The men started up and looked, and their hearts went cold. They knew it at once for the head of Guido Candilia, their brave comrade. Picking it up, they found a paper tied to the tongue protruding from the dabbled lips. It was the message he had borne with him, and on the back of it was scrawled in rough characters in Arabic the words, " Death to all Infidels ! "

After this something like despair settled upon the garrison. Day followed day, week followed week, until two months had gone by. Food was getting low, ammunition was almost spent, and many lives had been lost in beating off the almost daily attacks of the enemy. There could be but one end, if succour did not come soon : the defenders would be so worn from toil and weak from hunger that some day, thin as skeletons, they would be unable to resist an attack and the infidel hordes would pour in over their feeble bodies. Day after day the brave commander turned his eyes to the sea, closely scanning the rim of weltering waves for some sail which spoke of an attempt to rescue him. Surely some rumour of what was happening had gone across the waters to his proud masters in their palaces at Genoa, or to the windy towers of Rhodes, where the Knights of St John kept their unceasing vigil against the forces of the evil Prophet and his infidel people ! If such news had reached them, why did they not send succour to brave men holding out for the honour of Christianity and the fame of Christian knighthood ?

Now sixty days had passed, and never the sight of

the red flag flying from the peak of a vessel had gladdened the eyes of the Genoese. At length the commander made a resolution, and he called his captains and the remaining men-at-arms about him.

"Look you," he said, "there is but one way for brave men to meet the death that shall be ours whether we stay or go. Soon we shall be too weak to lift our swords or our arquebuses. The quartermaster tells me there are but three rations left for each of us, and after that there is but starvation and the deaths of toothless old dogs. I will not die thus," and there was a light in the dark eyes and a ring in the resolute voice that found an echo in the breast of each of his listeners. "We will eat our remaining rations in one meal, so as to give us strength, and at dead of night we will sally forth and fight our way toward the sea. We may all find death—we shall probably be overwhelmed ere our feet are wetted by the sea waves; but if fate is kind to us some may win through and seize a galley, cast it loose, and make an effort to escape in the confusion and the darkness. At any rate, whether we live or die that is my resolve—I will not starve like a rat in a trap, and those who will follow me shall go forth with me to-night."

There were some three hundred men remaining, and they took little time to make up their minds to follow their brave commander. All that day they were busy, quietly destroying or rendering useless all weapons and other articles which might, if captured, be of service to the enemy, and three hours before midnight they sat down to their last meal. They ate everything that was in the place, and then, with swords ready and the locks of their arquebuses well oiled, they sat in groups whispering together, waiting for the signal to be given by the brave Pietro Bembo.

It came at length, and the men ranged up four abreast behind the sea-gate. They heard the soft noise of the well-oiled chains as the portcullis rose and the bridge sank down across the moat. Then the first files went forward, stepping softly over the planks, with Pietro Bembo at their head. Suddenly there was a cry in the darkness ; a broad spear whizzed in among the advancing men, and there came the thud of naked feet, shrill cries of warning, of exultation, as the living walls of the enemy pressed against the little column of doomed men. No light was needed to show where to strike : every Christian face, pale in the darkness, was a target for a hundred spears, and the whites of rolling eyes in dark-skinned faces were the points where the Genoese thrust their swords and the arquebusiers fired their balls, ere, in the deathly press, no more room was given for their cumbersome weapons and men slew and tore and thrust with sword or long knife.

Slowly the stream of white faces thinned, bitten away on each side by the great shadowy mass that surged upon it. There was never a chance of the white men wetting their feet in the salt waves of the sea ; they fought and found death almost beneath the walls of the fortress they had so bravely defended. Soon the last brave form sank amid the darker waves, the great sea of savagery surged over all, and with yells of triumph the Berbers rushed into the fortress.

Kheyr-ed-Din, riding up in the dawn, passed the long line of dead Christians, now stripped of every thing of value, and said not a word. Entering the fort, he went through its chambers, noting the strength of the walls and the emplacements of the culverins, and bombards. Then, passing out again to his tent on the seashore, he ordered men to bury the dead and to clean out the fort. Meanwhile the Berbers had disappeared; they had performed their part of the bargain and had vanished like a cloud of locusts. Kheyr-ed-Din was content; at the expenditure of a few pieces of gold and a dozen or two of lives he was in possession of a place of great strength, which should become the nucleus of possessions that were to place himself and his brother on an equal footing with the Sultan of Tunis or any other petty chieftain on the African coast who wished to take heavy toll from the wealth obtained by braver men than themselves.

The aim of the brothers was now to capture two or three points on the coast and oust the native chieftains from their possessions, thus making themselves little potentates on the land as well as world-famous leaders on the sea. For this reason Uruj again collected a great part of their fleet and sailed to Bougie, determined to capture that place as an offset to the success of his brother in taking Jigelli. He landed his pirates and laid siege to the town from a respectful distance, for the garrison had been heavily reinforced with artillery since the last assault and the fortifications had now been completed. Uruj tried surprise attacks by night, but with no success, and days went by with nothing of good result to show to the impatient fighter. He sent for more men, and determined to make one more vigorous effort by night to gain a footing on the walls.

But meanwhile the commander of the garrison had

not been idle. He had got wind of the intention of Uruj to attack him and had instantly dispatched a fast brigantine to Spain informing the authorities of his position. For once the 'powers that be' bestirred themselves. A fleet was got together under a good captain, and well equipped with arms and men. The vessels sailed betimes, and reached the neighbourhood of Bougie on the day when Uruj was to attempt his great attack. A spy was sent ashore to ascertain the position of affairs, and on his return the admiral made his dispositions.

So headstrong was Uruj and so lacking in all foresight that he left his fleet drawn upon the shore with the most meagre guard. The last thing which he expected was an attack from the sea so soon after the opening of his second attempt on Bougie. While he was assembling his men for his great effort, however, the Spanish admiral, under cover of the darkness, was advancing with muffled oars to the attack on the pirates' flotilla. The Spaniards reached the boats without being seen, and the first knowledge of their presence the pirates had came to them in the midst of their fierce attacks upon the walls of the fort, amid the blinding flashes of the cannon and the roar of exploding charges. Suddenly cries arose: "The boats are on fire! The boats are on fire!"

They turned to find flames wrapping many of their galleys, amid the shrieks and cries of the manacled slaves upon the benches. Uruj rushed down with a body of men to see what was the meaning of all this; he was met by a murderous fire from the arquebuses of the Spaniards, but notwithstanding this he launched the galleys which were as yet untouched, and proceeded to engage the Spanish fleet. In the darkness, however he could do very little, since it was not the plan of the Spanish admiral to fight just then. While, therefore, Uruj was drawn away with a great number of his men, the Spaniards in the fort sallied out and inflicted heavy losses on the pirates left on shore.

When, after a vain pursuit of the Spanish vessels, Uruj returned, dawn was breaking and showed him the enormous extent of his losses. Half the number of his flotilla were but charred and blackened hulks on the seashore, and some hundreds of his men had been killed by the sallying Spaniards. In a great rage, and filled with bitter chagrin at the sense of being defeated a second time, Uruj drew off his forces and went to consult with his brother, Kheyr-ed-Din, at Jigelli. The two brothers sent an embassy to the Sultan of Tunis, asking if he would help them with men and ships to break down the stubborn Spaniards at Bougie. But the Sultan was incensed at their desire to be independent of him, and returned a haughty answer, refusing all assistance.

Soon after this a party of Moslems landed at Jigelli and craved audience of Uruj. They were an embassy from Algiers, where, for six years now, the Spaniards had held down the pirates, dominating the town from the strong fortress called the Peñon, which they had built at the mouth of the harbour. Algiers was one of the principal cities of refuge to which the Moors of Spain had fled, where knight and artisan, once ejected from their homes in Spain, had banded together to prey upon the ships of Spain in revenge for the miseries they and their forbears had endured. So successful had been the forays and raids of the Algerines that the merchants and princes of Spain had had to suffer the loss of many rich argosies, and thousands of their compatriots had been haled into captivity, until at length Count Pedro Navarro had been sent to inflict punishment upon the corsairs. He had succeeded too well for the Algerines. With his heavier guns he knocked the place about the ears of the pirates, battered and burnt some of their vessels, and, then, at the point of the sword, exacted an oath from the ruling personages promising loyalty to the Spanish Crown and the cessation of all piratical expeditions.

Relying less on the loyalty of the Algerines than on their fear of absolute ruin, Navarro caused a strong tower to be built on a rocky spit, or *peñon,* which lay on one side of the harbour, and from this point the town and its turbulent population of Moors, Moriscoes, and Arabs, land thieves and sea robbers to a man, could easily be held in check by the guns placed in the tower. For six years this intolerable state of things had lasted. How the townspeople lived during that time is a mystery, seeing that the stoppage of their staple business of sea-robbery must have meant starvation for most of them. As it was, they had at all times "to walk their ways warily"; they were compelled to see their galleys "rotting before their eyes and never dared to mend them; they had viewed many a rich prize sailing by and never so much as ventured a mile out to sea to look her over." The putting out of any but the smallest of fishing-boats would have brought the roar of cannon and the shattering ruin of a shot from the watchful gunners in the Peñon tower. Thus, the brilliant summer sun looked down on the decaying .timbers of bleached galleys lying on the shore, on a listless life through all the narrow streets of the city, of moody men who strolled gloomily up and down the strand with eyes straining away toward the dancing waves of the sea, which they must furrow no more while that white tower with its gaping gun embrasures barred their way.

Then a happy thing happened—the death of the King of Spain, Ferdinand the Catholic, whose ruthless hand had hurled the Moors from their beloved land of Andalusia, and who had followed them and their descendants even to this their place of refuge, and imposed a heavy tribute upon them. Immediately they received news of this event the Algerines refused to pay further tribute to the Spanish Government, and to aid them in beating down the strong fortress of the Peñon they called in a neighbouring Arab sheikh named Salim, who at the head of his wild clansmen attempted to storm the fort. But it was a hopeless task, and the Algerines soon recognized that other methods would have to be used. The result of a council of war was that an embassy was sent to the renowned corsair, Uruj. His fame for invincible courage had already spread throughout the ports of the Mediterranean, and if he could be prevailed upon to help he could bring the naval force and artillery as well as the courage and resource necessary to destroy the Spanish fort.

Uruj, in his castle at Jigelli, received the appeal with joy, and he instantly set forth by land with six thousand men, accompanied by a fleet of sixteen galleots and three barques laden with stores. On his way he settled a little difference with a man who in earlier years had been one of his boon companions and most trusted officers—Kara Hassan. This man had broken away from his former chief, with a following by whose aid he had induced the corsairs of the little port of Sherstel to accept him as their leader. There he had settled down, looking forward to successful piracy in a small way to support him in some dignity and comfort. Uruj had never forgiven Kara Hassan for renouncing his loyalty to the brothers Barbarossa. He appeared with his host before the little town, which submitted unconditionally. Indeed, Kara Hassan seems to have thought that no ill-feeling really existed between himself and his former master, and went out to welcome Uruj with all friendliness. Uruj, however, greeted him with objurgations and insults; high words arose, and the interview suddenly terminated by the silencing of Kara Hassan by means of an axe. Uruj had him seized and decapitated on the spot.

A few days later Uruj entered Algiers, and sent a message to the Spanish captain of the Peñon, offering him and his garrison a safe conduct to the coast if they would surrender. The Spaniard was very short in his reply. "I make no treaties with robbers," he said, "and neither the threats nor the proffered courtesies of a pirate would avail aught with a Spanish gentleman." Thereupon Uruj, for the space of twenty days, battered at the Peñon with his field pieces, and knocked off several chips of stone, but did little other damage.

The Algerines were in the meantime discovering that if they needed help from Uruj and his Turks against the Spaniards they stood in as great need against the corsairs themselves. The insolence and high-handedness of the pirates were not to be borne by the magnates of Algiers, many of whom were proud of their descent from the great families of Moorish kings and princes. Black looks and fierce glances began to take the place of smiling friendliness; the sheikh Salim, indeed, was even less discreet, and began to talk loudly and to threaten. When, therefore, one day the news was bruited abroad that Salim had been strangled in his bath by order of Uruj, the Algerine notables and the kinsmen of Salim saw that there was no hope for them unless they took instant and active measures to put an end to the despotic corsair's power.

Accordingly they entered into a conspiracy with the Spanish soldiers of the Peñon, and arranged for a general rising on a certain day. Uruj, however, by means of spies was kept informed of all that went on, and when the time was ripe he invited the ringleaders of the plot, twenty-two in number, to accompany him and his Turks to the mosque. When the priest had finished his ministrations there was the sound of a great crash, as the doors of the mosque were flung together. At the same time the corsairs, who swarmed in the building, threw themselves upon the conspirators, and, binding them with the turbans off their own heads, they led them before Uruj, who angrily reproached them with disloyalty and ordered their instant execution. The twenty-two unhappy men were immediately led into the street in front of the mosque, where their heads were struck off by the swords of the pirates.

After this there was no more thought of resisting the corsair, who was now virtually master of Middle Barbary. Certainly the handful of Spanish soldiers in the Peñon were still too strong for this pirate king, and in spite of the thousands under the command of Uruj they still held out. An expedition sent by the King of Spain to eject the pirate from his recently won kingdom failed dismally. Don Diego de Vera, with some fifteen thousand men, set out to punish this saucy rascal, but hardly had de Vera thrown up entrenchments before the town when Uruj issued forth at the head of his army, and such terror was in his name, and so little confidence had the Spaniards in themselves, that the pirates sent the Christian army hurrying back to their ships, after killing three thousand of them.

No better success attended the attempt of a local ruler, the Prince of Tinnis, who conceived the idea of thrusting out the usurper. He raised a great army against Barbarossa, and brought it toward Algiers. Uruj, gathering a force of fifteen hundred picked men, went out against him, and, disdaining the use of cannon, thrashed the forces of Tinnis and pursued them into their own city of Tenes, capturing the place. The Prince fled to the hills, and Uruj became ruler of his land. This success whetted the pirate's appetite for still further territory, and he moved on to Tlemcen, where the Sultan was the last of a long line of well-known kings. This potentate was conquered by the mere terror of the name of Barbarossa, for he fled without waiting to meet the foe.

With the fall of Tlemcen Uruj became master of a territory as large as the modern French colony of Algeria, and his exploits made many of the rulers about the Mediterranean quake in their shoes. Here was a man, a mere pirate, who feared neither God nor devil, who scattered the veteran forces of the King of Spain with as much ease as he put to flight the rabble army of an

African princelet. He had gained a kingdom as large as any one of the important States of Italy; his ships were everywhere, and their depredations caused enormous loss and injury to merchants in every port in Spain, France, and the merchant States of Genoa, Naples, and Venice. It was felt that this pirate king was becoming a menace to Christendom itself.

The victories of Uruj had had the result of bringing him within seventy miles of Oran, where the Spaniards ruled in force. The Marquis de Comares, Governor of Oran, had seen with shame and indignation the victorious advance of Uruj toward his province, and he sent a passionate appeal to his master, King Charles of Spain, begging to be allowed to lead an army against the corsairs of Algiers. The request was granted, and Comares launched a body of ten thousand veterans against the pirates.

Uruj got word of the proposed expedition against himself, which, indeed, had been organized with a zeal and energy unusual in Spanish affairs. He was at Tlemcen with but fifteen hundred of his pirates when he heard that Comares was marching against him. There was little time to lose, and therefore he made a dash by night, hoping to reach Algiers and to obtain larger forces before the Spaniards should get to Tlemcen. But the Marquis of Comares was well served by his scouts, and swiftly came the Spanish army in the track of the corsairs.

Mile after mile the pursuit was kept up. The Spaniards were hot upon the scent and would not be shaken off. At length word was brought to Uruj that a mile ahead was a river, the passage of which would be a difficult matter unless the Spaniards could be delayed. If he were caught while crossing, it might be disastrous to him ; but if he could win across without being attacked, he would be able to reach a place of safety before the Spaniards could do him much harm.

"Take the treasure chests," commanded Uruj, "and scatter their contents in the way of the Spaniards. That should delay them ; they will squabble over the spoil."

They did as he commanded: rings and bracelets, necklaces and jewelled belts lay on the sand of the desert, flashing back to the sun the glowing colours of amethyst, ruby, pearl, and dull-red gold. The Turks swept on toward the river ; the Spanish general, mounted on his charger and surrounded by his staff, came on at the head of his straining army. Some one pointed to the jewels lying before them.

"Trample them down!" shouted Comares. "Advance! advance! The man who stops to pick up one of those gewgaws shall be slain!"

Unflinchingly, therefore, the Spaniards swept over the glittering line of riches and kept up the hot pursuit of Uruj and his pirates. The latter had already reached the river, which ran between steep banks, difficult to descend. The men began to file across the treacherous ford. Half were already across when the cry arose from the rear: "The Spaniards are on us! The Spaniards!"

Uruj was already safe on the farther bank, but at the cries of his rearguard he turned, and with a few chosen spirits and his lieutenant, Venalcadi, he dashed back into the stream and regained the other side. There he found the Spaniards dealing death in the ranks of his men, who had turned at bay against overwhelming numbers. A stone corral, used for the herding of goats, stood on the bank, and into this Uruj leaped, ordering his men to line the sides against the enemy. Then began one more fierce battle between Moslem and Christian. Time after time the latter tried to sweep into the corral and overwhelm the pirates, only to be thrust back or slain by Uruj and his men, who fought desperately, knowing that no quarter would be given to them. Uruj, well set up and robust though but one-armed, his turban gone, darted hither and thither with the joyful light of battle in his eyes, shouting words of encouragement and advice and bringing the terror of his name and presence and the sharp edge of his streaming scimitar to the aid of this or that much-pressed little knot of his men.

At length Uruj engaged in combat with a Spanish lieutenant, who was armed with a long pike. The pirate tried to close upon his enemy, but the man, by name Garzia de Tineo, was deft with his weapon, and, shortening it, he thrust it into the corsair's neck. Uruj stumbled, and instantly another soldier struck him on the head with a sword, causing him to fall headlong. Leaping upon him, de Tineo with one stroke sheared the pirate's head from his body.

With the death of their leader the few remaining pirates yielded, and those who had crossed the river fled and scattered. All was open for the conquering march of the Spanish commander, who could have seized Algiers and thus, perhaps, have changed the course of history. But Comares seemed to think his task was completed with the death of the elder Barbarossa, little knowing that Kheyr-ed-Din, the younger of the brothers, was yet, by his political wisdom and craft, to join the power of the greatest pirate of the Mediterranean with the forces of the Grand Turk, and thus to form a rock of strength on the sea upon which the might of all the Christian princes would break in vain.

It is by reason of the fact that Kheyr-ed-Din was more of a political chieftain than a great corsair that his story as a whole lies outside this record of pirates and their doings. He became the greatest organizing seaman of his age while in the service of the Sultan of Turkey, and while consolidating and extending his own power as ruler of Algiers, he led the fleets of the Grand Turk to victory after victory. He was the chosen leader of a group of pirate captains numbering among them such famous names as Dragut Reis, Salih Reis, Sinan the Jew of Smyrna, and Agdin Reis, whom the Spaniards called Cachadiablo, or 'Goblin.' Under the leadership of these men the Algerine galleots intensified and extended the ill-fame which for the next three hundred years they were to possess throughout the seas which washed the shores of Europe.

The pirates became bolder every year. No merchant ship could count upon making a journey in peace in any part of the Mediterranean, and the galleys of the corsairs were known even beyond the Straits of Gibraltar, where they waylaid the treasure ships coming from the Indies, laden with the gold, jewels, and precious spices of tropical lands. During the life of Kheyr-ed-Din and many times afterward the princes of Christendom made half-hearted attempts to attack the growing power of the pirates. Tunis was besieged and captured by Charles V of Spain in 1535, and in October 1541, at the head of a great fleet, the same monarch entered the roads of Algiers. The pirates seemed in desperate straits, but the very elements betrayed His Most Catholic Majesty and heavy autumnal gales put confusion into the Spanish army and destroyed a hundred and fifty ships. The attempt ended in tragedy, and, chased and scattered by renewed tempests, the remains of the Spanish fleet staggered home, leaving Algiers more defiant than ever. Only with the battle of Lepanto in 1571, when the Turkish fleet was annihilated, was a supreme blow struck at the corsairs ; but the Christian Powers did not follow up their success, and Algiers continued to be the chief of numerous nests of pirates along the shores of Northern Africa.

It is a curious fact that the more famous corsairs were renegades ; that is to say, they were men born of Christian parents who, having, as a rule, been captured in youth by pirates, had later been received into the ranks of the corsairs. Many a man, pining in his prison or sickening of his forced labour, resolved to renounce both race and religion to escape his misery, so that Abbot Diego de Haedo, a Spanish writer who has left a description of the corsairs as he knew them in Algiers in the sixteenth century, could say that in his time "the main body of the corsairs are renegadoes from every part of Christendom, all extremely well acquainted with the Christian coasts."

It seems probable that the fighting qualities and excellent seamanship of the pirates were at their best during the sixteenth century. At that time they were undoubtedly monarchs of the Mediterranean. Haedo thus describes the state of things in his day : "While the Christians with their galleys are at repose, sounding their trumpets in the harbours, and very much at their ease, regaling themselves, passing the day and night in banqueting, cards, and dice, the corsairs at pleasure are traversing the east and west seas without the least fear or apprehension, as free and absolute sovereigns thereof. They here snap up a ship laden with gold and silver from India, and there another richly fraught from Flanders; now they make prize of a vessel from England, then of another from Portugal. Here they board and lead away one from Venice, then one from Sicily, and a little farther on they swoop down upon others from Naples, Leghorn, or Genoa, all of them crammed with riches. And at other times, carrying with them renegadoes as guides, they very deliberately, at noonday, or just when they please, leap ashore and advance into the country without dread some ten, twelve, or fifteen leagues; and the poor Christians, thinking themselves secure so far from the sea, are taken unawares; many towns, villages, and farms are sacked; and infinite numbers of men, women, and children, and infants at the breast are dragged away into a miserable captivity. With these wretched people roped together and loaded with their own valuable substance the corsairs retreat leisurely, with eyes full of laughter and content, to their vessels. As is too well known, in this manner they have utterly ruined and destroyed Sardinia, Corsica, Sicily, Calabria, the neighbourhoods of Naples, Rome, and Genoa, all the Balearic Islands, and the whole coast of Spain: in which last more particularly they feast as they think fit, on account of the Moriscoes who inhabit there; who, being all more zealous Mohammedans than are the very Moors born in Barbary, receive and caress the corsairs and give them information of what they desire to be informed of. Insomuch that before these corsairs have been absent from their abodes much longer than perhaps twenty or thirty days, they return home rich, with their vessels crowded with captives and ready to sink with the weight of wealth; with scarce any trouble thus reaping the fruits of all that the avaricious Mexican and greedy Peruvian have been digging from the bowels of the earth, and the thrifty merchant has been so many thousand leagues to procure."

It was only on lucky days that the corsairs put to sea. and a saintly man or a book of omens would be consulted to learn if the occasion was propitious. The favourite sailing days were Fridays and Sundays. The crews were warned, all was made shipshape, arms were lashed in their places along the quarters occupied by the men, the anchor was weighed and set in its appointed place, and then a gun was fired, the chained slaves upon their benches were made to dress their oars, and the good galleot began to draw away from the shore. "God speed us!" cried the crew, waving hands at wives and friends on shore; "God send you a good prize!" came the call from the crowd, and away went the ship on business that the merchants of Genoa, Naples, and Malaga fervently thought to be under the protection of Satan himself.

The corsairs had various methods of attack. When they sighted what looked like a fairly good cargo-vessel, they ran up a foreign flag so as to quieten any suspicions which the quarry might have. Then they would gradually work their way toward their victim until the merchantman would be able to look upon the deck of the corsair and to know from its packed crowd of men the character of the stranger. With prayers to saints and blows on the backs of their slaves the merchants would strive to get away. But too late! The guns on the forecastle of the galley were revealed by now, and renegade gunners were pitching shot with terrible effect among the rowers and crew of the trader. The crowd of cut-throat corsairs could be seen with muskets primed and scimitars flashing, as they stood ready to board as soon as the steersman had run their galley alongside. Then with the shock of the colliding vessels came the roar of battle; the evil faces of the pirates surged forward and their tigerlike figures climbed and crawled over the sides, their horrible war cries and execrations striking the palsy of fear into the hearts even of brave men.

When in the early part of the seventeenth century sails took the place of oars the corsairs quickly made themselves masters of the new fashion, and thereby extended the terror of their name to remoter lands. In 1617 a fleet went far west of Gibraltar and pillaged and devastated Madeira, bringing back over a thousand wretched captives. In 1627 a German renegade, who had assumed the Moorish name of Murad, led three pirate ships to Denmark and Iceland, bringing home some hundreds of prisoners; and a Fleming in 1631 came down on the English coasts, burning and robbing. Passing to the Irish coast, this daring rascal sacked Baltimore, and took over two hundred men, women, and children. "It was a piteous sight," says Father Dan, a priest who was at Algiers at the time, and left a narrative of the sufferings of the Christian captives to whom he was allowed to minister for a while, "to see them exposed for sale, for they parted the wife from the husband and the father from the child, selling the husband here and the wife there, tearing from her arms the daughter whom she cannot hope to see ever again." Again, in 1638 a renegade from Iceland led a fleet of corsairs to the shores of his native land, and there ravaged and burnt, just as his ancestors had done along the shores of the Mediterranean six hundred years before. Eight hundred Icelanders were brought away in captivity on this occasion.

Sailing-ships did not require hundreds of slaves for their crews, but nevertheless the number of captives taken did not diminish. There was naturally no lack of employment to which they could be put, on shore, and the demand was always equal to the supply. According to the character of their masters they were treated with brutality or humanity, but the lot of the majority was wretched in the extreme. The Christian nations, instead of combining to extirpate the whole of the evil traffickers and pirates, were accustomed to send consuls to reside at Algiers and Tunis to protect their miserable compatriots as much as possible and to negotiate ransoms for those whose friends could afford to pay them. Charitable bodies were formed in Christian countries to collect funds wherewith to ransom poor captives, the most famous of these being the French order of priesthood known as the Redemptionist Fathers. These priests, clad in white robes with a cross in blue and red upon the breast, went boldly to the strongholds of the brutal pirates and bargained for the release of French slaves.

The corsairs as a body varied considerably in strength

from time to time, and they never represented a force which could have defied any determined efforts of the Christian Powers to destroy them. At the end of the sixteenth century the Algerines possessed in all about forty-six galleys and brigantines, and the same number seems to have existed in 1634, when Father Dan wrote his experiences. A century later, namely, in 1719, they had only twenty-five galleons (sailing-vessels), of eighteen to sixty guns each, besides caravels and brigantines; but what the Algerine potentates lacked in men and ships they made up in insolence, and the poltroonery of the Christian kings and statesmen encouraged this behaviour.

England was one of the chief sufferers. Sir Thomas Roe, our ambassador at Constantinople from 1621 to 1628, reported that in one cruise alone the corsairs had captured forty-nine British vessels, and during the year 1622 four hundred British ships were taken. Appeals were constantly made for redress by ruined merchants, and the wives and daughters of imprisoned Englishmen piteously implored the Government to obtain the release of husbands, fathers, and brothers. All the European nations, in truth, suffered from the pest, but it was often a matter of 'policy' for them to be friendly with the corsair potentates—especially those of Algiers—in order to benefit from the losses inflicted on other trading States by the depredations of the pirates.

Indeed, the submissiveness of European States to the arrogance of the pirates of the Mediterranean during three hundred years makes a story of shame in which England is as much implicated as any other nation. All the chief Governments, including that of the United

States, paid from time to time huge sums as blackmail, so that their merchant vessels might go unmolested by the Algerine sea-robbers. The consuls and representatives sent by civilized States to the Court of the Dey were treated with insult, and forced to enter the presence of the ruler by bending under a wooden bar. Every affront was swallowed by these representatives, and if one had too much spirit to put up with the contumely showered upon him, the interests of his nation suffered, and he had either to submit to the Dey or be recalled.

No attempt was made to put an end to this humiliating condition of things until 1816, when Lord Exmouth was sent to Tunis, Tripoli, and Algiers to demand that Christian slavery should cease in those dominions. His firmness gained the success of his mission at Tunis and Tripoli, but it was not until he had fiercely bombarded Algiers for several hours, during which even British women served at the guns with their husbands, that the Dey was forced to submit, and to give an undertaking that in future Christian prisoners taken by piracy or in land raids should be exchanged instead of being enslaved. Here again the work was not completed; instead of making a clean sweep of the whole horde of pirates, the British Government allowed them, under conditions, to remain, with the result that in a few years their insolence and their depredations were as bad as ever.

In 1830, however, the day of retribution came. As the result of a dispute between the Dey and the French consul, during which the Dey was guilty of insufferable truculence and insolence, the French Government laid siege to the town, conquered it, and ultimately occupied the whole of the territory under the rule of the Dey. Even the story of this conquest is not without its dark side, but at any rate the power for evil of the Mediterranean pirates was now destroyed for ever.

V: The Buccaneers of the Spanish Main

I: The Narrative of Stephen Hooper, of Bristol, who was sold into Slavery in the West Indies, afterward became a Pirate, and was with Sir Henry Morgan at the Sack of Panama

I WAS born in the city of Bristol, a noted seaport in the West of England, in the year 1643. I was descended from parents noted rather for their industry than their birth. My father was a mate on board a merchantman trading to the Savannahs, having the reputation, as I have heard, of a very good seaman. Yet did he ever make little money, though my mother was a person of an industrious and saving character, who brought me up and bred me in the exercise of virtue. She also gave me as good a schooling as was within her means, and I was an apt learner. That I ever fell away from her good teaching and became the friend and companion of evil-living pirates and murderers was more by reason of harsh circumstances than of inclination, as I think the judicious and discerning reader will avow when he hath read my narrative. My mother happening to die when I was but a boy of twelve, and just after my father had departed on a voyage, I was placed in the care of my father's half-sister, the wife of a small ship's chandler. For some time I was treated well by my aunt and continued my schooling as usual, in which I made great progress. My aunt expected my father to return home within a little while, but as time elapsed and no news of him came, her treatment, which had always been sharp and grudging, now became harsh and tyrannical. The little money which my father had left with my mother, and which had been entrusted to my aunt, was soon consumed, and when at last the owners of my father's vessel informed us that they feared it and the crew had been lost, my lot became hard indeed.

My aunt not only begrudged every morsel I ate, but treated me with the greatest harshness, beating me unmercifully and availing herself of every opportunity of punishing me, by reducing my meals to bread and water in solitary confinement. In all this she was countenanced and assisted by my uncle, a man named John Palmer, who, while my aunt was a veritable virago in visage and voice, covered up his character, which was as cruel and oppressive as hers, by an unctuous manner of bearing and a soft and plausible voice. At length my sufferings became more than I could longer endure, and I ran away, intending to go to an uncle's, a brother of my dear mother's, who lived on a farm near Gloucester. But I was found and brought back, and punished severely, so that for fourteen days I lived on nothing but bread and water, saw no human being but the ugly and cruel face of my aunt, and nought else but the damp footings of the wall just outside the gratings of the window of my cellar prison.

When at length I was released, I was sent upon an errand by my uncle to a ship in the roads, where I was to take some stores, and on my way back, being forced by my hunger, I stole a ham from a shop, but such was my ill-luck that I was detected and hurried to the magistrate's house. As the result of inquiries my uncle and aunt were summoned to appear, and they overwhelmed me with reproaches, and alleged that in spite of their care and expense on my account, I wished to ruin their reputation by bringing shame and scandal upon them. As the shopkeeper whom I had robbed had recovered the ham undamaged (for such was my awkwardness that I had been unable to get away with my plunder and had not even been able to set my teeth in it), and, out of respect to my relations, would not press the charge, the magistrate, Sir John Mawksley, allowed my uncle Palmer to take me away on condition that he gave me a severe physical chastisement and arranged to send me out of the country. The sequel, to shorten a long story, was that when I was a lad of but twelve and a half years, I found myself in the schooner *Mary of Berkeley*, on my way to the Caribbee Islands, where, as my uncle Palmer had promised me, I should have an opportunity of making my fortune on the plantation of an Englishman named Saunders, who was a friend of my uncle's.

We had very good weather until we came into the vicinity of the Bermoothes, where a great storm assailed us, whereby we were thrown out of our course. At the end of eight days the storm abated, and we shaped our course for Guadeloupe, but we could not keep on this tack, and therefore made for the island of Tortuga, where we anchored in the port of Cayona. Here the captain began to sell his cargo, though I had heard we were due to sell this at Guadeloupe, and began to take on board great quantities of tobacco, which is much grown there. One day a Spanish planter came on board the ship and sat drinking with the captain, who, after a while, called me into his cabin.

"This gentleman here," he said, pointing to the planter, "is in need of a strong lad to help about his house in the island. You had better bind yourself to him." Saying which, he pushed a paper and a quill toward me.

"But," I said, "my uncle said I was going to an Englishman in the island of Guadeloupe."

"Your uncle left you in my hands," replied the captain, with an oath. "He doesn't want a thief in his family, and I have sold you to this gentleman for three years. It will make a man of you. Sign and get ashore!"

I was but a boy and I was astounded at what he said: to think that my relative had sent me out to be sold like any slave was a piece of news which confounded me. I was in a mazed condition, and I signed the agreement without another word and accompanied my master on shore.

I found that my master, who was named Garcilasso, was what they called a bucanier, or buccaneer, more than a planter. A buccaneer was one who hunted wild bulls and cows, and smoked their meat for sale to the crews and masters of vessels which called at Tortuga who needed stores of meat. The word cometh, as I have been informed, from a Caribbee Indian word *boucan*, which is flesh or fish preserved by smoking. My master knew no English and I knew no Spanish, but I was quick to learn what my master wished me to do, and in a few weeks I picked up enough Spanish to understand a good deal of what he said. At that time he was collecting guns, powder and shot, and other stores, for the purpose of going to the neighbouring island of Hispaniola, or, as it is now called, Santo Domingo, where was great plenty of the wild cattle. With some twenty other men we shortly set sail, and having landed on the island we took to the woods for the hunting. We went to a village in a wood where were other buccaneers, all of whom were a mongrel sort of people, some born of white European people and negroes, and called mulattos, and others of negroes and Indians, and called alcatraces. My master was a creole, that is, he was born of Spanish parents in the Caribbees. The country was very beautiful, but the life was one of unremitting toil and of a disgusting character. I had to keep in the village and look to the food of my master and his partner, a mulatto named Corbo, and when the carcases of beasts were brought in I had to help flay them, cut up and smoke the meat, and boil down the fat for tallow, and to prepare the hides. Here I spent two wretched years, revolted not only by the work and the brutality of the people about me, but subject to the cruel treatment of my master and his partner. As the time of my apprenticeship approached its termination, they redoubled my work, if that were possible, and drove me to slave for them night and day with blows and curses innumerable. This is their usual practice, as I saw and knew from the cases of other white servants in the village. Many were Frenchmen and Spaniards who had been inveigled from comfortable homes in Europe, whom they worked unmercifully because they wished to get all the labour out of them that they could before their three years were expired. Some fell sick of a disease called coma, which was a sort of despair from which they surely died, since it was the effect of brutality in treatment and want of rest. Some tried to escape, but when they were recaptured their fate was worse than before.

At length my masters, having secured all the hides, smoked meat, and tallow they required, returned to Tortuga to sell the results of their labour. Here they spent their gains prodigally, giving themselves up to all manner of excess, vice, and drunkenness. Men bought hogsheads of wine, staved them in the street and called their friends to sit around and drink; they threw wine at passers by or asked them to partake also; so that you soon saw many men lying like logs about the causeway, utterly dead to all that went on about them. Quarrels and bloodshed were frequent in these bouts of drunkenness, and it was in one such dispute that my master lost his life. If, however, I thought my fate would be better from this circumstance I was quickly undeceived, for his partner, Corbo, took me to his plantation and there forced me to work with his slaves in the tobacco field. He told me he would have full return for the food he gave me and that he did not care whether I lived or died. At length, when my three years were nearly expired, he sold me to Miguel Fontences, a great planter who was known to be the most cruel and savage of all on the island. But, wonderful to relate, he took a fancy to me to have me about the house, where I worked as a servant of all work. He had a Spanish wife, who though of a fierce and ungovernable nature when angry, was often kind and generous. I could, however, never count on what treatment I should receive, getting lashes when I expected fair words, and careless or kind speech when I thought I might get blows. I spent five wretched years there, and then my master lent me to a pirate, one named Alvarez, who had been, with many others, inflamed by the exploit of the buccaneer named Pierre le Grand, who, being tired of occupations upon land, had recently gone pirating and had taken a great Spanish ship and fifty thousand pieces of eight. With Alvarez I went on three cruises, which were very successful, for we took six trading vessels, two of which were plate ships. The profit I gained for my master was very great, and, indeed, the whole island was at that time riotous with the success gained by many pirates among the vessels of Spain.

There was a man among us on the *Campeador*, which was Alvarez's ship, who was reckoned to be the boldest and coolest among us. He was a Frenchman named Francis Lolonais. In his youth he had been transported to the Caribbee Islands, as a servant or slave. Being out of his time he came to Hispaniola, where he joined for some time with the hunters or buccaneers, and afterward became a common mariner on the *Campeador*. Alvarez was a friend of the governor of Tortuga, Monsieur de la Place, and he recommended Lolonais to Monsieur, who patronized the young Frenchman, insomuch that he gave him a ship in which he might seek his fortune. I went with Lolonais on his two first voyages, in which he was very successful. By this time I was my own master, and had already got together a little money from my shares in the expeditions I had made with Alvarez, and I made still more when I went with Lolonais. We sailed from Tortuga to the coast of Campeachy, and there fell in with a great ship, the *Viuda de Malabar*, which was carrying great wealth of silver and goods to Spain. Though the Spaniards fought well, they were overwhelmed by the fierceness with which we dashed upon them, and we gained the ship and all its gear. In the second voyage we captured two merchantmen, and sacked a town in Granada, named Ciudad de la Perla, which had a garrison of a hundred men. Here we made above four thousand pieces of eight in money, besides much plate and many jewels, in all, to the value of thirty thousand pieces of eight. In this adventure I received a severe cut on my right arm which severed a muscle, so that, as our ship's surgeon said, 'I should never be able to split a Spaniard's skull to his chine again,' by which words he humorously referred to an action of mine which had recommended me to the pirates on the second voyage I ever made.

With the money I had now made I bought a small plantation, and though I was but twenty-two years of age I thought to settle down and earn a modest competence as a planter. But, as you shall hear, my friend Captain Henry Morgan drew me forth again later to share some of his famous exploits among the idolatrous and haughty Spaniards. Through several of the crew who sailed with Lolonais, I heard of all that befell them on their next ill-fated expedition. A huge storm drove them on shore when they reached the coast of Campeachy. All the men were saved, but the Spaniards were watching them as they struggled ashore, and killed most of them when they came up into the forest. The pirates fought valiantly, but they were outnumbered, and Lolonais only saved himself by hiding under the bodies of his dead shipmates. When the Spaniards quitted the place he crawled forth, killed a half-breed and assumed his dress, in which he made his way into Campeachy town. There, as he walked about, he saw the Spaniards making fires and drinking and rejoicing together. He asked a slave the reason of this. "It is because a renowned pirate named Lolonais has been killed," was the reply. "Why do they rejoice," asked Lolonais, "seeing there are many pirates to take his place?" "He has harassed and injured them vastly," answered the slave, "and his cruelties against them have been such that the Spaniards would rather choose to die or to sink fighting than to be taken by him." Which was very true, for he loved blood for its own sake, and would torture his prisoners before he slew them. Lolonais also heard that several of his men were made captive by the Spaniards, and that these also averred that he was dead.

Lolonais mingled with certain low slaves and assumed an ascendancy over them, so that he got them to promise that they would throw in their lot with him, thinking that he also was an escaped slave who wished to leave the mainland. He made certain proposals to them, and many promises, and one night they stole a canoe and some food and put to sea. Fortune favoured them in this venture, and I myself saw and greeted Lolonais on the very day on which he landed at Tortuga again. He was in low straits then, being discredited by reason of the loss of his ship and by his coming back in such poverty. In a little while, however, I heard that he had got a small coasting brig with twenty-one very common rascals to man her, with which he set forth to retrieve his fortune. He made for a town in Cuba, thinking to gain wealth there, but the governor at the Havannah having received word that pirates were menacing the place, sent a ship to the relief of the town, with ten guns and ninety men. It had been told the governor that the pirates were commanded by the ill-famed Lolonais. At this the governor swore passionately, but he gave the captain of the relief ship a great negro to serve for a hangman, and charged him "not to return into his presence without having totally destroyed the pirates, except Lolonais, who was to be brought alive to the Havannah."

When the Spanish captain arrived near the town threatened by the pirates all seemed quiet, and the Spaniards lay at anchor in the river Estera, near the town. Lolonais was aware of their coming, and conceived a stratagem to take the vessel. Toward two o'clock one morning the watch on the deck of the Spaniard heard the sound of oars in the water on one side, and thinking fishermen were about the officer called out to them:

"Boat a-hoy! Have ye heard anything of the pirates hereabout?"

"Nay," came the answer as if from a fisherman; "neither pirates nor aught else."

The Spaniards were content with this reply and thought that indeed the pirates had fled at the rumour of their approach. But just as dawn was breaking over the river there came other sounds of rowing, and the noise of men climbing by the chains into the forepart of the vessel. The Spaniards were caught napping, the pirates were all aboard ere the full ship's company had tumbled up from their bunks. Then began a fierce fight; the Spaniards fought manfully, and when they had been forced to retreat to the poop they levelled their guns at their assailants and slew several. Nevertheless, the fierceness of the pirates was such that half the Spaniards were already slain or wounded, and the other half were driven down the hatches. Lolonais warped the vessel out of the river, where, indeed, it should never have been placed, and when he was at sea again he stood by the hatches with Moses van Vin, his lieutenant, a vile Dutchman whom I could never abide for his greedy and treacherous ways, and ordered the Spaniards to come up. The poor wretches came up, indeed, but only to have their heads struck off when they had made five steps along the deck. Lolonais slew the captain with his own hand, mocking him beforehand with his defeat. The negro who had been named executioner cried for mercy. Lolonais told him to confess all he knew, which the poor wretch did, telling him how angry the governor had been and what had been his charge to the Spanish captain, and the office he himself had been given, which was to take off all the pirates except Lolonais. At this Lolonais smiled grimly, but the negro was slain with the rest. One only of the Spaniards did Lolonais spare, and him he sent back to the Havannah to the governor with a written message, as thus :

"I shall never henceforward give quarter to any Spaniard whatsoever ; and I have great hopes I shall execute on your own person the very same punishment I have done upon them you sent against me. Thus I have retaliated the kindness you designed to me and my companions.

"FRANÇOIS LOLONAIS"

After this Lolonais sailed to Maracaibo, where by good

hap he surprised a ship laden with plate and other merchandises, outward bound. With this prize he returned to Tortuga, where he was received with joy, for now his success had caused his former failure to be forgotten.

Greatly elated with this good fortune which had befallen him, Lolonais now contemplated still greater exploits. He designed to equip a fleet sufficient to transport five hundred men and necessaries, and with this force he aimed at taking Maracaibo itself. When once he had published his intention abroad he had no difficulty in getting over four hundred men in a little while. At length, having finished all his preparations, he set sail with his fleet, which consisted of eight vessels, the crews numbering six hundred and sixty persons. Good fortune was with them at first. A Spanish ship which Lolonais captured off Punta de Espada had forty thousand pieces of eight aboard her, and jewels to the value of ten thousand more. Another, with military pay on board to the amount of twelve thousand pieces of eight, also contained great store of powder and ammunition and a vast number of muskets.

Lolonais thereupon went forward to Maracaibo, which is a prosperous city built on the western side of a great lake. The town is defended by a fort in which are mounted sixteen great guns. The pirates having landed a league off the fort, advanced by degrees toward it; but the governor had espied their landing, and had placed an ambush to cut them off behind, while he should attack them in front. Lolonais was too wary, however, and he defeated the ambush, which fled into the city. Then, after a fierce battle of three hours, he became master of the fort without any other arms than swords and pistols the great guns of the Spanish being useless to resist the pirates. The people of Maracaibo, hearing of the capture of the fort, fled with precipitation to a town farther inland called Gibraltar, and the pirates, entering the city two days later, found plenty of victuals, as flour, bread, pork, brandy, wines, and poultry, with which they made good cheer. Little wealth, however, was to be found, and therefore Lolonais sent out some men into the woods to capture any of the fugitives they could find. That very night, indeed, his men returned, having sought to good purpose, for they brought money to the value of twenty thousand pieces of eight, several mules laden with goods, and twenty prisoners.

Fifteen days did the pirates stay in Maracaibo, and then they made for Gibraltar. Here, however, they were valiantly withstood by the governor of Merida, the chief town in those parts, who had fought in Flanders, and it was only by an old trick that Lolonais enticed the Spaniards from their fortified batteries. He pretended to turn and draw off in confusion, whereupon the Spanish soldiers rushed out in disorder. By this means Lolonais defeated the enemy and seized the town, in which, however, he found little gold or silver. The pirates threatened to burn the town if a ransom of ten thousand pieces of eight were not paid, and on this sum being rendered to them they returned to Maracaibo, where they likewise collected a tribute of twenty thousand pieces of eight and five hundred cows.

Thereafter the pirates sailed to Hispaniola, and arrived there in eight days. They landed in a port called Isla de la Vacca, where they unladed their whole cargazon of riches. Having made an exact calculation of all their plunder, they found in ready money two hundred and sixty thousand pieces of eight : this being divided every one received his share. Those who had been wounded received special sums for the loss of their limbs. Then they weighed all the plate uncoined, reckoning ten pieces of eight to a pound. The jewels were prized roughly, either too high or too low, by reason of the men's ignorance. This done, every one was put to his oath to swear that he had not smuggled anything from the common stock.

The whole dividend being finished they set sail for Tortuga. Here they arrived a month after, to the great joy of most of the island ; for, as to the common pirates, in three weeks they had scarce any money left, having spent it all in things of little value, or in dissipation or gambling.

In a little time Lolonais determined upon another expedition, and now he need take no great care to gather men to serve under him, more coming in voluntarily than he could employ. He resolved to make a second voyage to Nicaragua, there to pillage as many towns as he could. He set off with six ships and seven hundred men, and took his course to the Continent, toward the Cape Gracias à Dios. But a great storm drove them into the Gulf of Honduras. Here they landed and pillaged far and wide, but getting little for their trouble among the poor Indian villages situated there. At length they assaulted the Spanish town of San Pedro, where the townsmen defended themelves with great obstinacy. But hitherto they had obtained very little profit.

At length, receiving tidings that a large Spanish ship

was expected in the Gulf, Lolonais repaired his ships and cruised about waiting for the enemy to come. When the ship had come, they found it was a much larger vessel than any of their own, being mounted with forty-two guns. Lolonais assaulted her with great courage; but the Spaniards defended themselves so well that they forced the pirates to retire. The smoke of the powder continuing thick, however, like a dark fog, the pirates stole back with four canoes crammed with men, and boarding the ship with great agility they overpowered the Spaniards. But little did they find in her, for she was almost wholly unladen of her goods.

Then Lolonais called a council of war and told the men that he intended for Guatemala: hereupon they divided in several sentiments, some liking the proposal, and others disliking it, especially a large party of them who were but raw in these expeditions, and who had imagined at their setting forth from Tortuga, that pieces of eight were gathered as easily as pears from trees; these were for turning back, while others affirmed that they had rather starve than face their creditors in Tortuga without money in their pockets. The major part, however, separated from Lolonais and the rest, and began to make their way homeward.

Lolonais, thus left by most of his companions, remained alone in the Gulf of Honduras. His ship being too great to get out at the ebb of those seas, he sustained great privations from the want of provisions, so that he and his men were constrained to go ashore every day to seek sustenance, and not finding anything else, they were forced to kill and eat monkeys, lizards, and other animals such as they could easily get at.

At last in the latitude of the Cape of Gracias à Dios, near a certain little island called De las Pertas, his ship struck on a bank of sand, where no art availed to get her off again, though they unladed all the guns, iron, and other weighty things as much as they could. Hereupon they were forced to break the ship in pieces, and with planks and nails build themselves a long boat in which to get away. But considering that their work would be long they began to cultivate some pieces of ground; they sowed French beans, which ripened in six weeks, and many other fruits. They had good provision of Spanish wheat and bananas. Thus they feared not hunger in these desert places, and employed themselves upon the boat for five or six months. When it was finished they cast lots who should go in it, as it was not large enough for all. It was first resolved to go to the river of Nicaragua, to see if they could capture some canoes from the Indians, in which the remainder of their comrades could be brought away.

Lolonais, with half his men, set sail in the long boat, and in a few days arrived at the river. But their approach had been perceived by some Spaniards and Indians, who together laid an ambush, and setting upon the pirates when they had landed, so took them by surprise that the greatest part were slain on the spot. Lolonais, however, escaped aboard the boat with a few others, and, getting away, was still resolved to look for canoes with which to go back for the men left in the Gulf. But now Dame Fortune had turned her back upon this bold leader, and death only was to be his portion. For, landing one day upon the coast of Darien, where there were large numbers of wild Indians, or braves, he and most of his men were seized. Two only escaped as by the skin of their teeth, and one, who ultimately reached Tortuga again, told me a year afterward how he had to look upon the fate of his comrades from the shelter of a tree, expecting every moment that he himself would be discovered and haled to the same doom. Lolonais and the others were tied to stakes, and brushwood was placed about them, and then lighted, and so miserably did these men perish, while the Indians danced about them yelling with glee.

Having now given a compendious narrative of the exploits of Lolonais, I will relate the great action of Captain Henry Morgan when he took and fired the great city of Panama. In this I myself took part, as shall be related in its proper place.

Captain Henry Morgan was born in the principality of Wales; his father was a rich yeoman or farmer, of good quality. Young Morgan had no inclination to the calling of his father, and therefore left home and joined a ship going to the Barbados. When he landed in that island he was sold by the captain of the vessel to a planter, with whom he served his time. Afterward he betook himself to Jamaica, where he joined a pirate ship and performed three or four voyages with profit and success. It was at this time that I fell in with Morgan, for on his happening to call at Tortuga with the pirate ship, I gave him information as to a certain Spanish town on the mainland which he and his master, Captain Mansvelt, had a mind to attack. They wished me to go with them as a guide, but I had just bought my plantation and could not leave care of it to anyone else; they promised, however, that if they succeeded in gaining wealth, I should have my share. Which voyage turning out successfully, Morgan visited me later and gave me my share of the spoil they had gained.

Morgan was of a sturdy and robust make, with a broad face, brown hair, and hard brown eyes. He was well-spoken, with a quick manner of speaking and a masterful look. There are some who speak evilly of him, charging him with fraud and treachery in the division of spoil, but I speak of him as I found him, fair in his dealings and careful in redeeming his promises.

After his fourth voyage he joined stocks with other men in Jamaica and bought a ship, with which he made a very triumphant voyage to the coasts of Campeachy, whence he returned with several prizes. I shall not relate at length all the exploits of Captain Morgan at this time. It will suffice to say that in all his attempts, until the time of his great assault upon Panama, he was successful. At the taking of El Puerto del Principe the results were small, amounting to no more than fifty thousand pieces of eight, in money and goods, which caused general grief to all, since it would not have enabled the men to face their creditors in Jamaica. But he more than made up for these deficiencies at Puerto Bello. As he had himself told his men when some had spoke against assaulting the strong town with their slender forces, small numbers, if they be full of courage, may succeed where larger numbers of mean spirits may fail. " If our number is small," said he, " our hearts are great ; and the fewer persons we are, the more union and better shares we shall have in the spoil." And indeed the booty was great, for when, at the Deadman's Island, or Cayo del Muerto, they made a dividend or division of the spoil, they found they had two hundred and fifty thousand pieces of eight in ready money alone. At Maracaibo, also, which most men might have thought was no better than an empty wine-skin after Lolonais had sacked it two years before, he yet found a trifle of spoil, though no more than twenty-five thousand pieces of eight in money and jewels. But there was a huge quantity of merchandise and slaves, all of which raised the value of the booty to five times the amount of ready money.

Captain Morgan now perceived that Fortune favoured him, by giving success to all his enterprises, which occasioned him, as was natural to a man of ambition, to aspire to greater things. He undertook, therefore, to equip a new fleet, for which he assigned the south side of Tortuga as a place of rendezvous, writing letters to all the expert pirates there inhabiting, and to the planters and hunters of Hispaniola, informing them of his intentions and desiring their appearance, if they intended to go with him. I also received a letter in which Captain Morgan invited me to go with him, but as I was now no fighting man, he asked whether I would be his man of business, as he knew that I had a knowledge of reading and writing and figures. As my plantation was doing well and I had a good overseer, an Englishman whom I had befriended, named Nat Parsons, I wrote in reply to Captain Morgan accepting his offer, and when the time came I left my affairs in the hands of Nat Parsons and went to the rendezvous. There I was received with much friendliness by the Captain, who took me aside and told me that I was to be a sort of secretary to himself, to keep the necessary accounts of the expedition, and especially to keep a list of the booty which might be made. He bound me by an oath to do this office honestly, threatening me with severe punishment if I deceived or defrauded him or any of the company. As some of the Captain's enemies have asserted that he cheated over the division of the spoil taken at Panama, I declare here that neither I nor to my knowledge did Captain Morgan retain anything that was not due to us.

We weighed anchor off the Cape of Tiburon on December 16, 1670, and came to the island of St Catherine, off the coast of Cuba, three days later. In the capture of this place from the Spaniards we suffered some little tribulation, but the island was taken with small loss. Here we found little money, but much powder and ammunition, which to us were almost as valuable as money.

The object of the present expedition was the capture of Panama, a rich and old city of the Spaniards on the western coast of Darien, beyond the high Cordilleras. For the purpose of approaching this place a narrow but difficult neck of land had to be passed, lying between that part of the Spanish Main called the Carib Sea, and the Pacific Ocean. The land was filled with high mountains, rocky cliffs, thick forests, and tortuous paths, and the best way to approach the city was by a river named Chagres, which flowed down from the mountains into the Carib Sea.

At the mouth of the river was a strong town, also called Chagres, which had a castle built on a high mountain, and at the foot of the mountain was a strong fort with eight great guns, commanding the entry to the river. It was necessary that this fort as well as the castle should be captured by Captain Morgan, before he could hope to take his expedition in boats up the river Chagres to the great and rich city of Panama. Accordingly, the Captain sent his second in command, or vice-admiral, Captain Brodeley, with four hundred men, to take the town of Chagres, he himself remaining at St Catherine.

The Spaniards made a very courageous resistance, but after our men had burned down portions of the palisading around the fort and had thus made a breach, the Spaniards who remained alive cast themselves down into the sea rather than ask quarter for their lives. Out of three hundred and fourteen men wherewith the castle was garrisoned, only thirty remained alive. Our men lost about a hundred, besides seventy wounded. From the prisoners they learned that the Spaniards at Panama had already received notice of Captain Morgan's projected expedition against their city, a deserter from our side having reached the governor of that city. It was also declared that the governor of Panama had placed several ambuscades along the river of Chagres; and that he waited for us in the open fields about Panama with three thousand six hundred men.

When Captain Morgan received news of the capture of the castle of Chagres he immediately set forth with the rest of his forces, and in eight days we had reached Chagres. Never shall I forget the great roar of acclamations which greeted us as we sailed toward the town. Already when we were afar off and our men on shore had seen the English colours on our masts they had begun shouting, and the joy and gladness with which Captain Morgan was received when he landed were beyond description. After repairing the castle and settling the command of the garrison, Captain Morgan set forth with twelve hundred men for Panama. We were accommodated in thirty-two canoes, and there were five boats laden with artillery. We took little provisions with us, for the Captain hoped to provide himself sufficiently from the Spaniards who were lying in ambuscades upon the way.

The first day we sailed six leagues, and then a party landed to seek victuals in the neighbouring plantations. None, however, could we find, the Spaniards having fled, carrying all they had with them. This was the first day of our journey, and most of us had to be content with only a pipe of tobacco, so great was the lack of victuals. Next day, about evening, we came to a place called Cruz de Juan Gallego. Here we were compelled to leave our boats, for the river was dry for want of rain and many trees had fallen into the channel from the thick forests upon either bank. Next morning Captain Morgan set apart one hundred and sixty men who were to guard the boats while the rest of us went forward on foot. He charged these men on no account to leave the boats, for he was in great fear lest the Spaniards should issue from the forests, which at that place were of an almost incredible denseness, and overwhelm them if they separated. After a very meagre breakfast for most of us we set forth upon our march, but the way was woefully difficult. The great trees were so close together, and the creepers and climbing plants grew so thickly about them, that we had the utmost difficulty in getting forward. At length, seeing how long and dilatory would be our progress, Captain Morgan thought it more convenient to return and transport the lighter boats or canoes, although it might be done only with great labour, to a place farther up the river called Cedro Bueno. Here many of us re-embarked upon the river while others marched along the bank. We still could not find any food, the country in this part being so wild that it seemed not to hold any plantations or farms.

The fourth day a large party of us landed, the country being more open; the rest went by water, being conducted by other guides who always went before them to discover, on both sides of the river, the ambuscades of the Spanish. I was in one of the canoes on this day, and about noon we came to a place called Torna Cavallos: here the guide of the canoes cried out that he perceived an ambuscade. His words caused infinite joy to all of us in the boats, for we hoped now to find some provisions to satisfy our extreme hunger. Having come to the place, we found nobody in it, the Spaniards having fled, nor had they left anything behind them but a few old empty wine-bags made of skin, with the hair outside. There were also a few crusts of bread scattered on the ground where the Spaniards had eaten. We were very angry at this, and the men swore that they would eat the Spaniards themselves when they met them. They tore down the light huts which the men of the ambuscades had made. Many of us began to cut up and eat the leather bags, to allay the craving of our stomachs, and quarrels arose among several as to who should have a portion of this tough meal. I myself procured a portion, and for all that the leather was so distasteful it did ease my pain for a little while. By the bigness of the place of the ambuscade, we conjectured that about five hundred Spaniards had been there.

Having stayed the pangs of our hunger in the manner described, we proceeded farther, till we came about nightfall to another post, called Torna Munni. Here had been another ambuscade, but the place was more barren even than the former. We searched the neighbouring woods, but could not find anything at all to eat, the Spaniards having been so provident as to strip the place of everything that might provide us with sustenance. That man was happy that had reserved since noon any little bit of leather to make his supper of, drinking after it a good draught of water. Some who have never been out of their mothers' kitchens may wonder how we could eat and digest these pieces of skin, so hard and dry as they were. Whom I answer that, could they once experience what hunger, or, rather, famine, is, they would find the way as we did. We first sliced the leather in pieces, then we beat it between two stones, and rubbed it, often dipping it in water to make it more supple and tender. Lastly, we broiled it, having picked out as many hairs as we could. Having thus cooked it, we cut it into small morsels and ate it, helping it down with frequent gulps of water, of which, by good fortune, we had plenty at hand.

The fifth day, about noon, we came to a place called Barbaçoa. Here at a little distance were several plantations, but all as bare of food as if locusts had swept through them. After searching a long time, however, the men found a grot which seemed to have been lately hewn out of the rock, in which had been concealed two sacks of meal, wheat, and like things, with two great jars of wine. The discoverers would have consumed these things almost at once, but word being carried to Captain Morgan, he, knowing that some of the men were now very weak from hunger, caused what was found to be very carefully divided among those who were in greatest necessity. Those that were still too feeble to march were put into the boats, while the others walked.

The sixth day we continued our march, howbeit we were constrained to rest very frequently, both by reason of the ruggedness of the way and the extreme weakness of many of the men, who endeavoured to relieve their hunger by eating leaves of trees and green herbs, or even grass, but this only added to their misery. This day at noon we arrived at a plantation where there was found a barn full of maize. This was immediately brought out and distributed among us all, and there was sufficient for all of us to have a good allowance. But many of the foolish fellows retained not their share for long; for, reaching an ambuscade in about an hour, many threw away their maize, believing that now they would find all things in abundance. But in this they were much deceived, for no food or living thing was discovered in the place where the Spaniards had been stationed. On the other side of the river, however, they saw about a hundred Indians, who all fled away. Some of the men jumped into the river to cross it with the intention of seizing some of the Indians, but in vain; for, being much more nimble than our men, they not only got away, but shot and killed many with their arrows, hooting at them and saying: "*Ha, perros! a la savana, a la savana!*" —" Ha, ye dogs! Go back to the plain!"

When night arrived we had reached a spot where it would be necessary to cross the river, in order to continue our march toward Panama. We rested on the ground beside the river, though the sleep of most of the men was not profound. I heard many of the men railing and reviling against Captain Morgan, inasmuch as he had not brought proper stores of provisions with us. Some swore they would turn back next day, while others said they would rather die of hunger than go back from their undertaking. Others laughed and jested, saying that the croakers ought to have stayed in Jamaica or Tortuga, and worked in the tobacco fields with the nigger women. Then I heard the word which one of the guides sent round to comfort the men, which was to the effect that 'It would not now be long before we met with people from whom they would reap some considerable advantage.'

The seventh day, in the morning, the men made clean their arms, and every one discharged his pistol, or musket, without bullet, to try their firelocks. This being done, we crossed the river, and at noon we arrived at a village called Cruz. While yet far from the place we perceived much smoke from the chimneys, the sight whereof gave us great joy, and hopes of finding people and plenty of good cheer. Thus the men went on as fast as they could, the hungry and thin faces of the most miserable lighting up at the prospect. Others called to their friends as to what they would choose to eat when they reached the village. "Smoke is coming out of every chimney: they are making good fires to roast and boil what we are to eat." I verily believe some of the foolish fellows believed that good fortune was about to provide them with a Lord Mayor's feast.

At length, having arrived all sweating and panting at the village, which had three streets, we ran and looked into every house, but found not a single person, but only good fires, which we wanted not, and a few cats and dogs. These, of course, were soon killed and devoured. There were also some jars of wine, which, being drunk, caused great sickness among the men, owing to the starved condition of their stomachs. Many were so sick that we could make no further progress that day, but remained until the next morning.

Cruz is but eight leagues from Panama, and is the last place to which canoes or boats can proceed, for which reason Captain Morgan was forced to leave his canoes and to land all the men, though never so weak. The next day two hundred of the stronger men were sent before the body of the army to discover the way to Panama and to get news of any ambuscades. The path was very narrow, so that only ten or twelve persons could march abraast, and often not so many. The men had a rencontre with some Indians some miles upon the way, at a place where, if the Indians had been more dexterous in military affairs, they might have defended the passage against all our army. That evening a great rain fell, which caused us to march the faster, and to seek for houses to preserve our arms from becoming wet ; but the Indians had set fire to every hut. However, after diligent search, we found a few shepherds' huts, though nothing to eat in them. These not holding many men, we placed in them a few as a guard, who kept the arms and powder of the rest. As for us who remained outside in the fields, being dressed as we were in nothing but a pair of seamen's trousers or breeches, and a shirt, without either shoes or stockings, we had much ado to shelter ourselves under trees from the rain, which lasted with great violence until the morning.

Just before dawn we recommenced our march, and continued in the cool of the day, for the clouds still hung over our heads, though the rain did not fall. At last, having reached the top of a high mountain just behind the city of Panama, we saw the South Sea stretched out before us as far as our eyes could carry. The sudden sight took my breath away, as it did for many others, but we were all filled with joy at having reached almost the end of our tedious and miserable journey. We could decry but one ship and six boats, which were making for the little islands of Tavoga and Tavogilla, lying far out toward the south.

That afternoon we came to a vale where we happily found many cattle. Here we instantly set to work, and while some killed and flayed cows, horses, bulls, and asses, of which latter there was the greatest store, others kindled fires and got wood to keep them supplied. Such was our hunger that we could not wait to cook the meat properly, but having cut the flesh into convenient pieces or gobbets, we threw them into the fire, and ate them only half roasted. We then set forth again, and in a little while we came in sight of the highest steeple of Panama, whereat we rejoiced mightily. All the men showed signs of extreme joy, casting up their hats into the air, leaping and shouting, just as if they had already seized the town. They shot off their muskets and pistols to show their delight, which was a foolish thing to do, seeing that they had been better advised to retain their bullets for the rascally Spaniards.

At the noise thus made some fifty horsemen appeared from the city, as if to observe our movements, but they did not venture within musket shot. When they went away the big guns in the city opened their fire upon us, but it was only waste of ball and powder. We could hear the great shot ripping and thudding among the trees some hundred yards before us, for we were not within reach of this cannonade. Having placed sentinels about our camp, we opened our satchels and fell to eating very heartily the pieces of bulls' and horses' flesh which we had reserved from the afternoon. Afterward we laid ourselves down easier in mind and body than we had been since we started from Chagres.

Next morning we advanced in the direction of Panama by an irksome and difficult way whereby we should avoid ambuscades. At length we came to the top of a little hill, and suddenly discovered the people of Panama drawn up in battle array. They seemed so numerous that fear struck the hearts of many. But as we talked among ourselves we began to realize that, having got so far, we must either fight with resolution or be slain ourselves, for no mercy could we expect from an enemy whom the English had always despoiled and used harshly whenever they had met them in these parts. Captain Morgan went among his men rallying their spirits, and telling them that though the Spaniards might have more artillery they had not the stout hearts which alone would win a hand-to-hand conflict. Thereafter he divided his men into three battalions, and sent forward a body of two hundred buccaneers who were very dexterous in the use of their muskets.

Our guides had taken a way which compelled the Spaniards to meet us at a very disadvantageous place for them, namely, where the land was low-lying and boggy. As soon as the band of buccaneers drew nigh, the Spaniards sent out their horsemen against them, who came forward crying out "Viva el Rey!"—"God save the King!" but the ground being full of quags they could not wheel about as they desired. The buccaneers kneeled down, and taking careful aim poured a full volley of shot among the horsemen, each bullet finding its stopping-place in the body of an enemy. The Spanish horse were thereby thrown into confusion, whereon the infantry essayed to support them. But the buccaneers were so quick and accurate in their shooting, that the Spaniards durst not advance.

Hereupon we saw many negroes running forward driving great black bulls before them, whom they goaded in order to make them break up the body of our marksmen. The most of the bulls fled away, being frighted by the firing. A few broke through the musket men, but all these were shot dead. By this time all three battalions of our men were engaged with the enemy, who, for all his efforts, could not make head against our fire. The battle continued two hours in a very lively manner. The greatest part of the Spanish caballeros were already killed, and those that survived now fled, leaving the infantry to make what head they could. But the efforts of these were also in vain, for we pressed forward upon them so closely and searched them so mercilessly with our shots that at length, firing a final volley, they threw down their weapons and scattered, running to find hiding-places in the town.

Captain Morgan would not command us to follow immediately, since we were very wearied with our many privations and exertions, and he had no knowledge of what the strength of the Spaniards in the city might be. At length a Spanish captain was brought to him, who told him of the preparations which had been made in the town to receive our attack, from which it appeared that trenches had been dug and batteries raised to defend the town. Captain Morgan now reviewed the men and counted the dead and wounded. We had lost a considerable number, but not so many as the Spaniards, of whom we counted six hundred lying dead, besides the wounded and the prisoners. After resting awhile we went forward once more. Though they had lost greatly, our men were nothing discouraged. On the contrary I heard many speak with pride at perceiving what huge advantage they had obtained against a stronger enemy. All of them swore that they would finish the business as they had begun, and would fight till not a man was left. In this spirit they resumed their march upon the city.

When our ranks came within sight of the walls the great guns which the Spaniards had mounted upon them belched forth, some with great shot, others with musket-balls, and still others with clouds of little fragments of iron. They fired incessantly at the advancing men, so that unavoidably we lost numbers at every step, for the bits of iron were flying in all directions, maiming, wounding, and killing.

Again and again did our men dash against the walls, yelling and shouting, while the Spaniards replied with their guns and muskets. At length, after three hours of fighting, our men gained a footing at one place and pressed forward so impetuously that soon the Spaniards fled from their guns. Then our men went through the nearer parts of the town, killing all who opposed them, and looting where they found goods worth the taking. But the inhabitants had transported most of their wealth to remote places. As soon as the first fury of their entrance was over, Captain Morgan assembled all the men, and told them that he had learned that the Spaniards had poisoned all the wine in the city. He accordingly forbade the men to drink any. This, however, was only a device which he had hit upon, for he feared that if his men gave way to drinking, the Spaniards who were still at liberty, and who greatly outnumbered us, would get courage to come and overwhelm us while we were helpless in wine.

Next day, about noon, from the place where we had encamped outside the city we suddenly saw great clouds of smoke and flame rising from some of the chief buildings. Many of the Spaniards and some of our men did what they could either to quench the flames, or, by blowing up some houses and pulling down others, to stop the conflagration but these efforts had little success. All the houses of the city were built of cedar, very curious and magnificent in appearance, and were adorned inside with hangings and pictures, and being of such material, many streets were soon involved in the destroying element. The fire increased so that before night the greater part of the city was destroyed. I was very busy at that time at my duty of keeping an account of all booty that was brought in, and I had little time to attend to much that was said by the men who continually came and went from my apartment in a villa where Captain Morgan had made his headquarters. But I heard that some of the men charged the Captain himself with having caused the city to be set on fire, which was a very foolish thing to say, seeing that by such means he stood to suffer as great loss in booty as any of them. I have no doubt it was as the Captain alleged: that the Spaniards themelves had set fire to their town, permitting it rather to become a prey to the flames than to fall into the hands of pirates.

Next morning Captain Morgan sent a company of a hundred and fifty men to Chagres to announce the success of our expedition. We often saw whole troops of Spaniards running to and fro in the fields as if about to rally, but they never had the courage to attack us. Captain Morgan also dispatched two troops of one hundred and fifty men each, well armed, to go into the country and search for inhabitants who had escaped. He had already sent a ship out to sea to bring back any boats which had fled from the city with fugitives and riches on board, and this soon returned with three boats they had taken. But these prizes, together with two hundred prisoners captured in the vicinity of the town, we would willingly have given up for one galleon which escaped, richly laden with all the king's plate, jewels, and other precious goods of the richest merchants of Panama. On board were also the religious women of the nunnery in the town, who had with them all the ornaments of their church, consisting of much gold and silver plate, rich vestments, and other valuable property.

In the ports of the islands of Tavoga and Tavogilla our men found several boats laden with very good merchandise; all which they took and brought to Panama, where they made an exact relation to me of all that they had captured. We also found there, two days later, a good ship newly come from Payta, laden with merchandise and with twenty thousand pieces of eight.

Every day Captain Morgan sent forth parties of two hundred men to scour the country round to find fugitives, and these troops soon gathered many prisoners and much wealth. The prisoners of good standing were subjected to some violence to make them confess where they had hidden their riches, and too often, I fear, the tortures were made excessive ; but the men were disappointed at not finding more loot ready to their hands, and they could hardly be stayed in what they did.

Captain Morgan having now been at Panama three weeks, he commanded all things to be prepared for his departure. He ordered beasts of burden to be collected, on which to carry our spoil to Cruz, where we could descend the river to Chagres.

At this time I was able to be of great service to the Captain. I had seen for some days past certain of the more truculent and ambitious fellows among our men colloguing together with great secrecy when they thought they were not observed. When I approached they separated or began joking and jesting together. I took occasion to overhear what they were speaking about, and much to my surprise learned from this and that that they had made a plot to desert the Captain with some three hundred other men. I made the Captain aware of what I had learned, and he put certain spies to work in whom he had great reliance. In a few days we had as pretty a conspiracy exposed as ever one could imagine. The conspirators, at the head of whom was a man named Michael Macmanus, a turbulent Irishman, designed to seize a certain ship then in the port of Panama, and in it to go cruising in the South Seas, a-pirating, until they had secured as much wealth as they desired, when they would return home by way of the East Indies.

For this purpose they had already gathered and hidden much provisions, with a sufficiency of powder, bullets, and all other ammunition ; likewise some great guns belonging to the town, some muskets, and other things. With these they had designed not only to equip their vessel, but to fortify themselves in some island which might serve them for a place of refuge. When Captain Morgan had possessed himself of their plans he sent immediately to the vessel which they had designed to take, and caused the mainmast to be cut down and burned, together with all other boats in the port, whereby all the plans of the rascals were frustrated. When Macmanus and his friends found that their designs had been discovered they were mightily enraged, and began to murmur against Captain Morgan, and I verily believe it was these men who began the rumours and suspicions which afterward arose concerning Captain Morgan's division of the spoil taken in the city. They knew also that I was in the confidence of the Captain, and joined me in their anger and rage against him.

We left Panama on the 24th of February, 1671. To carry the spoil taken from the city it was necessary to collect a hundred and seventy-five beasts of burden, and thus we set forth, the animals being laden with silver, gold, and merchandise, the prisoners, six hundred in number, walking behind, the whole surrounded by our men. Nothing was to be heard but lamentations, cries, and doleful sighs of so many women and children, who feared that Captain Morgan designed to transport them into other countries as slaves. Moreover, the prisoners endured extreme hunger and thirst, which misery Captain Morgan designedly caused them, to excite them to seek money to pay for their ransom.

At the village of Cruz, on the banks of the river Chagres, an order was published among the prisoners to the effect that within three days every one who desired should produce their ransom, under the penalty of being transported to Jamaica. In the course of such three days many were ransomed, but others failed to get money, and they were accordingly forced into the boats, weeping and lamenting.

Half-way down the river Captain Morgan commanded us all to be disembarked and mustered, and caused every one to be sworn that they had not concealed anything; nor kept back spoil, even to the value of sixpence. This done, Captain Morgan, knowing that these reckless fellows would not let an oath stick in the way of their private interests, commanded every one to be searched very strictly, both in their clothes and satchels, and elsewhere. That this order might not be ill taken by his companions he permitted himself to be searched, even to his very shoes. To this effect, one was assigned out of every company of thirty men, to be searcher of the rest. The search being over we set forth again, and arrived at the castle of Chagres on the 9th of March. Here we found all things in good order, excepting the wounded men whom we had left at our going forth to Panama; for of these the greatest number were dead of their wounds.

At this place we made a dividend or division of the spoil which we had brought back, every man in each company receiving what was his due, according to a set of rules which Captain Morgan had framed before ever we had set forth. But murmurs began to arise, some of the men saying that the division was not done according to rule, but according to the will and pleasure of Captain Morgan, who was retaining much more than his proper share.

Macmanus took a chief part in this discontented mur-

muring. He came one day with three others of his fellow-plotters, to wit, Jake Nutt, Frederick Hatton, and Mivvy Stevens, and spoke as follows, rolling his eyes as he did so, and throwing some sparks of his rage at me, who stood beside the Captain : " Look 'ee here, Captain, this sharing is not thought honest by many of us. Here we have been given but two hundred pieces of eight a head. After all the labours and troubles and dangers which we have been exposed to, we get no more than a miserly pittance that will suffice for but one good carouse in Kingston ; and as for the duns who will meet us when we show face there, they will laugh at us for fools at bringing so little home with us. What are you going to do about it, Captain ? "

The Captain answered with great coolness that the sharing had been done honestly ; that the booty which had been gained had been, in spite of all the toils and dangers which had been suffered, very disproportionate to the number of men who had to share in it, but that strict account had been kept of all that had been obtained.

" Strict account ! " cried the rascal. " Do you think that that squint-eyed little chandler's man of yours could keep an honest account if he tried ? " By these opprobrious words he referred to me, whose name for probity had at any rate ever been higher than his own, and so I roundly told him, adding that if his muddied wits could understand them my accounts were open to his view.

" Aye," retorted he, adding abusive words which I will not repeat ; " do ye think I haven't heard of two sets of accounts being kept by huckstering rogues before now—

one for exhibition and the other for private use? But you, you are but the tool of the Captain—you rogue! Look'ee here, Captain, you're not dealing honest by your old mates who have sailed with you in many a good ship out of Kingston, and shared many a broad doubloon over the wine-barrel. You have learnt old Mansvelt's lessons badly. He was ever straight and honest, as you know. Come now, share the plunder honestly."

The Captain replied that he had dealt in perfect honesty in the matter of the division, and could in no way amend or alter anything which had been done.

"Then I tell you, Captain, you will never get me sailing with you again," returned Macmanus, "nor many another bold boy who thinks as we do. You are keeping the best jewels for yourself, that I'll swear, and you shall rue this to the day of your death."

Macmanus and his fellows got half the army to believe in their rascally suspicions, and they held aloof in surly dudgeon. Captain Morgan nevertheless went on his way undisturbed by lowering looks and murmurs. He ordered the ordnance of the castle of Chagres to be carried on board his ship; then he caused most of the walls to be demolished, the edifices to be burned, and as many things ruined as could be done in a short time. All these matters having been completed, he went aboard his own ship and put to sea, the part of the army that remained faithful to him following him in three vessels, the others remaining on shore vowing all kinds of vengeance on those who followed the Captain, so that it was thought at one time that the two factions or parts would have fallen to blows upon the very shores or in the boats.

We reached Jamaica in safety, where, when all things

were arranged, I parted from Captain Morgan, who thanked me for my services to him, and made me a present over and above my due share. With this amount of money I retired to Tortuga, where I lived for some time in quiet on my plantation. Then some of the Macmanus faction coming to the island, they tried to raise bad feeling against me, so that I felt I should not have any peace of my mind or my life if I stayed longer in those parts. I accordingly sold my plantation secretly, and with my wife and children took ship for Virginia, where I have since made my home.

Thus ends the narrative of Stephen Hooper, who, as pretty well appears from his own story, was mainly concerned to write his own adventures, and did not trouble to continue the history of the man who was the most famous, as he was the most sagacious, of all the pirates of the Spanish Main. It will be interesting to give in a few words an account of the later life of Captain Henry Morgan.

Despising the threats of his former companions, who had suffered many privations in returning from Chagres, owing to the fact that they could procure no stores, Morgan settled down in Jamaica and lived the life of a private gentleman. There he made himself acceptable to the society of the place, which did not find it expedient to look too closely into the antecedents of newcomers. He courted and married the daughter of a wealthy merchant, and for some years passed an almost uneventful existence.

The hatred of the men who believed that he had defrauded them was, however, always very bitter against him, and they were constantly seeking for an opportunity to revenge themselves upon him in some way. When, therefore, they heard that he designed to retire to the island of St Catherine, there to set up an estate, they determined to waylay and murder him. But their plans came to naught in a very curious manner. It happened that at this time a new Governor, Lord Vaughan, came from England to Jamaica, and one of his first actions was to arrest Henry Morgan, by royal warrant. On Morgan asking an explanation, he was answered that his Majesty, King Charles II, had received many complaints of the grievous injuries and damage which Morgan, as a buccaneer, had inflicted upon Spanish subjects and possessions, and it was to answer for these crimes that he was to be shipped to London.

What happened when Morgan reached London is not known with any certainty, no records having survived of his trial. But it is evident that he ingratiated himself with his easy-going monarch, and we next learn that he was knighted by the King and appointed to be Commissioner for the Admiralty at Jamaica. Returning to the West Indies, he became a respectable official under the Crown, and in 1680, when the Governor of Jamaica at that time, Lord Carnarvon, returned to England, he left Morgan as his deputy, until the new Governor should assume control. During that period of high office Morgan took the opportunity of putting an end to much of the annoyance he was doubtless subjected to from his old associates in a very effectual way. He had them seized, and hanged them out of hand as desperadoes too notorious to need public trial!

After this we lose sight of certainty in the life of Morgan,

It appears that in the reign of James he was thrown into prison for some reason now unknown, and what was his subsequent fate history does not relate. She has not even troubled to record when or at what place this 'prince of pirates' died.

II : Blackbeard

IT is evening, still and windless. There has been no breeze all day, only the stifling heat of the direct rays of the sun beating upon the ship's deck, making the pitch sizzle in the seams, and the brasswork as hot to the hand as if it were fire itself. The good ship the *Great Allen* lies heaving on the oily flood. She is some weeks out of New York harbour, bound for Jamaica, with wine, silk, and other merchandise, Christopher Taylor commander. As the coppery orb of the sun sinks beneath the waves far to the west, the clouds draw slowly across the sky, and in a little while thin rain begins to fall, not the tropical rain that betokens a wind to come in its wake, but a steady, even downpour that may continue for hours.

The Captain gives a last look round before he descends to his cabin. He knows he is in dangerous waters, and that a few miles to the west of him is Turk's Island, where Vane, the pirate, has been known to clean his ship. He bids his mate, whose watch it is, to keep his eyes and ears open and to call him instantly should anything untoward occur. The figure of the first mate goes to and fro on the quarterdeck, lit up now and then as he passes the light gleaming up from the companion-way. The sailor watching on the forecastle is only a shadow in the gloom, and the figures of other men of the watch are to be made out only by a keen eye, as they huddle beneath shelter from the rain.

Seven bells are struck, and the silence descends again almost tangibly as the last note dies away. The mate still walks up and down; sometimes—a matter of habit—he looks up at the invisible rigging, and then steps to the binnacle. He whistles softly for a wind, but the sea is still and oily, and the vessel slowly swings this way and that to all points of the compass as the lazy currents heave beneath her.

Suddenly the mate stops in his walk, goes quickly to the side, and stands in an eager, listening attitude. He strains his sense of hearing, and faintly over the water, from what direction he cannot tell, comes the soft, regular sound of dipping oars. For a moment he thinks he is dreaming, then, curving his hands round his mouth, he shouts: "Boat ahoy! What boat is that?" There is no reply: only the sound of the dipping of muffled oars in the water.

The Captain down below has heard the cry and comes running up half dressed. "What is it?" he asks.

"There's a boat somewhere about," is the reply. "Listen, sir; they're oars, or I'm a Dutchman."

For a moment Christopher Taylor, the commander, listens, and then, swiftly coming to a decision, cries:

"They are sweeps, not oars! They are island pirates or I'm much mistaken! Pipe all hands on deck, and serve each man with pike and cutlass!"

The mate rushes to the fo'c'sle, and the clear, long-drawn scream of the boatswain's pipe breaks forth. Up the hatchway swarm the men. Lighted lanterns are handed up and hurriedly fixed—battle lanterns whereby the crafty enemy may be seen—and men gird on cutlasses and seize their pikes. Meanwhile a grinding noise is heard on the larboard quarter, there is a sudden burst of yells and outcries in various tongues, and up from the main and mizzen channels streams a crowd of pirates, their fierce eyes gleaming in the dim, uncertain light of the lanterns as they clamber over the sides and leap on the deck. The Yankee sailors fling themselves upon the cutthroat crew, and for some tense moments the yells die down, giving place to the panting and stamping and fierce ejaculations of men in deadly physical combat. Here and there is a groan, a sudden cry checked by rising blood, the thud of falling bodies, the shout of exultation. The pirates force the sailors back, still manfully fighting, but fighting in vain now against their quicker and more practised opponents. Still the sturdy forms are to be seen in the dim light, now thrusting fiercely with the pike or aiming a vengeful blow with a cutlass, while the flash of a musket or pistol reveals for an instant the fierce, sweat-glistening face of friend or foe. Men locked in each other's hold struggle and stumble over the bodies of the dead or wounded, their fingers clenching the throats or thrusting at the eyes of each other.

The American sailors, hard-bitten men who have sailed the seas for years and won their way through many a tropical storm, make one more rally. Led by their doughty Captain, who, though wounded, still makes his bold voice heard above the din, the men press together and throw themselves upon their enemies, who give way a little. For a moment it looks as if even now the crew may thrust the rascals overboard, when suddenly, with a shriek which curdles the blood, over the side of the ship and into the midst of the pirates bounds an object which sends terror into the hearts of the sailors. It seems to be no more than a horrible face, with fierce, wild eyes and gleaming teeth, the head and features surrounded by immense bushes of black hair and beard. On the top of this is a broad hat, hung from the rim of which are lighted tapers which flicker as the horrible face dances here and there, and show up the whites of the gleaming eyes, the gnashing teeth, and the red mouth. In the dim light cast by the ship's lanterns and the tapers beneath the hat, the cooler sailors can see that the face is, indeed, attached to the body of a man, on whose breast dangle three brace of pistols hanging in holsters.

Startled by this creature's horrible appearance and his shriek, the sailors give way, and next moment with a rush the pirates have swept the men to the hatchways, down which they tumble in a heap. As they are driven back a hideous voice begins to cry all manner of fearful threats and imprecations, mingled with oaths in Spanish and English.

" 'Tis the fiend Blackbeard," says one old sailor, as he picks himself up and feels a bruise along his arm. " He dresses himself up like that and, by the Lord Harry, he's frightened us like a pack o' giggling girls."

Groans alone come in reply to him, or muttered curses, as men nurse their wet wounds or think of the end in store for them.

In this way Captain Teach, commonly known as Blackbeard, got possession of the big ship the *Great Allen*, in which he made most of his later voyages, after changing her name to the *Queen Anne's Revenge* and mounting forty guns upon her. The morning after her capture, the vanquished crew were ordered to tumble up from below and to make the vessel ship-shape, which they did by tossing the dead pirates and their own dead ship-mates overboard, and slushing down the bloodstained deck. The same day they were sent ashore on a desolate, sandy island, with a keg of water and one case of biscuits, there "to frizzle till they were done," as Blackbeard told them, while they saw their good vessel sail away with the black flag at her peak, and the rascally faces of the pirates grinning and jeering at them over the sides.

Many were the crews and passengers which Captain Teach, or 'Blackbeard,' marooned in this way. Sometimes the unfortunate men thus deserted suffered untold agonies of hunger and thirst ere they sank down and died, their flesh to be cleaned from their bones by land-crabs, while the gulls screamed overhead. Sometimes, however, better luck befell them, and a passing vessel, catching sight of their signals, sent a boat to bring them off.

Edward Teach was a Bristol man born, and took to the sea when young. He sailed out of Bristol on board a privateer which some merchants there fitted out during the French wars. He exchanged from one privateer to another, always as a common sailor, distinguishing himself by personal bravery and reckless daring. About the end of the year 1716 he joined a well-known pirate in the West Indies named Captain Benjamin Hornygold, by whom he was put in charge of a big French Guineaman which the pirates had captured. After a successful cruise in this vessel he was put in a sloop, and went on a voyage as consort to Hornygold himself. Then Teach and his friend and captain fell out. Hornygold was becoming afraid of his profession, and was for taking advantage of the King's proclamation which had just been published at Providence, promising the King's mercy to all pirates if they surrendered by a certain date.

Teach laughed at all such "lily-livered rogues" as thought of pardon and mercy; he was for the 'skull and cross-bones' till Davy Jones claimed him, and so he roundly told Hornygold his opinion of him and sheered off in his sloop. Hornygold, however, went to Providence, and when Captain Rogers, the Governor, arrived there, he surrendered to him at his pleasant villa outside the quaint old town.

On board his big ship, the *Queen Anne's Revenge,* Teach sailed up and down the Western seas and made his name and his deeds known and feared from Sandy Hook to Trinidad. Ship after ship fell to him. Sometimes his victims tried to make a fight of it, but often they scuttled away in their boats as soon as the pirate unfurled his black flag; whereupon Teach would put a prize crew aboard under his mate, Israel Hands, to take the vessel to their port of refuge, or, if he did not think this worth while and the ship was of no great value, he would take the goods out of her and scuttle her, or set her on fire. More than once Teach had a brush with one of his Majesty's men-of-war, and came off with no damage. Once, indeed, the vessel opposed to him found she had to do with an enemy who was better armed than herself, and Blackbeard had the satisfaction of seeing the man-of-war abandon the engagement and take to flight.

One day Teach fell in with a little sloop of ten guns called the *Revenge,* and on challenging her found that she was the ship of a foolish planter turned pirate, named Major Bonnet, who owned property in the island of Barbados. The Major had got tired of a humdrum existence on land, and though himself quite ignorant of seamanship, he had got one or two reckless spirits to join him, and had sailed the seas, picking up weaker vessels than his own, but fleeing with terror from anything which threatened trouble. Teach sailed with the Major for a few days, but finding how ignorant he was of a maritime life he put one of his own mates, a man named Richards, aboard the sloop, and took the Major on board his own ship, telling him that as he was such a green hand, it would be better for him not to risk his life on his own vessel, but to live easy. This arrangement, however, did not continue long, and Bonnet left the pirates a little later, though his sloop was not restored to him. He resumed his feckless existence, with what ending—whether he ultimately swung on a gibbet or died quietly in his bed—history does not appear to have recorded.

It is quite evident that Teach was one of the type of roaring, ranting pirates who to personal bravery and daring added something of the melodramatic in his manner of life generally. He cultivated the natural ugliness of his appearance, and doubtless enjoyed all the terror which his repulsiveness excited in those who came in contact with him. The beard which gave him the cognomen by which he was generally known was quite natural, and he allowed it to grow to an inordinate length, so that ultimately, it is said, it reached to his eyes and almost to his waist. The ends he was in the habit of twisting into tails with bits of ribbon and fixing them about his ears. He would roar and rage with great appearance of fury, making fearful declarations of his powers of evil and injury, and claiming that he was a son of Satan himself and a past master in all wickedness. Once, indeed, being in drink, he told his men that he would give them an idea of what life in his parents' home was like. Accordingly, with two or three others, he went down into the hold of his ship, and, closing up all the hatches, he filled several pots full of brimstone and other evil-smelling combustibles, and set them on fire. Then he told his companions to wait and see how long they could live in an atmosphere that was native to him and which would have to be their own before long. So there the rogues sat, the livid light from the burning brimstone playing frightfully on their evil faces, the men sobered for the moment, and becoming more concerned, indeed, as they felt the acrid fumes burning their throats and making them gasp for air. At length, when some of them were ready to faint, and others swore they could stand it no more, Blackbeard laughed uproariously, telling them they were lily-livered rogues, not at all fit for promotion as yet. Ever afterward he twitted them with their weakness, at the same time impressing them with the fact that while they had suffered he had enjoyed the experience.

It appears that when the pirate and his crew were not in pursuit of some merchant ship or in the midst of the excitement of a fight they spent their time in drinking, gambling, or quarrelling. Enforced inactivity often caused the men to indulge in thoughts of mutiny. This appears from the fragment of a diary which was kept by Blackbeard, and was discovered after his death. In this he briefly records the events happening day by day. Thus, on such a day the rum had all run out, and the men were somewhat sober; whereupon apparently some took to quarrelling and others whispered plots, and there was talk of the party breaking up. "So," says the diary, "I looked sharp out for a prize." On another day it is recorded that a prize was "took with a great deal of liquor on board, so kept the company hot, then all things went well."

On one occasion the rovers sailed up the coast to Carolina, taking a brigantine and two sloops on their way. Then they lay off the bar of Charlestown for some time, causing a great flutter in the hearts of the inhabitants of that town, the seafaring portion of whom speedily enlightened the authorities as to the identity of the rogue who was so flagrantly displaying his black banner before their very eyes. The townspeople wondered what the pirate would be at, but they were not long kept in suspense. Blackbeard's design was to blockade the port, capturing the ships which entered or left it. Thus, a ship which cleared the harbour the first day, bound for London with some distinguished colonial passengers, was forced to come under the pirate's quarter and to submit to a prize crew being placed aboard. The next day they took another vessel coming out of Charlestown, and also two pinks (small, narrow-built trading vessels) going into the harbour, as well as a brigantine with fourteen negroes aboard. All these captures, says the quaint old record, being done in the face of the town, struck a great terror to the whole province of Carolina, so that they abandoned themselves to despair, being in no condition to resist the force of the pirates. There were eight sail in the harbour, ready for the sea, but none dared to venture out, it being almost impossible to escape the hands of the rascals. The inward bound vessels were under the same unhappy dilemma, so that the trade of the place was totally interrupted. What made these misfortunes heavier to them was a long, expensive war the colony had had with the natives, which was but just ended when these robbers infested them.

On the fourth day John Gills, the ship's carpenter, who was also the ship's surgeon, came aft to Captain Blackbeard as he sat beneath an awning on the quarterdeck, and, twisting the quid from one side of his mouth to the other, said:

"See, 'ere, Captain, we're run out of medical stores, and if so be any one of the chaps was to lose his appetite I couldn't physic him. What's to be done?"

Blackbeard thought for a moment; but Israel Hands, who stood beside him, said:

"Let's take the chest out of the *Frontiersman* [the passenger ship for London]. That'll have all we want in it."

"No, by the Lord Harry, we won't!" cried Teach. "We'll get it out of those long-faced hucksters and pig-eaters ashore. I'll send and demand a thumping good medicine chest, or I'll threaten to blow up the ships I've got, and make all the ladies and gentlemen take a short walk along a plank!"

His decision was acted upon. Richards in his sloop, the *Revenge*, was signalled to come aboard, and he received his instructions from Blackbeard. Very soon the little vessel was darting away toward the harbour mouth, while the passengers on board the *Frontiersman* wondered, in the midst of their wrath and anxiety, what further roguery and daring the pirate intended. One of the members of the town council, a Mr Samuel Wragg, happened to be on board the outward-bound ship. He was a dignified little man, in sober, snuff-coloured coat, blue waistcoat and breeches, and as he walked up and down the deck with his wife upon his arm, both setting a brave example to the rest of the colonials aboard, he wondered to what lengths the ruffians would go.

Arrived at the mouth of the harbour, Richards, with four other pirates, to wit, John Carnes, Dick Stiles, Ed. Salter, and Jim Blake, got into a boat and rowed themselves to the quay, accompanied by a Mr Marks, one of the prisoners, a highly respectable townsman, whom they took with them to back up their demands. Black looks met them from the mariners, ships' officers, and townspeople who had quickly assembled on the quay, but, bringing their pistol butts well into view and hitching their cutlass belts forward, the five pirates, with Mr Marks in their midst, roughly elbowed their way through the crowd, and tramped along the cobbled street to the Court-house, where the magistrates would then be sitting.

Rumour of their coming preceded them every step of the way, and at the windows and doors of every log-built house of the lesser folk and the stone-built mansions of the town dignitaries necks were stretched and mouths were agape to see the men whose insolence and truculence did not stop short of walking barefacedly into the town which they had outraged.

To the three magistrates seated upon the dais of the court, with the royal arms of England above their heads, the pirate captain made his demand, prefacing his remarks with nothing of the deference and respect which people usually showed when entering the presence of the justices, representatives of the majesty of the law which dwelled far across the tumbling wastes of water in distant Westminster.

THEY WERE SENT ASHORE "TO FRIZZLE TILL THEY WERE DONE"

"Look 'ee," said Richards, glowering horribly at the three dignified and bewigged gentlemen above him, "we want a medicine chest, see? None of your footy little playthings, but one with everything needful for sailor men in it. The Captain sends me and he bids me tell ye, that if such a medicine chest is not down at the quayside within two hours, and we who've come ashore to bring his message are not allowed to leave without violence, why, d'ye see, he'll make the people walk the plank that are aboard the ships he's taken and the ships he'll set afire. Scc?"

"Who is your master, you rascal?" asked one of the justices, a dignified old man with a choleric countenance.

"Who is my master?" echoed the pirate. "Why, curse ye, none's my master!"

"Who sent you, then, with this insolent message?"

"Why, who else but Captain Ed'ard Teach, or Blackbeard, as you land swabs call him."

The old gentleman was seen to get very red in the face at the impudent answers, and he seemed about to burst out in some angry words, but his two fellow justices murmured warning words, and one of them, turning to the pirate, said:

"We will consider your message and will let you know our decision in an hour."

"Mind ye," said the pirate, turning to leave, for the lure of the wineshop called him and his comrades, "no dirty tricks, or your friends out there will suffer for it. We'll leave ye this man," indicating Mr Marks, "to tell ye that Captain Blackbeard and his men are not fellows to be bamboozled."

The five pirates tramped out of the Courthouse, leaving

the justices to stare blankly at each other at the unheard-of affront put upon them.

While the dignitaries considered the matter, and heard all that Mr Marks had to tell them, Richards and the others went from wineshop to wineshop, in the sight of all people, " who," says the record, " were fired with the utmost indignation, looking upon them as robbers and murderers, but durst not so much as think of executing their revenge upon them for fear of bringing more calamities upon themselves, and so they were forced to let the villains pass with impunity."

Only black looks greeted the five pirates where they passed, and though they were served with wine when they asked for it, if looks and wishes could have killed, their drink would have poisoned them. The five rogues took no notice, however, and laughed and jested and jeered without hindrance, but it was only the fear of the pirate ship outside the bar that kept many a sturdy citizen from trying conclusions there and then with the insolent rascals. In two hours Richards and his men went to the Courthouse again to learn the answer of the magistrates and to reclaim Mr Marks. The latter, who was waiting for them, told them that the town councillors had decided to give them the medicine chest they desired, and that it was probably on its way to the quayside at that moment. The pirates then betook themselves to their boat, and found, indeed, that a chest was awaiting them, filled with the finest medical stores the town could produce, and amounting in value to between three and four hundred pounds.

Thereupon the men went aboard the sloop with the chest and their prisoner, and, putting out to sea, came soon to Captain Teach and told him of the result of their mission. Whereat Blackbeard laughed uproariously, and going aboard the *Frontiersman* he invited the Captain and the chief passengers to drink with him, which they did, though with no alacrity or enjoyment. After giving them one or two villainous toasts, he told them that they were free, after which he returned to his own vessel. The Captain of the *Frontiersman* then headed back for harbour, followed by the other ships which had been captured by the pirates outside the town. It was very necessary that the *Frontiersman* at any rate should return to the port ere she set forth on her long voyage across the Atlantic, for Blackbeard had stripped her of stores and valuables of every kind. Altogether, out of the ships he had captured in the five days he had 'held up' Charlestown he took £1500 in silver and gold coin, besides provisions and other goods.

Blackbeard sailed away south, and for some days nothing happened. Then it was noticed that Blackbeard and Hands were often in very secret talk; sometimes they would be joined by Richards, and all three were very mysterious and resented any jesting inquiry on the part of the other pirates as to what they were talking about. A few days later the rumour went through the pirate crew that they were going to Topsail Creek, a lonely inlet in the South Carolina coast, to clean and refit. As they neared the creek Blackbeard, who seemed to be in liquor and was very hilarious, ordered the helmsman to steer for the narrows at a place where, as the more sober of the crew recognized, there would be a considerable risk of grounding. Sure enough the big ship did ground on the sand there. Blackbeard knocked down the steersman, calling him a lubberly fool, and stamped about the sloping deck swearing and ranting for some time. Then, through the speaking trumpet, he ordered Hands in the *Revenge* to come to his assistance in order to get him off. Captain Hands, in his eagerness to fly to the relief of his dear captain, was not sufficiently wary of the shoals thereabout, and he also grounded. Then there was cursing and confusion, indeed, and the heated language which was interchanged between Blackbeard and Hands seemed to be all quite seriously meant.

As a matter of fact, however, the whole thing had been planned between Blackbeard, Hands, and Richards. Blackbeard had by this time secured a fair amount of booty, and many of the crew had hinted that it was about time a division was made. The Captain therefore determined to break up the company bit by bit, except for some fifteen or twenty who were his special friends, in order to secure the best part of the wealth for himself and his intimates.

The day following the grounding of the *Queen Anne's Revenge* and the sloop *Revenge,* Teach, together with Hands and Richards, went aboard a second sloop they had with them, leaving some of the crew, who vociferously complained, to guard the two grounded vessels. As yet it appeared that none of the men had an inkling of what was really happening, but when the crowded sloop containing the bulk of the pirates stopped at a lonely sandy island some considerable distance from the shore and about twenty miles from where the other ships had grounded, there were black looks upon the faces of many of them. Suspicions had begun to work, and they looked at one another in doubt and hesitation.

Then came Hands, who ordered a boat to be lowered, which was done. "Now, you, Venner, Solomon, Nye" —he sang out some names, and with a rough gesture indicated other men—"get into the boat."

There arose angry murmurs, questions, replies; there was scuffling and men gripped each other. Seventeen was the number of the men Hands had told to get into the boat, but the sloop held some forty more; and these forty, with knives or clubbed pistols, forced the seventeen down the side of the ship into the boat, some with bleeding heads, black eyes, or wounds in the body, all of which they ignored in their rage, while they poured all manner of vituperation and threats upon Blackbeard, Hands, Richards, and their treacherous shipmates. They were rowed, by a strong crew, to the little island and forced ashore, without biscuit or water. Then the boat was pulled back, the rowers came aboard, and the boat was swung up. The sails of the sloop were unfurled and bellied in the wind as she took the seaward breeze and slipped away from the island, where the seventeen men, standing on the edge of the sea, shook clenched fists and roared their rage.

It is not known what were Teach's doings immediately after this. He disappears for some time, and when history knows him again he turns up at Bath Town in North Carolina, with about twenty of his men, and they surrender to his Majesty's proclamation and receive certificates of pardon from the Governor of the province, one Charles Eden, Esquire.

What had Teach done with the other twenty men, and how had he disposed of the plunder he had amassed? It is probable that he had made an ostensibly honest partition of the booty with the whole forty, and had persuaded half of them to leave the ship by ones and twos, so as not to create suspicion by landing a large number, at places along the coast, retaining about him only the score or so of kindred spirits on whom he could rely. But whether he had dealt honestly with these is a moot point, and when and where he found a hiding-place for his wealth is unknown. Just before the engagement wherein he found his richly deserved death one of these men asked him whether, in case he should be killed, he had told the young woman he had lately married where he had buried his money. He replied that 'nobody but himself and Satan knew where it was, and the longest liver should take all.'

Teach, therefore, after having buried his booty in some hiding-place, pretended to turn honest, and we may now imagine him as leading a roaring life ashore, a penitent pirate enjoying the pardon of his Majesty, which was granted to all sea-robbers on that coast who surrendered to the royal mercy within a certain time. It appears, however, that as a matter of fact he was anything but a reformed robber, for, as the old record has it, his submission was not done from any real reformation of manner of thinking, "but only to await a more favourable opportunity to play the same game over again." Meanwhile he cultivated the acquaintance of the Governor of the State, Charles Eden, and the Governor's secretary, a man named Knight, both of whom he found to be willing tools, eager to share in any spoils which he might gain.

We need not suppose that Blackbeard gave a thought to the seventeen men he had marooned on the desolate island, where, there being neither bird, beast, herb, nor water for their sustenance, they must have perished miserably if Major Bonnet, the planter turned pirate, had not taken them off two days later. As it seems that Teach had taken the sloop *Revenge* from Major Bonnet, it is possible that he and the marooned men may have joined forces in the hope of having vengeance upon the common enemy; but, as it happened, retribution was to be made by other hands.

After some time ashore Blackbeard, in June 1718, went to sea again upon piratical deeds intent, and robbed several vessels of their goods and valuables. Then, returning to Okerecock Inlet, in North Carolina, he assumed a mode of living, which burdensome as it was to the traders and inhabitants of those parts, appears nevertheless to have been carried out with the connivance of Governor Eden and his secretary. Teach's manner of dealing was to lie at anchor in the coves, or to sail from one inlet to another, trading with such sloops as he met for the plunder he had obtained. He would often take stores from the traders without any show of trading, and a black look or an attempt to withstand him would be met with a blow; at other times, when he was in a good-natured mood, he would make the skippers presents for the goods he seized.

Sometimes he went ashore among the planters, inflicting himself and his men upon them, their wives and families, whether they liked it or not. Here also he could be brutal, robbing his victims of their most precious belongings, for which he would or would not make any return according to the mood in which he found himself. He often proceeded to bully the Governor himself; not that Charles Eden ever resisted him or objected to his demands, the man being a weak tool enough and perfectly submissive, but merely because he wished to show himself the Governor's master.

Needless to say, these various outrages ended by stirring up hatred and in uniting all minds against the pirate, and the traders, shipmasters, and better-class planters resolved to submit to his oppression no longer. They therefore, with as much secrecy as possible, sent a deputation to Virginia to lay their grievances before the Governor of that colony, and to solicit an armed force from the men-of-war lying in St James's River.

The Governor of Virginia was a man of a different mould from the huckstering traitor at North Carolina, and he quickly concerted measures with the captains of the two English men-of-war, the *Pearl* and *Lime*, then lying in the river. Governor Spottswood hired two small sloops, the vessels most suitable for work in the shallow creeks along the coast, and the English captains agreed to man them. The command of this little expedition was given to Mr Robert Maynard, first lieutenant of the *Pearl*, and the story of his bravery, resource, and determination is a stirring one. The sloops were well manned, and furnished with ammunition and small arms, but they had no guns mounted.

We cannot do better than recount the events of the actual engagement in the words of Captain Charles Johnson, who early in the eighteenth century published a volume of collected histories of pirates and highwaymen.

"Blackbeard had heard several reports [of the expedition sent from Virginia] which happened not to be true, and so gave less credit to a warning sent by Knight, the Governor's secretary. Nor was he convinced till he saw the sloops advancing down the inlet. Then it was time to put his vessel in a posture of defence. He had no more than twenty-five men on board. When he had prepared for battle he sat down and spent the night in drinking with the master of a trading sloop, who, it was thought, had more business with Teach than he should have had.

"Lieutenant Maynard came to an anchor, for the place being shoal and the channel intricate there was no getting in where Teach lay that night; but in the morning he weighed, and sent his boat ahead of the sloops to sound, and coming within gun-shot of the pirate, received his fire; whereupon Maynard hoisted the King's colours and stood directly towards him with the best way that his sails and oars could make. Blackbeard cut his cable, and endeavoured to make a running fight, keeping a continual fire at his enemies with his guns. Mr Maynard, not having any, kept up a constant fire with small arms, while some of his men laboured at their oars. In a little time Teach's sloop ran aground, and Mr Maynard's drawing more water than that of the pirate, he could not come near him; so he anchored within half gun-shot of the enemy; and in order to lighten his vessel, that he might run him aboard, the lieutenant ordered all his ballast to be thrown overboard and all his water barrels to be staved in and then weighed and stood for him. . . .

"As Mr Maynard's sloops were being rowed toward Blackbeard (the sloops not being above a foot high in the waist, and the men being consequently all exposed), the pirate fired a broadside charged with all manner of small shot. The sloop the lieutenant was in had twenty men killed and wounded, and the other sloop nine. This could not be helped, for there being no wind, they were obliged to keep to their oars, otherwise the pirate would have got away from him, which, it seems, the lieutenant was resolute to prevent.

"Blackbeard's sloop fell broadside to the shore; Mr Maynard's other sloop, which was called the *Ranger*, fell astern, being for the present disabled. So the lieutenant, finding his own sloop had way, and would soon be on board of Teach, he ordered all his men to go below, for fear of another broadside, which must have been their destruction and the loss of their expedition. Mr Maynard was the only person that kept the deck, except the man at the helm, whom he directed to lie down snug; and the men in the hold were ordered to get their pistols and their swords ready for close fighting, and to come up at his command, for which purpose two ladders were placed in the hatchway for the more expedition. When the lieutenant's sloop boarded the other, Captain Teach's men threw in several new-fashioned sort of grenades, viz. case-bottles filled with powder and small shot, slugs, and pieces of lead or iron, with a quick match in the mouth of it, which, being lighted from without, the flame presently runs into the bottle to the powder, and as it is instantly thrown aboard, generally does great execution, besides putting all the crew into confusion. But, by good providence, they had not that effect here, the men being in the hold. Blackbeard, seeing few or no hands aboard, told his men, 'that they were all knocked to head, except three or four, and therefore,' says he, 'let's jump on board and cut 'em to pieces.'

"Whereupon, under the smoke of one of the bottles

just mentioned, Blackbeard enters with fourteen men over the bows of Maynard's sloop, and were not seen by the lieutenant until the air cleared. However, he just then gave a signal to his men, who all rose in an instant and attacked the pirates with as much bravery as ever was done upon such an occasion. Blackbeard and the lieutenant fired the first shots at each other, by which the pirate received a wound, and then they engaged with swords, till the lieutenant's unluckily broke, and as he stepped back to cock a pistol, Blackbeard with his cutlass aimed at his head. Just at that moment one of Maynard's men gave the pirate a terrible wound in the neck and throat, by which lucky interposition the lieutenant came off with only a small cut over his fingers.

"They were now closely and warmly engaged, the lieutenant and twelve men against Blackbeard and fourteen, till the sea was tinctured with blood round the vessel. Blackbeard received a shot into his body from the pistol that Lieutenant Maynard discharged, yet he stood his ground, and fought with great fury till he received five-and-twenty wounds, five of them by shot. At length, as he was cocking another pistol, having fired several already, he suddenly fell down dead; by which time eight more out of the fourteen had dropped, and all the rest, much wounded, jumped overboard and called out for quarter, which was granted, though it was only prolonging their lives a few days. The sloop *Ranger* now came up and attacked the men that had remained in Blackbeard's sloop, till they likewise cried for quarter.

"The lieutenant caused Blackbeard's head to be severed from his body, and hung up at the bowsprit end; then he sailed to Bath Town, to get relief for his wounded men.

"After the wounded men were pretty well recovered, the lieutenant sailed back to the men-of-war in St James's River, in Virginia, with Blackbeard's head still hanging at the bowsprit end, and fifteen prisoners, thirteen of whom were hanged. One, it appeared, was taken out of a trading sloop by Blackbeard the night before the engagement, and he was let off, not being considered to be as criminal as the others. The only other that escaped the gallows was Israel Hands, the master of Blackbeard's sloop. The aforesaid Hands happened not to be in the fight, but was afterward taken ashore at Bath Town, having been sometime before disabled by Blackbeard, in one of his savage humours, after the following manner: One night, drinking in his cabin with Hands, the pilot, and another pirate, Blackbeard, without any provocation, privately draws out a small pair of pistols and cocks them under the table. This being perceived by the fourth pirate, he withdrew and went upon deck, leaving Hands, the pilot, and the captain together. When the pistols were ready Blackbeard suddenly blew out the candle, and, crossing his hands, discharged the weapons at his company in the dark. Hands, the master, was shot through the knee and lamed for life, but the second pistol did no execution.

"'What did you mean by that?' yelled Hands. 'Do you want to kill us?'

"'Kill ye?' laughed Blackbeard. 'Why, yes, you lubbers. If I didn't kill one or other of you now and then you would forget who I am!'"

Hands was tried and condemned, but just as he was

about to be hanged a ship arrived from London with a proclamation prolonging the time during which his Majesty's pardon was to be extended to pirates who surrendered to his mercy. Hands claimed the benefit of this dispensation and was let off. Later he was seen in London begging his bread along the streets.

VI: The Last of the Pirates

I: The Story of Captain Kidd

TO most people the name of Captain Kidd carries with it all the romance connected with pirates and piracy. It conjures up visions of a reckless sea-rover who, flying the 'Jolly Roger' at the peak of his swift frigate, pursues for some glorious years his wicked trade of levying toll from rich, fat nabobs on passing East Indiamen. At last, retiring to a lonely island in the tropic seas, he there orders three of his men to dig a hole in some secluded spot wherein to conceal ironbound chests containing ill-gotten gains. When these have been let down, with a few shots from his pistol he slays the men who are filling in the hole, and buries their bodies where they fall above his secret hoard.

It is a pity to have to record that, so far as such visions relate to the Captain William Kidd known to history, they are utterly without basis in fact. Kidd was far from being the typical pirate. He seems to have begun the voyage which ended in his undoing with intentions which were quite honourable, and it was only ill-luck, the murmurs of a mutinous crew, and favourable opportunity which forced him to do those things which branded him as a pirate and brought him to the gallows.

It was in 1695 that a ship was launched at Deptford called *The Adventure Galley*. She was chartered by highly placed people to scour the West Indian seas in order to put down pirates, and at the same time to enrich her owners with the plunder taken from the pirates themselves. It is stated that the owners included King William himself, but however this may be, it is certain that Lord Bellamont, then Governor of Barbados, and Lords Romney and Shrewsbury, were among the capitalists who had stakes in this hazardous little investment, which at the same time was of such doubtful morality.

Casting about for a suitable commander to place in charge of *The Adventure Galley*, Bellamont bethought him of a man whom he had met in the West Indies, named Captain Kidd, or Kid, who had commanded a privateer in those seas, who knew the haunts and habits of the pirates, and who, moreover, had the reputation of being a good seaman and a bold leader. To give the affair a legal appearance, the King's commission was procured for Kidd, whereby "our trusty and well-beloved Captain William Kid," was given "full power and authority to apprehend, seize and take into custody, certain wicked and ill-disposed persons, to wit, Captain Thomas Too, John Ireland, Captain Thomas Wake, and Captain William Maze, or Mace," who had associated themselves for the purpose of committing "many and great piracies, robberies and depredations on the seas upon the ports of America, and in other ports, to the great hindrance and discouragement of trade and navigation, and to the great danger and hurt of our loving subjects," etc. etc.

It was at the end of April 1695 that Kidd sailed out of Plymouth Harbour, having under him a crew of eighty men. His ship carried thirty guns and was well found in every respect. All things, indeed, promised well. He proposed, in the first instance, to sail to New York. On the way he took a small French ship, which, on arrival

"I WOULDN'T BE SHIPMATES WITH SUCH AN UNSOCIABLE SWAB AS YOU, AVERY"

at New York, was declared to be a lawful prize, and the proceeds from this enabled Kidd to add to his stores. He also engaged a larger crew, and when he left New York he had a hundred and fifty-five men on board. They were a rough and reckless company, for they were employed, not on a wages basis, but on the principle that each should be entitled to a share of whatever booty was taken.

Nine months after he left Plymouth Kidd arrived at Madagascar, where was the hunting-ground of pirates who preyed on the growing East India trade. But misfortune dogged him from the beginning. He could find no pirates in the seas about Madagascar, and no better success attended him when he extended his cruise to the coast of Malabar. Meanwhile his crew became discontented by reason of the continued non-success, and sickness also came among them. Fifty of them died from cholera within the first year. Added to this, the ship had become foul and leaky and the stores were giving out. It is pretty evident that in the last few months of this period Kidd had a difficult task to keep his men under control, bitterly disappointed as they were.

By commission other than that empowering him to fight and seize pirates, Kidd was authorized to capture French ships. Just about this time he came up with a vessel which looked like a trader. Kidd hoisted French colours, whereupon the trader ran up a similar flag. When the vessels had approached each other, Kidd hailed the stranger in French, and was answered in the same language. On this Kidd ordered the Captain to come aboard, whereupon it turned out that the master was a Dutchman, but that the ship belonged to native owners.

The man who had replied to Kidd's challenge in French was a Frenchman, but only a passenger. Kidd told the latter that he would have to seize the cargo, and that he, the Frenchman, would have to consider himself to be the captain. Kidd's motive in acting in this way was obvious. He did not wish to do anything which was illegal, but his failure to capture a prize and the grumblings and mutinous spirit of his men forced him to get possession of some booty or other. By seizing the cargo of the native-owned vessel under the colour of the ship's being French he satisfied his men and salved his conscience, though it was by means of a falsehood.

Some time afterward they came up with a Dutch vessel. The appetite of Kidd's men had been whetted by the money they had received from the sale of their first prize, and they stood talking together when they saw the Dutch ship, and were for attacking her. One of them named Moore, a gunner, was deputed to urge the Captain to seize the Dutchman, and he went up to Kidd and told him that the men thought the ship ought to be taken, seeing how emptyhanded they were after more than a year at sea.

"Go back to your place," replied Kidd. "I am no pirate and I will not become one for any of you."

"But, Captain," said the other; "you need not fire a shot. I have a plan for taking her that will save your reputation and yet satisfy the men. For you must remember that in this matter you must allow us to have a voice, seeing that we stand to lose so much. This is my plan. Get the Captain of the Dutchman aboard us, and make him sign an affidavit that you have not taken his vessel. Let us go aboard her and take enough to satisfy the men, and then leave her."

"I will do nothing of the kind," replied Kidd. "Get on deck and let me hear nothing more of it."

Moore went away in a sullen humour, and Kidd, going on deck soon afterward, found many of the men gathered about the long-boat, preparing to swing her out.

"What does this mean?" he cried, striding toward them.

The men gave him black looks; then one or two murmured: "If you can't take what's offered you, we will."

"I tell you, you mutinous dogs," cried Kidd angrily, "that if any of you launch that boat and go to that ship, not one of you shall come aboard this vessel again, for I'll shoot you when you come alongside."

The men hung back at this, rage and baulked cupidity flushing their faces. Kidd walked toward the wheel and told the man there to keep the ship a point or two away from the Dutchman. He saw the men about the long-boat gradually break up, talking in groups, but they now seemed to have no design to go after the other vessel. As time went on it was evident that Kidd's refusal rankled in the minds of the men, who went about their work slowly, and whenever they looked at him it was with angry eyes, and lips which muttered curses or abuse. The atmosphere for three days was electrical, and the situation culminated in a tragedy.

On the afternoon of the third day Kidd passed by where Moore, the gunner, was standing upon the deck, talking in low tones with one of the other men. Their talk ceased as the Captain came up to them, and their looks darkened. This irritated Kidd, who felt that he could no longer brook the mutinous spirit abroad.

"That plan of yours," said Kidd, "do you think it would have saved your fool's neck from the rope?"

"What plan, sir?" replied the other, insolently pretending ignorance. "I never had a plan or spoke to you of a plan."

"You lying rascal!" shouted Kidd. "Is that your scheme now?"

"And if I am a lying rascal," retorted the other, "you've made me so. You have brought me to ruin and many others of us."

"Have I ruined you, you dog?" roared the Captain, completely losing control of himself. He looked about for a weapon, seized a wooden bucket standing by, and as Moore dodged to get away, he swung it round and hit at the man. It fell full upon his skull, and the fellow went down like a log.

"Here, carry this fool to his bunk," said Kidd to the men standing near. "A little blood lost will bring him to his senses."

But Moore never recovered consciousness, and the first mate came to Kidd next morning to tell him that the man was dying. Indeed, Moore died during the day, and a gloom sank upon the ship, which did not lift for some days after the body, sewn in a hammock and weighted with a shot, had been launched to its grave in the sea.

The net result of this incident was to cause Kidd to realize that the men were in a dangerous mood, which might lead to open mutiny unless he found something to satisfy them. Ill-fortune favoured him, for a little time afterward they fell in with a trading vessel, the *Quedagh Merchant,* which Kidd chased. Having come up with her, he found there were two Dutchmen aboard and one Frenchman, all the rest being natives. To quiet his conscience and to give a legal justification to his action, he seems to have again taken the view that the finding of a Frenchman aboard made the ship a French prize. He seized the vessel.

There was a very rich cargo on board the *Quedagh Merchant,* and after Kidd had put the crew and passengers ashore at different parts of the coast he sold off a large portion of the goods, realizing by this means nearly ten thousand pounds. As favourable opportunities offered he disposed of the whole cargo, and when the division of the profits was made, each man's share came to two hundred pounds, Captain Kidd's proportion being about eight thousand pounds, the number of shares falling to him being forty.

Soon afterward Kidd, having placed some of his men on the prize, sailed for Madagascar, where he fell in with a pirate ship named the *Resolution,* commanded by Captain Culliford. Kidd proposed to seize this vessel under his commission, but, on broaching the design to his men, they demurred, and on pressing it they threatened to mutiny and to shoot him. Culliford and his men appear to have expected nothing less than capture at the hands of Kidd, and were agreeably surprised when he and his men fraternized with them.

Kidd's vessel was now so leaky that he had to keep the pumps going almost continually. He therefore shifted all his guns and stores to the *Quedagh Merchant,* making a division among his men of all the cargo which remained.

He now proposed to return and render an account of his expedition to the wealthy men who had fitted him out, but when the crew learned of this most of them left him, not caring to return to humdrum methods of existence. A good many joined the pirate Culliford, while others strayed off into Madagascar. Kidd was left with about forty men.

With these he sailed for New York, where Lord Bellamont, the chief of Kidd's friends, was now Governor. Kidd hoped to be received with favour, seeing that, after all, he had brought back a very good return for the money laid out upon the expedition. Greatly to his surprise, however, as soon as he came to anchor he was boarded and seized, together with all his papers and effects. His crew were also imprisoned, and as soon as a ship was ready to sail to London all of them were sent there to stand their trial at the Old Bailey.

It is evident that Kidd's irregular proceedings in the Eastern seas had raised up powerful enemies against him, but as he had been sent out by other equally powerful friends, and as persons in high places had found the capital for his expedition, it was sought to punish him without bringing to light the names of those who were associated with him in the enterprise. His doings on the Indian seas had frightened the merchants trading there, and they caused questions to be asked in Parliament, and some investigations were accordingly made into the commissions which had been given to him. The result of all this was to incense Lord Bellamont and the other highly placed men against Kidd, since the investigations made them appear to be aiders and abettors of a man whose dealings were very like those of a pirate.

In May 1701 Captain Kidd and nine of his crew were brought to trial at the Old Bailey. All of the accused were found guilty except three, who proved that they were apprentices and therefore not free agents. There were two trials. At the first the men were charged with acts of piracy on the high seas, but it appears that Kidd was charged only with the murder of the gunner, Moore. This was in order to prevent him going into the question of his commissions, whereby he might have been able to make some very awkward revelations as to the noble lords who had been behind him.

Kidd admitted that he had killed Moore, but he pleaded that he had been greatly provoked, and that, in any event, he was Captain at the time, and if he had not dealt severely with the man the condition of affairs might have ended in open mutiny. The trial was a one-sided affair. Kidd had had all his money taken from him, so that he had none to enable him to fee counsel to plead on his behalf, nor was he permitted to use the ship's papers, for these had also been taken from him. It was evident that the dice were heavily loaded against him. He had offended his noble friends very deeply in his efforts to gain a good return for them, for his actions had stirred up enmity against them in other influential quarters, and to avoid disclosures which would prejudice their honour and reputation, his once good friends, now his bitterest enemies, were resolved that he should die.

In the second trial Kidd was charged with acts of brigandage on the high seas, but he answered that he went out in a laudable employment and had not committed any acts of piracy, having taken French vessels only, as he was empowered by one of his commissions to do. He called one Colonel Hewson to speak as to his reputation, and this man gave him an excellent character. The Colonel stated that Kidd had served under his command, and had been in two engagements with him against the French, in which he fought as well as any man he ever saw; that Kidd had also engaged a French captain who had a squadron of six sail under his command, while Kidd had but one ship. But these things had happened several years before the present unhappy business, and only indicated to the respectable minds of the jury that a brave man could become a villain, if opportunity offered.

When sentence of death was passed upon him and his companions, Kidd said: "My lord, it is a very hard sentence. For my part I am the innocentest person of them all, but I have been sworn against by perjured wicked people."

Even at the end the wretched business of hanging was bungled. The rope by which Kidd was being hanged broke, and he fell to the ground, still alive. He and his six fellow prisoners were hung at Execution Dock. The names of the others were Nicholas Churchill, James How, Gabriel Loff, Hugh Parrot, Abel Owen, and Darby Mullins. Execution Dock was situated in a dirty and gloomy portion of Wapping. Originally the gallows were erected at low-water mark, and the bodies of malefactors were left hanging until the tide had washed over them three times, when they were cut down. In the seventeenth century, however, the gallows were removed above low-water mark, and the bodies of sea-rovers who had been executed were suspended in chains on high gibbets along the shores of the Thames, as a reminder to all sailormen coming and going on the river that they should obey their captains and not go a-pirating.

Such was the fate of Captain Kidd and his six companions. For many years their bodies, hung in iron cages to keep the dried flesh and bones together, swung and twisted at the end of the chains in winter rains and summer sun, a perpetual horror beyond the gloomy mudbanks of the river.

II: Captain Avery, "the Successful Pirate"

IT was in the harbour of Corunna that one day in the spring of the year 1696 two English ships lay at anchor, waiting until certain Spanish officers should come aboard. The ships were the *Duke* and the *Duchess,* both of Bristol, belonging to merchants who had fitted them out to help the Dons in guarding the coasts of Peru, which was one of the Spanish colonies. They had called at Corunna to take on board certain stores and the officers before-mentioned who were going on duty in South America. Each ship carried thirty guns, and a crew of over a hundred and thirty hands.

Captain Gibson was commander of the *Duke,* and John Avery was his mate. Gibson was the ordinary sea captain of his time—red of face, somewhat full of habit, his speech larded with oaths and abuse; not a man of great wits or keen intelligence, but one of honesty of purpose, filled with a desire to do his duty by his owners, and a fairly competent seaman. He had the vice of his time, a vice as common among the nobles of the land as among the poor 'tarry-breeks' of Bristol and London—he drank to excess whenever he had an opportunity.

His mate, John Avery, was a man of a different stamp both as to mind and body. Slender of build, long in the head, he had the air of one of the men whom Cæsar disliked—thin men, who think "too much: such men are dangerous." Avery had dark hair, a sallow face, and eyes which were constantly on the move, seeing all and missing nothing that might be turned to his advantage. John seemed to be a popular mate with most of the men; some he had sailed with before, maybe, but though he got his orders done smartly it seemed to be by reason of his lively manner of addressing those under him. He did not swear at them and promise them all manner of personal injury if they did not tumble up smartly or do this or that in record time; he appealed to their good nature and their vanity, praising one, half mocking another. He was not known to the captain, but the owners had put him aboard, saying that he was a man who had worked for them to their satisfaction on other voyages and was one in whom they had confidence. The captain had been satisfied with his work during the trip from Bristol to Corunna. Avery seemed to get all the work out of the men that was necessary, though his manner of doing this was not a usual one. In fact, Captain Gibson had sometimes thought that Avery was too familiar with some of the hands, but he had not troubled himself as to this so long as the mate carried out his duties.

If Captain Gibson had been a little keener-witted he would have seen that Avery was indeed dangerously familiar with some of the bolder spirits among the crew. At night, for example, when it was the mate's watch on deck, he could have been seen confabulating with some half-dozen of the watch in the shadow of the long-boat swung amidships. This had gone on from the third day out of Bristol. Avery had a persuasive voice, in the tones of which raillery and scorn were mingled with a repressed fierceness. At first the men had laughed awkwardly, or replied with bravado, as if they knew the mate was talking freely, but were willing to show that they could be as bold in their talk as he. Later, they laughed less, but the talk sank to whispers, and only one or two at a time were seen with Avery at night in the lee of the long-boat. Thus things stood on the third night of their stay in the port of Corunna, where, as was the habit of Spaniards then and now, business seemed to proceed very slowly and was generally being deferred until an indefinite 'to-morrow.'

Avery was an abstemious man for the mate of a ship. He had not often joined the Captain in his nightly potations in his cabin while on the voyage, and only once had he sat ashore with him. For his part, the Captain found nothing else to do when the ship was in port but to sit drinking the hours away in some little 'ordinary,' or public-house, near the docks. A boat's crew went ashore for him every evening at a fixed hour, and brought him aboard again and put him in his bunk. This day, as it happened, the Captain had returned on board early in the day, and in the evening he sat alone in his cabin, where, as a great favour, Hewittson, the second mate, was allowed to join him in drinking. There they sat, hardly saying a word, pushing the bottle from one to the other as their mugs became empty. At the beginning of the evening the Captain had cursed Avery for an unsociable dog, but as the rum soaked deeper into his brain his wits worked less and his tongue was tied.

When it was time to turn in he sent Hewittson away, and having undressed, he got into his bunk and incontinently fell asleep, dead to everything about him. It was the first mate's watch that evening, and the second mate and most of the other watch turned into their hammocks at the usual time, though some of the men wondered before they went to sleep why Goodsell, Saunders, Meakins, and one or two others in their watch still kept on deck. However, the men went to sleep without resolving this query, and by nine o'clock the ship was to all appearances sunk in slumber.

It was a quiet night, bright with stars. There were several ships lying in the bay besides the *Duke* and *Duchess*. Lights glimmered on the vessels, and here and there in the houses on shore, but every moment one or other of these was extinguished, and silence seemed to settle more and more deeply upon the sea, the harbour, and the shipping. Borne across the water came broken voices now and then as people passed along the quay to their homes, and a snatch of a sailor's chorus came from a ship or two in the bay, or from some 'ordinary' where the leave men were turning out to find their boat. The water heaved gently, and the ships at anchor swung slowly as the tide made out to sea.

By and by the sound of an approaching boat was heard aboard the *Duke*, and Avery, looking over the side, saw a ship's long-boat coming toward him through the gloom. "What boat is that?" he sang out. The sound of oars ceased as he called, and a gruff voice replied:

"Is that the *Dook*? Is your drunken boatswain aboard?"

"Ay, he's aboard and waiting for more company," was the reply.

These words were a signal agreed upon. On receiving the answer the men in the long-boat made fast to a rope and scrambled over the sides of the ship. There were sixteen of them, and they hailed from the companion vessel, the *Duchess*. Out of the darkness the forms of some dozen men came together, and Avery's voice was heard to say: "We are all on deck, lads. Now, secure the hatches without noise. You, Dickson, stand over the fo'c'sle hatch, while six others of you weigh the anchor. The others will trim the sails."

The design Avery had broached to his fellow conspirators was nothing less than to seize possession of the *Duke* and to sail away under the 'Jolly Roger,' to prey upon traders in the high seas off the coast of India. He had got most of the crew of his own ship to come in with him, and sixteen of the crew of the *Duchess* had also listened to his persuasions.

So sure was Avery of being able to hold his own against any ship then in the harbour which might have attempted to stop the execution of his plan that he did not slip the anchor, but, without hurry or confusion, he had it weighed leisurely, though he ordered that no chanty should be sung as the men slowly walked round the capstan and the chain clanked through the hawsehole.

The sound of the weighing of the anchor carried plainly over the quiet sea, and roused the Captain of the *Duchess* from a semi-drunken sleep. He came up after listening confusedly for some moments, but only in time to see his companion ship glide from her anchorage a hundred yards away and under full sail slip rapidly seaward. Putting his hands round his mouth he hailed her, but the only reply he received was mocking laughter. "This is rank piracy!" he cried in a rage, and considered whether he should follow and give the rogues a shot or two. By this time his mate stood beside him, and having consulted together they decided to ask the aid of a big Dutch frigate of forty guns which lay a quarter of a mile down the bay. Thereupon the Captain ordered a boat to be lowered, and getting into it he was rowed to the Dutchman, whose commander, Mynheer van Gracht, he awoke, and told him that it appeared that the rascally crew of the *Duke* had seized their ship and run away with her. The *Duchess* was not strong enough to hope to bring the absconders to reason, but the *Graaf Hendrik*, as the Dutch frigate was named, with its forty guns, could easily make them lower their flag and heave to. But the Captain's words were all in vain; the spare little Dutchman was all politeness, but he was under orders from his Government and could not spare the time, nor had he the power to chase the English vessel. "But, man," cried the Captain of the *Duchess*, "there's a thousand pounds in the hands of those rascals. The owners would willingly pay you five hundred to get back their ship. If I was only fast enough, and had but five more guns, I'd go after the rogues myself." Mynheer van Gracht, however, would not be moved, and at length the English captain, with some stinging reflections on Dutchmen's want of spirit, went over the side to his ship, railing and cursing at large.

By this time Avery, on board the *Duke*, was rapidly lengthening the distance between himself and the harbour. The wind drew steadily from the south-east, and he caused every stitch of sail to be set, to take advantage of the favourable breeze. He walked the quarterdeck with a man named Jonathan Harris, whom he designed to make second in command, the glances of both of them passing from the fast disappearing lights of the shore to the canvas bellying above their heads. Suddenly, one of their fellow conspirators ran up the steps and saluting the quarterdeck, said:

"The Cap'n below is ringing his bell like a muffin man ashore."

Avery, together with Harris and another man named Rose, went to the companion leading to the cabin, and the shutter being pushed aside they descended to the Captain's room. They found him sitting up in his bunk with a comically puzzled and frightened look on his red face. The noise of working tackle above his head and the motion and creaking of the ship had awakened him, but his rum-sodden wits could give him no explanation of the unexpected sounds he heard.

"What—what's the matter?" he asked, peering at Avery in the dim light of the swinging oil lamp.

"Nothing," said Avery with assumed indifference.

"But—but there is, I tell ye!" cried the Captain, catching some sense of fright even from Avery's cool demeanour. "Is the ship adrift? Has there been a storm? Something's the matter with the ship. Does she drive from her anchorage?"

"No, nothing's the matter, I tell you," replied Avery. "We're at sea, that's all, with a fair wind and good weather."

"At sea!" cried the Captain, his eyes almost jumping from his head. His hands gripped the side of the bunk. "Why, how can that be?"

"Come, come!" said Avery, with a laugh. "Don't be in a fright. Put on your clothes and I'll let you into a secret." Then he went on harshly. "Come, hurry out o' that. You must know that I'm Captain of this ship now, and you must walk out of this. I am bound to Madagascar, with a design of making my own fortune, and that of all the brave fellows joined with me."

Half dazed, the Captain climbed out of his bunk and began to put on his small clothes, muttering to himself some not very complimentary things about Avery and "all thieving piratical rascals" like him.

"Don't be frightened," said Avery. "We mean you no harm if you behave reasonable. Look ye, if you have a mind to make one of us, we will receive you into our company, and—who knows?—if you turn sober and mind your business more and your bottle less, perhaps in time I may make you one of my lieutenants. If not, well, there's a boat alongside and you shall be set ashore."

"I'll go ashore," said the skipper with alacrity; and now that he saw he was not to be throttled or otherwise made away with, he regained something of his spirits. "I wouldn't be shipmates with such an unsociable swab as you, Avery, for all the gold in the sea. So this comes o' your refusing to drink with your Cap'n—while he was trustin' you, you was conspiring to turn pirate and seize the ship. If I ever ship another mate like you, Avery, who won't take his tot o' rum every night like a man, well, I'll——"

"Stow all that tackle, you old fool," said Avery, "or I'll cut your tongue out before I put you ashore. Now, then, look alive—no, you don't take your papers," he went on, as the skipper made to go to his sea-chest for the ship's documents. "Nothing more than the clothes you stand up in—not even a dram to keep the cold out."

Grumbling bitterly, the old man was turned out of his cabin, the door of which Avery locked, and in a few moments Captain Dawson, the second mate, and eight of the imprisoned crew who would not join the pirates had clambered down into the long-boat of the *Duchess*, which was still alongside, and amid the mocking messages of the pirates they began their long pull back to land.

Avery, thereafter, made a good passage to Madagascar, from which island he proposed to sail the Indian seas on the look-out for merchant ships. Near the island they fall in with two small sloops, manned by men who had run away with the vessels from the West Indies. These were bent on the same design as Avery, and they were induced to ally themselves with his larger force, since they were not strong enough alone to possess themselves of any considerable prizes. The three ships therefore set off together.

One day, when off the mouth of the river Indus, the masthead look-out man spied a sail, upon which they gave chase. Coming up with her, they found her to be a tall ship, like a Dutch East Indiaman. Avery fired a shot across her bows, whereupon she hoisted the colours of the Mogul, but still kept on her way.

"Her decks are crammed with people," said Harris, who was looking through the glasses at the big vessel; "and it seems that she intends to defy us. They are making ready some guns on the larboard quarter."

"Let her have all the shot we can give her," said Avery.

"Nay, for my part, captain," said Harris, "I'd close with her and board her. Nothing like the pike and pistol."

"I tell you we'll pepper her well first with our cannonade," repeated Avery, and he gave orders to clear the guns of the starboard quarter. Harris glanced at Mimms, the second mate, and the thought was in both their minds that Avery was not the bold and reckless fighter they had thought him to be. The same view was held by many of the gunners, one, indeed, a white-haired old seaman who had been with Morgan at Panama, saying, " This 'ere firing at a ship a mile off wasn't Henry Morgan's way. A broadside at close quarters and then boarding-irons and cold steel ! Is our man afraid of 'em ? "

A hail came from one of the sloops : it was the Captain, and he said that he and his friend in the other sloop would bring the Mogul ship to. Then the two of them raced off, and it was a delight to the crew of the *Duke* to see them, while at the same time they envied them, and grumbled as they loaded their guns and rammed home the charges. The sloops dashed away like hunting dogs after a boar, one on each side of the lumbering Mogul. Little balls of smoke spat from the sides of the tiny vessels ; then, still racing alongside the big ship, they closed, one on the bow and the other on the quarter. Faintly over the heaving water came the shouts and cheers of the pirates as the grappling irons held and word was given to board the Mogul. Keen eyes on board the *Duke* saw and envied the men swarming black upon the bulwarks of the big ship. Then there came a cry. " She's struck ! She's struck ! " It was true ; the great yellow banner at the peak suddenly became limp and flapped weakly as it was hauled on deck.

Instantly orders were given to brace the yards on the *Duke*, and soon the ship was flying toward the big prize, all the men of the crew crowding into the forepart and craning their necks to see all they could as they gradually neared the tall ship.

When at length Avery got on board her, he was astounded at the richness of the prize which had so unexpectedly fallen into his hands. He had hoped for nothing better than a few thousand pounds' worth of merchandise —silks and spices, with some quantity of skins or feathers perhaps; but as, accompanied by Mimms and Captain Heron, one of the sloop masters, he went through the cabins of the Mogul ship, his eyes glistened with greed.

The name of the vessel was the *Kootab-u-Din* and she was one of the Great Mogul's own fleet. She had on board a company of great magnates and officials of the Court, who were in the service of their mistress, the Princess Fatma, daughter of the great Aurengzebe, or Mogul Emperor. This lady was making a pilgrimage to Mecca, and besides the personal riches of herself and the princes and functionaries journeying with her, she had a rich present to lay before the shrine of Mahomet.

All that day and the next day the boats of the *Duke* and the two sloops were busily engaged in transhipping the rich plunder to their own holds. There was much joy among the pirates, many of whom delighted to rig themselves up in the magnificent robes which formed part of the booty, and to hang round their necks the gold chains and jewels. Fortunately the weather kept fair, which enabled them to clear out everything of value from the Mogul ship, including the stores and provisions. After this the pirate vessels drew away and let the native ship go free. As, however, the princess and her attendants had not even the necessary food wherewith to continue their journey, they had to put back to Bombay, where their arrival, and the fact of their having been stripped of everything of value by English pirates, soon spread through the land.

The news created a great stir among the English merchants, and the despoiling of one of their princely personages excited the subjects of the Mogul against the English settlements. The East India Company, then but lately established, had much trouble in soothing the irritation felt by the Mogul and his people. The news of the bold action of Avery and the great booty seized by him gave rise to extravagant tales in England. It was the common belief that Avery, after taking wealth to the value of a million pounds from the Mogul ship, also seized the Hindoo princess and married her, while her female attendants were shared as wives among his crew, and that he then went to Madagascar and took possession of the island, where he erected forts and towns, built a fleet of ships, and founded a stable government, living meanwhile in great happiness with his Indian wife, by whom he had several children. It was even said that his growing power as an Eastern potentate began so to disturb the English Government and the East India Company that schemes were considered for fitting out a squadron to put down his power, while others were for offering him and his companions an Act of Grace and inviting them to England with all their treasures, so as to gain his friendship for the benefit of the European trade with the East Indies.

Such tales probably emanated from the fertile brains of literary hacks living in their bare garrets at Islington or Shoreditch, who, poor rogues, made up by the vivid wealth of their imagination for the starvation and penury of their actual existence. The writer possesses a pamphlet which is the product of one such scribbler's pen. It is a small brochure of sixteen pages, brown with age, which was written in London in 1709, and sold at the price of one penny. It purports to be *The Life and Adventures of Captain John Avery, the Famous English Pirate (rais'd from a Cabbin Boy to a King) now in Possession of Madagascar. Written by a Person who made his Escape from thence, and faithfully extracted from his Journal.* This too veracious person is supposed to have been a certain Dutch gentleman, named Adrian Van Broeck, who while on a voyage to Batavia was captured by John Avery and taken to Madagascar. The narrative leaves Avery at the dizzy height of almost imperial power, having circumvented a plot and defeated all his enemies, yet sending a beseeching letter to the Governor of the East India Company making an offer of "some Millions" in consideration of being suffered to return home to his own country, for which he had a great inclination to do some service.

Leaving all such visions of illimitable wealth and power to the yearning brains which produced them, we will continue with the true narrative of Captain Avery's further adventures, which, indeed, led him to but poor circumstances and a miserable conclusion.

After leaving the Mogul ship the three pirate captains determined to make their way to Madagascar. "We've got enough here, lads," said Avery, "to set us all up as gentlemen for the rest of our lives. But there's more where this came from, and I'm one that's going to keep under the Jolly Roger till I've got ten times what we've got now. But you see, lads, we'll want a place to store our plunder, and what better place than a stronghold in the forests north of Point de Miramir, there, where the beach shelves and there's a creek made for our boats and a nice deep ten fathoms where the ship can be tucked comfortably near to hand, yet hidden by the trees from keen eyes at sea ? What say you ? "

Captains Heron and Martin were quite agreeable and said so. " Then it's agreed," returned Avery. " We'll go ashore there—make a bit of a strong fort and keep the plunder there all safe and sound till we think it time to share it out. We can always leave a few hands to guard it while we go for more."

Two days afterward there came a bit of a squall. The night was very dirty, and Avery kept on the quarterdeck, continually peering into the darkness to see that the two sloops were still in sight. " Look you," he said to Harris, with a sly grin, " 'twould never do for us to lose either o' them sloops. They've got some of the plunder aboard—them ropes o' pearls that Heron's got are worth a Jew's eyes—and we'll have to hit on some plan to get all the booty aboard this craft, d'ye see ? " Harris agreed, and suggested that next day when the sea went down they should hold a council on board the *Duke* and get the sloop captains to bring their stuff aboard for safety.

This was accordingly done, and when the bottle had passed round the cabin table for some time between Avery, Harris, and the Captains of the sloops, Avery began to talk in the most persuasive tones he could command. He called attention to the danger of storms, by which they might all be separated from each other ; together, he said, the wealth they now had was sufficient for all, but no one wished to lose a single gold button of it, and he suggested that as his ship was the most seaworthy, and being well armed was less in danger of being snapped up by any vessel likely to be sailing in those seas, the plunder they had aboard the sloops should be sent aboard his ship for safety. If they thought well of the idea, he would order the carpenter to make a big chest large enough to take all the valuables, and three different locks should be fitted to it, of which they should respectively hold the keys. Then, in case they were separated by dirty weather, they could all make their way to Miramir.

The proposal was put forward with such seeming honesty and good nature that the two sloops' captains, after a few moments, agreed to the suggestion. On the next day they sent the plunder which they had to Avery's ship, and saw it stored in a big chest with three different locks, the keys of which they held severally, so that the chest could not be opened without all of them being present.

During the next two days the ships kept within easy hail of each other, but as they bowled along before a favouring breeze Avery became very affable with his crew, sending them grog in the fo'c'sle and inviting two or three of them at a time into his cabin. Here, while the bottle circulated, he told them that all the wealth which had been taken out of the Mogul ship was now under their own hatches, and that when divided among all of them, including the crews of the sloops, each man would get so much, but that if it were divided among the crew of the *Duke* alone each man's share would be more than double the amount. Some of the men looked at each other very sourly or doubtfully, until Morgan's old gunner, Tompsett, suddenly thumped his fist on the table and said: "Then, Cap'n, in the name o' thunder, let's give 'em the slip and share it all atween ourselves!"

Avery seemed startled for a moment, and then grinned, and only Harris, who was sitting by, knew that this had been the very thought that all Avery's talk had been leading up to. For a little while Avery would not hear of the idea, but Tompsett became emphatic, and the other men joined in to support him. Avery with apparent reluctance allowed himself at length to be persuaded, the rest of the crew were sounded, and it was finally decided to bilk the sloops' crews of their share.

When, next morning, the sloops' men looked round the waste of waters for a sign of the *Duke* there was not a spar of her to be seen. They heaved to and waited, but as the day wore on they realized the trick which Avery had played upon them, and curses both loud and deep and threats of the direst revenge were launched against the traitor and his crew.

Avery and his men, very satisfied with themselves, now held a council, and it was resolved that as they now had sufficient to make them all easy for the rest of their lives they should go to some country where none of them was known and settle down. This was the vision they held before their simple eyes, though each knew in his heart that, once ashore, with a wineshop or inn within easy call, and several brave fellows to share, any wealth they had would soon disappear down the throats of themselves and their thirsty friends.

It was decided that they should go to America, and that twos and threes of them should land here and there along the coast, so as to get away without any risk of being recognized and apprehended as pirates. The first place they arrived at was the Island of Providence, which was then but newly inhabited by white men. Here they determined to sell the ship, since if, as was originally intended, they went to New England, the *Duke* might possibly be recognized by some seaman or other. Ere long a purchaser was secured, to whom it was pretended that the vessel had been fitted out for privateering, but that, having had no success in their venture, the owners had sent instructions for the craft to be sold. Having got rid of the ship in this way, the pirates bought a small sloop, in which they betook themselves to the mainland.

By this time they had had a dividend of the booty, but Avery kept for himself the larger part of the jewels which had been taken. At every place at which the sloop touched some of the crew went ashore, with their share of plunder, with the idea of dispersing and finding a place where no one would suspect them and where they could settle down. At Boston, where some of them landed, Avery also went ashore, and made careful inquiries of some of the ships' agents dwelling there as to the possibilities which existed in the place of getting full value for his diamonds and other precious stones. He found, however, that, the place being no more than a trading town, with no luxury and not many people who dealt in anything but common goods, he would have great difficulty in selling his booty and might be suspected of having stolen the jewels. He accordingly suggested to the twenty of the crew who still remained with him that they should betake themselves to Ireland, where they could easily separate and find safety. This having been agreed to, they set sail in the sloop and made their way to the north of Ireland, and having sold the sloop and shared the proceeds they dispersed. Some went to Cork, and others to Dublin. Here, having quickly spent their illgotten gains in riotous living, and repenting of having thus wasted their substance, they yielded themselves up to the King's officers, and in course of time made peace with the Government for their misdeeds.

Avery found that his possession of the rich jewels was likely to become a burden, and that while he did not dare to sell them he was like to starve. Every day in his poor lodging he took them out, and the dazzling light and flashing beauty of them scared him, for it seemed inevitable that if he, a rough seaman, were found in possession of such wealth, he would be denounced as a pirate. He therefore determined to endeavour to get rid of them through persons of respectable standing and appearance, whom rich merchants would trust, and with whom they would deal fairly.

He accordingly made his way to England, and took a lodging at Bideford, in Devon, a quiet little village where nobody knew him, and where he passed under an assumed name, as a poor ship's captain taking a holiday. At this time Avery was not in good health, suffering from an internal complaint which weakened him greatly. From Bideford he sent private messages to one or two friends whom he thought he could trust. These came to see him, and one of them, a person of some standing as a business man in Bristol, promised to introduce him to certain reputable merchants in that town who dealt in precious stones.

A little while afterward two gentlemen came from

Bristol, bringing a letter from Avery's friend, and visited Avery at his lodging at Bideford. He laid the matter before them and showed them the jewels and some small gold vessels which constituted the whole of the booty he had received. After Avery had protested that he had obtained these things in a legitimate manner, and the gentlemen had asserted that they were men of honour and would deal fairly with him, Avery confided the treasure to them, receiving a few pounds in money for his more pressing needs.

Some weeks passed, but Avery received no news from his merchant friends, and his money was almost exhausted. In great anxiety of mind he wrote to them, urging them to complete his business and to send him some money. After he had written several such letters, a little money was forwarded, but the merchants said they found difficulty in disposing of the gems. Avery wrote frequently after this, but it was only after repeated applications that any money was sent him, and then the amount was very small, hardly sufficient to pay his debt to his landlord. At length, becoming weary of this penury and anxiety, the pirate went to Bristol and sought out the merchants, demanding that they should either give him the value of the jewels or return them to him. The merchants would do neither, and when, the discussion waxing hot, the Captain threatened them, they roundly told him they did not care for his threats; that indeed they had had it in their minds to denounce him to the Government as a pirate, for they had a shrewd suspicion that he had been proscribed by the same proclamation under which Captain Kidd had been seized and tried, whose body now hung on its gibbet on the bank of the Thames. In short, the respectable Bristol merchants showed, as the chronicler says, that they were as good pirates on land as Avery had been on the sea, and that they held him completely in their power.

As we have already said, Avery was in bad health and his spirits were very low. A suspicion seized him that the merchants had a scheme for delivering him to the police without reflecting upon themselves or revealing the existence of the jewels, and he became alarmed. On leaving the office of the rascally traders he took passage to Ireland, hoping to find old shipmates there who would relieve his immediate necessities. But his hopes were disappointed and he was reduced almost to beggary. At length he wrote to the merchants, throwing himself upon their mercy and asking them to make him one more payment to keep him from starvation. Months passed, but no reply came. Reduced to extremity, he now resolved to go back to England and make one last appeal to the men who had so cruelly deceived him. Though weak and ill, he joined a trading vessel as a common hand, and thus worked his passage back. He landed at Plymouth, whence he made his way slowly on foot to his old landlord's house at Bideford. Here, while resting for a few days, he fell sick and had to take to his bed, and though he fought desperately against his illness, in four days he was a dead man. When his landlord came to look through his effects for the wherewithal to pay the expenses he had been put to and to afford decent burial for the deceased, there was found not enough to provide a coffin, and the pirate who was worth thousands of pounds had finally to be buried by charity.

At the time when Avery was hiding in furtive misery

he had been made the hero of a play called *The Successful Pirate,* which was produced at Drury Lane in November 1712, and was designed to show the astounding wealth and power which this most fortunate of pirates was then popularly supposed to be enjoying. In this case, indeed, fiction was much stranger than truth, and the contrast between them, as defined by the eighteenth-century author from whose record the above facts have been derived, was very striking; "for while," says the writer, "it is said that Avery was aspiring at a crown, he wanted a shilling, and at the time when it was given out that he was in possession of such prodigious wealth in Madagascar, he was starving in England."

In the foregoing pages an attempt has been made to describe some of the more striking and picturesque figures in the 'Rogues Gallery' of pirates. There are many other portraits which could be added, but, in the main, the story of one pirate is very much like another. The circumstances of time and place may differ, but the motives and manners are very similar. There were brave men among the sea-rovers, as the present record has attempted to show, there were men, also, of uncommon gifts and many high qualities; but the average pirate was a man whose great motive was to get booty, by fair means or foul, from friend or from foe. And in the varying story of his attempts to gain his end there is scarcely any but can find some spice of attraction.

Piracy is still a profession among many of the seagoing inhabitants of China, but the last sea-rover at all well known to European peoples was Benito de Soto, a Portuguese. He was one of the crew of a slaver, and while off the coast of Africa, in 1828, he seized the ship, and proceeding to the West Indies he there pursued the ordinary life of a corsair. He seemed to delight in bloodshed and in torturing his prisoners. On one occasion he shut down the crew of a vessel in the hold and then set fire to the ship, while he stood by gloating over the scene. He fell in at last with a British vessel, named the *Morning Star*, and sent his mate aboard with orders to kill all the crew and passengers and then to scuttle the ship. The mate contented himself with locking up the crew and passengers, and then, having bored holes in the hull below the water-line, he left the vessel to its fate, confident that a few hours would find it and its load of prisoners at the bottom of the Atlantic. It happened, however, that the passengers were able to break from the round house where they had been incarcerated, and the crew having been released, all hands were set to pump the water from the ship. Next day the men were taken off by another vessel and safely landed in England. Soto proceeded to Cadiz, where, in the course of selling his ship, suspicions were aroused, with the result that he was seized and charged with murdering some of the crew of the *Morning Star*, and with other acts of piracy on the high seas. He defended himself with some ingenuity, but the proofs of his guilt were overwhelming, and he paid the penalty of his crimes on the gallows.

Thus died the last of the pirates, who in his brief career seemed to sum up the blood-thirstiness and violence of all who had gone before him.